Cook Up Comfort

160 cozy WW Freestyle™ recipes, with love from Chef Eric Greenspan

WW Publishing Group

Managing Editor: Valeria Bloom

Food Editor: Eileen Runyan

Writer and Project Editor: Alice K. Thompson

Contributing Editors: Lisa Chernick,
Leslie Fink, MS, RD

Nutrition Consultants: Laureen Jean Leyden,
Ariella Sieger

Recipe Developers: Terry Grieco Kenny,
Angela Nilsen, Carol Prager, Julia Rutland

Creative Director: Ed Melnitsky

Design Director: Daniela A. Hritcu

Designer: Rebecca Kollmer

Production Manager: Alan Biederman

Photo Director: Marybeth Dulany

Photographer: James Ransom

Food Stylist: Jerrie-Joy Redman-Lloyd

Prop Stylist: Bette Blau

Front cover:
Spaghetti with mozzarella-stuffed meatballs, page 116

Back cover:
Chef Eric Greenspan prepares Mac 'n' cheese with creamy squash sauce (recipe on page 119)

About WW

WW is a global wellness company and the world's leading commercial weight-management program. We inspire millions of people to adopt healthy habits for real life. Through our engaging digital experience and face-to-face group meetings, Members follow our livable and sustainable program that encompasses healthy eating, physical activity, and a positive mindset. With more than five decades of experience in building communities and our deep expertise in behavioral science, we aim to deliver wellness for all. To learn more about the WW approach to healthy living, please visit ww.com. For more information about our global business, visit our corporate website at corporate.ww.com.

Farfalle with sausage, broccoli rabe, and white beans, page 113

Crunchy
oven-fried
drumsticks,
page 140

Contents

About our recipes

While losing weight isn't only about what you eat, WW realizes the critical role it plays in your success and overall good health. That's why our philosophy is to offer great-tasting, easy recipes that are nutritious as well as delicious. Our recipes emphasize the kinds of healthy foods we love: lots of fresh fruits and vegetables, most of which have 0 SmartPoints value, and lean proteins, some of which have 0 SmartPoints and others that are low in SmartPoints. We also try to ensure that our recipes fall within the recommendations of the U.S. Dietary Guidelines for Americans—lower in saturated fat and sugar with plenty of fruits and vegetables, lean proteins, and low-fat dairy—so they support a diet that promotes health and reduces the risk for disease. If you have special dietary needs, consult with your health-care professional for advice on a diet that is best for you, then adapt these recipes to meet your specific nutritional needs.

Get started, keep going, and enjoy good nutrition

At WW, we believe that eating well makes life better, no matter where you are in your weight-loss journey. These tasty recipes are ideal, whether you're just getting started or have already reached your goals on the SmartPoints system. Unlike other weight-loss programs, which focus solely on calories, the SmartPoints system guides you toward healthier foods that are lower in sugar and saturated fat, and higher in protein. But this isn't a diet—all food is "in." Eating well should be fun, energizing, and delicious, so that healthy food choices become second nature. To get maximum satisfaction, we suggest you keep the following information in mind while preparing our recipes:

- On the WW Freestyle™ program, eating a mix of foods (rather than all zero Points meals) can help you avoid feeling bored or deprived. Remember, there's room for all SmartPoints foods in your plan—variety is key to a healthy and livable eating style.

- SmartPoints values are given for each recipe. The SmartPoints value for each ingredient is assigned based on the number of calories and the amount of saturated fat, sugar, and protein in each ingredient. The SmartPoints values for each ingredient are then added together and divided by the number of servings, and the result is rounded.

- Recipes include approximate nutritional information: They are analyzed for Calories (Cal), Total Fat, Saturated Fat (Sat Fat), Sodium (Sod), Total Carbohydrates (Total Carb), Sugar, Dietary Fiber (Fib), and Protein (Prot). The nutritional values are obtained from the WW database, which is maintained by registered dietitians.

- To boost flavor, we often include fresh herbs or a squeeze of citrus instead of increasing the salt. If you don't need to restrict your sodium intake, feel free to add a touch more salt as desired.

- Look for these symbols throughout the book to choose recipes that fit best with your dietary needs:

  Vegetarian: Recipes that contain no animal flesh foods or products made from animal flesh, though they may contain eggs and dairy products.

  Vegan: Recipes that contain no animal flesh foods, eggs, dairy products, or honey.

  Gluten free: Recipes that contain no wheat, barley, or rye, or any products that are made from these ingredients.

  Dairy free: Recipes that contain no milk from any animal and no products made from animal milk.

  Nut free: Recipes that contain no tree nuts or peanuts.

  Note: Recipes conform to the icon designations, but the "Freestyle it" tip and "Note from Chef Eric" serving suggestions may not.

- Recipe introductory headnote suggestions and "Freestyle it" and "Note from Chef Eric" tips have a SmartPoints value of 0 unless otherwise stated.

- For information about the WW plan, please visit ww.com/us/m/cms/plan-basics.

Calculations not what you expected?

SmartPoints values for the recipes in this book are calculated without counting the zero Points foods—fruits, most vegetables, and some lean proteins that are part of the plan. However, the nutritional information does include the nutrient content of these ingredients. This means you may notice discrepancies with the SmartPoints value you calculate using the nutrition information provided for the recipe versus the SmartPoints value listed for the recipe. That's because the SmartPoints values for the recipes that contain zero Points ingredients have been adjusted to reflect those ingredients, while the nutrition information provided includes the nutrition for all of the ingredients. For tracking purposes, use the SmartPoints value listed for the recipe. Also, please note, when fruits and veggies are liquefied or pureed (as in a smoothie), their nutrient content is incorporated into the recipe calculations. These nutrients can increase the SmartPoints.

Alcohol is included in our SmartPoints calculations. Because alcohol information is generally not included on nutrition labels, it's not an option you can include when using the handheld or online SmartPoints calculator or the WW app. But since we include the alcohol information that we get from our database in our recipes, you might notice discrepancies between the SmartPoints you see here in our recipes and the values you get using the calculator. The SmartPoints listed for our recipes are the most accurate values.

Choosing ingredients

As you learn to eat more healthfully and add more wholesome foods to your meals, consider these:

- **Lean meats and poultry**
  Purchase lean meats and poultry, and trim them of all visible fat before cooking. When poultry is cooked with the skin on, we recommend removing the skin before eating. Nutritional information for recipes that include meat, poultry, and fish is based on cooked skinless, boneless portions (unless otherwise stated) with the fat trimmed.

- **Seafood**
  Whenever possible, our recipes call for seafood that is sustainable and deemed the most healthful for human consumption so that your choice of seafood is not only good for the oceans but also good for you. For more information about the best seafood choices and to download a pocket guide, go to the Environmental Defense Fund at seafood.edf.org, the Monterey Bay Aquarium at seafoodwatch.org, or the Safina Center at safinacenter.org.

- **Produce**
  For the best flavor, maximum nutrient content, and the lowest prices, buy fresh, local produce such as vegetables, leafy greens, and fruits in season. Rinse them thoroughly before using, and keep a supply of cut-up vegetables and fruits in your refrigerator for convenient healthy snacks.

- **Whole grains**
  Explore your market for whole-grain products such as whole wheat and whole-grain breads and pastas, brown rice, bulgur, barley, cornmeal, whole wheat couscous, oats, farro, and quinoa to enjoy with your meals.

A welcome from Chef Eric Greenspan

To me, comfort food is about flavor, about authenticity, and about approachability. It's the kind of food you don't have to micromanage; it's the kind of food you can cook and share with joy. And that's why I'm so excited to introduce this fantastic collection of WW Freestyle recipes, both as an enthusiastic member of the WW community and as Brand Ambassador for WW Healthy Kitchen™.

What I love about the WW Freestyle program is it lets me be me. As a chef who's been called "the king of comfort food," you know I never want to sacrifice flavor. This book is proof that you can eat real food, that you can cook absolutely delicious meals, and do it all in a healthy way. That's because WW is about living better, making smart choices, and finding your own balance.

I've spent more than 20 years working in some of the world's top kitchens, opening restaurants of my own, and cooking alongside many of the most talented chefs in the world at food festivals and private events, as well as on television. I've learned a lot about making wonderful food along the way, but developing recipes for the WW Freestyle program presents an exciting challenge. I find that I am discovering new things and gaining insights every day. The WW Freestyle approach brings a fresh satisfaction to cooking at home for my family, and gives me confidence that I'm nourishing them with healthy meals. In the past, I would fall back on rich ingredients like butter and cream to develop flavor, and I didn't know much about portion control. WW Freestyle has taught me how to emphasize flavor in a healthy way that I can enjoy.

One of the reasons I started this journey is for my kids. I have a 5-year-old and a 2-year-old, and I want to keep up with them, now and in the future. I want to set a good example when it comes to healthy living. As my weight increased over the years, food—once a source of joy—became a source of self-doubt. I now know how to find balance; WW has given me back my love for food.

The energy and creativity that I've found in the WW community have been amazing. Hearing from other Members about what they do, how they cook, and how much they enjoy the program has been inspirational to me. Because no one can just flip a switch and suddenly be healthy; it's not an overnight transformation. You need support along the way, and you need tools and strategies to face the challenges. It's a community I'm thrilled to be a part of.

Happy eating, and let's keep the conversation going!

—Chef Eric Greenspan
@chefgreeny on Twitter and Instagram

Vegetable Tartines, page 61

WW Freestyle focus:
All about zero Points foods

Our newest program makes deciding what to eat much easier, with much less tracking, so you can focus on what really matters in your journey— nourishing your whole self while doing more things you enjoy. So what exactly are zero Points foods, and how can you make the most of them? We've rounded up the most important categories and given you a brief tutorial on each. Eggs, chicken, turkey, seafood, tofu, beans, yogurt, veggies, and fruit are all covered here. And you'll also find "Freestyle it" tips included for specific recipes throughout the book, providing you with recipe-specific swaps, additions, and more that can help you out in the kitchen. We hope it helps you savor every healthy bite!

Eggs

Eggs are one of the most versatile and exciting WW zero Points foods. From breakfast to dessert, they're delicious stars in their own right, and also do a fabulous job as backup ingredients in baked goods, casseroles, puddings, and more. You'll see a lot of eggs throughout this book, and not just in the breakfast chapter: They make a fabulous (and photogenic!) topper for all kinds of dishes, from sandwiches to salads and vegetable bowls, so we've turned to them often in our recipes.

Nutrition

Eggs are a zero Points food on the WW Freestyle program, so you don't have to track them. (If eggs are cooked with oil or butter, as they often are, you'll need to track the SmartPoints for that fat, however.) Eggs are a terrific source of protein, with 6 grams in a large egg and 8 grams in a jumbo egg. They also pack a number of important nutrients, including vitamins D and E, choline, and lutein.

The cholesterol and saturated fat content in eggs were once a concern for many; check with your doctor if you have any health issues that might be affected by egg consumption. The good news is that most nutritionists now agree that moderate egg consumption is fine for the majority of the population. Even better, advances in agriculture have actually lowered the cholesterol content of eggs, to about 185 mg today for a large egg.

FUN FACT

Duck, goose, quail, and even ostrich eggs are all WW Freestyle zero Points foods.

Buying & storing

Choosing which variety of egg to buy can be surprisingly complicated, with even a moderately sized supermarket offering you a number of choices. **Large** eggs are the most common commercial size and what most recipes call for, so you'll probably want to stock these. **Medium** eggs are a good size for two-bite deviled eggs, and **extra-large** or hulking **jumbo** eggs are preferred by some for breakfast staples like fried or poached eggs.

Certified organic is the only agricultural standard regulated by the USDA. Common terms you'll see in the egg aisle like **cage-free, free-range,** and **pastured** refer to a commitment to giving hens freedom of movement and/or access to the outdoors but have no agreed-upon definitions. **Omega-3** eggs come from hens fed a diet containing foods like flaxseed that are particularly rich in this nutrient, resulting in a greater concentration in their yolks.

Although eggs keep very well under refrigeration, fresher eggs will almost always taste better; try some from your farmers' market to experience the flavor of really fresh eggs. If buying from your supermarket, be aware that the **"sell by" date** is 1 month from when the eggs were packed, and the **"use by" date** is no more than 45 days from packing. Store eggs in their carton on a shelf in the fridge; storing them in an open plastic egg caddy leaves their porous shells exposed to moisture loss, and they may absorb odors from other foods.

FUN FACT

White eggs are laid by white-feathered chickens, and brown eggs are laid by brown- or red-feathered chickens. There's no difference in nutritional or cooking qualities between the two. A few unusual breeds of chicken lay blue, green, or speckled eggs.

No-recipe egg dishes

Perfect hard-cooked eggs

Place large eggs in a saucepan and cover by 1 inch with water. Bring just to a boil; remove from the heat and let sit, covered, for 10 minutes. Drain, cover with cold water, and let sit until cool enough to handle. Crack eggs against the side of the pan; one by one, peel eggs. Excellent over salads and veggie bowls, great in sandwiches or as a protein-rich topping for creamy soups.

Jammy eggs

These eggs will have soft, runny, "jammy" yolks. Follow the instructions for hard-cooked eggs (above) but let the eggs sit in the hot water for just 7 minutes before cooling. Peel these eggs very gently, as they're softer and more delicate than hard-cooked eggs. Jammy eggs are popular in noodle bowls, as a topping for ramen soup, or smashed open over toast.

Easy fried eggs

Heat 1 teaspoon oil or butter (add 1 SmartPoints for either) in a medium nonstick skillet over medium heat. When hot, crack two eggs into pan. Sprinkle with salt and pepper and cover. Cook for 2 minutes; uncover and use a spatula to separate the eggs if the whites have run together. For sunny-side up eggs, continue to cook, covered, until the yolks are set, 2–3 minutes; for over-easy eggs, carefully flip the eggs and cook for 1 more minute.

Poached eggs for everything

Fill a deep skillet half full of water, adding about 1 teaspoon of vinegar (white or cider) per cup of water. Bring to boil over high heat. Lower the heat so the water barely simmers. Crack an egg into a small cup and carefully slip the egg into the skillet. Repeat quickly with 2 or 3 more eggs (don't crowd the pan). Simmer gently until the whites are opaque and the yolks firm a bit, 4–5 minutes. Lift eggs out with a slotted spoon; drain them briefly on a paper towel–lined plate or transfer right to a dish. Excellent on top of sautéed greens, over salads, or in grain bowls.

0 SmartPoints deviled eggs

Split cooled, peeled hard-cooked eggs, remove the yolks, and mash them with an equal amount of plain fat-free Greek yogurt. Stir in a bit of finely chopped shallot and Dijon mustard. Season to taste with salt and a tiny bit of cayenne, and mound the yolk mixture back into the egg halves. Garnish eggs with chopped fresh herbs or a sprinkling of spice mix like Old Bay Seasoning, za'atar, or lemon-pepper seasoning.

FUN FACT

Telling a hard-cooked egg from a raw one is easy: Place an egg on the counter top and give it a spin. A hard-cooked egg will spin nicely, while a raw egg will wobble about.

Chicken breast

Our members never stop asking for more delicious ways to prepare chicken, and we think there's never been a better time to enjoy it. Not only are there more choices at the supermarket than ever—from farm to table to an ever-growing variety of cuts and prepared products available—but skinless chicken breast is now a zero Points ingredient on the WW Freestyle program. That means you can enjoy this versatile favorite every day without tracking it.

Nutrition

A raw 6-ounce skinless boneless breast packs 38 grams of protein with just 4 grams of fat and 204 calories. Four ounces of ground breast meat clock in with 25 grams of protein, 2 grams of fat, and 141 calories. Chicken breast is also high in a number of B vitamins, including niacin, as well as potassium, phosphorus, and selenium. Although chicken breast is a zero Points food, the way you prepare it, such as sautéing it in oil or marinating it and then grilling it, may add SmartPoints. Other cuts of chicken, like thighs and drumsticks, are delicious and also great choices for healthy eating, although they are not zero Points foods due to their slightly higher fat content.

Buying & storing

There's never been a wider range of chicken options on the market. Here's a glossary of basic terms applied to poultry.

Air-chilled After processing, chicken parts are usually chilled rapidly in ice water. Air chilling uses cold air, not water, with a few advantages: It reduces the risk of cross contamination, prevents water absorption to protect natural flavor without increasing weight, and conserves water.

Antibiotic-free Poultry raised in crowded conditions are susceptible to disease, so antibiotics are often administered in feed as a preemptive measure. Critics cite possible risks to humans from consuming "secondhand" antibiotics, as well as the overuse of these medicines contributing to antibiotic-resistant bacterial strains ("superbugs"). If these issues concern you look for poultry labeled antibiotic-free.

Free-range Poultry that's given access to the outdoors for some time each day can be labeled free-range. The USDA doesn't specify conditions or length of time, so the birds may or may not be exercising enough to significantly impact their quality of life or change the way they'll taste.

Hormone-free All poultry sold in the United States is required to be raised without added hormones, so any you buy will be hormone-free.

Kosher Chicken prepared under rabbinical supervision can be labeled kosher. The process involves salting the bird; some salt is infused into the flesh (something many cooks find extra tasty!).

Organic To be labeled organic, poultry must be raised by USDA-certified organic practices, never treated with antibiotics, and given access to the outdoors. It must be raised on certified organic feed free of animal byproducts and genetically modified grains.

Once you choose your chicken, follow a few rules to keep it fresh and safe: **Keep it cold.** Raw poultry should be stored at 40°F or below. **Avoid cross contamination.** Raw poultry and its juices should be kept away from other foods. After preparing it, wash your hands, countertop, cutting board, and other utensils with hot, soapy water. **Freeze it after 2 days if you haven't cooked it.** Chicken can be frozen in its original packaging for a few weeks. To freeze for up to 9 months, overwrap the store packaging with heavy-duty aluminum foil or plastic wrap and freeze. Thaw chicken in the refrigerator on a plate or rimmed tray to catch any juices.

No-recipe skinless chicken breast dishes

Poached chicken

Place chicken breasts in a deep skillet in a single layer. Pour in enough water to cover them and season the water generously with salt. Add a few smashed garlic cloves, some bay leaves, or herb sprigs, if you like. Bring to a simmer over high heat; lower heat and simmer until the breasts are no longer pink in the center, 10 to 15 minutes. Remove the breasts from the liquid (save liquid to use as broth). Use the poached chicken warm, room temperature, or chilled.

Lemon-garlic grilled chicken

Place chicken breasts between two sheets of wax paper and pound lightly with a rolling pin until they are ¾-inch thick. Place in zip-close plastic bag and add lemon juice, salt, pepper, and chopped garlic. Let marinate at least 20 minutes or up to 8 hours. Prepare an outdoor grill for medium-heat cooking or heat a ridged grill pan over medium-high heat. Remove chicken from marinade (discard marinade), spray each breast with nonstick spray, and grill until cooked through, about 3 minutes per side.

Crispy chicken cutlets

Place chicken breasts between two sheets of wax paper and pound lightly with a rolling pin until they are ¾-inch thick. Beat an egg with 1 teaspoon water until frothy. Dip breasts into egg, then roll in seasoned panko bread crumbs (calculate 1 SmartPoints value for each 2 tablespoons panko). Place skillet over medium heat and cover bottom with a thin layer of oil (calculate 1 SmartPoints value for each teaspoon). Add chicken and cook until coating is browned and chicken is no longer pink in center, 3 to 4 minutes per side.

Easy chicken burgers

Season about a pound of ground skinless chicken breast with salt and pepper and mix in a few tablespoons each of finely chopped onion and finely chopped parsley. Form into 4 patties, each about ¾-inch thick, and cook on a hot ridged grill pan just until cooked through in the center, about 4 minutes per side.

Bone-in roast chicken breasts

Preheat the oven to 375°F. Spray a baking pan with nonstick spray. Lay skinless bone-in split chicken breasts in the pan and sprinkle with salt, pepper, chopped garlic, and chopped fresh herbs (rosemary or thyme are good). Bake until meat is cooked through and an instant-read thermometer inserted into the center of the breast (not touching bone) registers 165°F, about 45 minutes.

FUN FACT

In 1980, about 10% of an average chicken's weight was breast meat. In 2007, chickens were about 21% breast meat.

Turkey breast

A whole roast turkey might be a once-a-year treat, but there are lots of reasons to turn to turkey breast year-round. Not only is it a nice change from chicken, but it's also got a distinctive rich flavor and meaty texture that make it an excellent replacement for other proteins like pork and beef. And since it's now a zero Points food on the WW Freestyle program, you don't have to track it, making it a deliciously convenient choice.

Nutrition

Skinless turkey breast is terrifically lean and packed with protein. A 6-ounce portion of raw skinless breast has 194 calories, 40 grams of protein, and just 4 grams of fat. Four ounces of raw ground skinless breast have just 144 calories, 25 grams of protein, and 4 grams of fat. Turkey breast also contains a number of important nutrients, including riboflavin, phosphorus, and selenium. Remember that although skinless turkey breast is a zero Points food, the way you prepare it, such as pan-searing it in oil or using an oil-based marinade on it, may add SmartPoints that you'll need to track.

What about other cuts of turkey, like thighs and drumsticks? These dark-meat pieces are delicious and, when served skinless, are also a great choice for healthy eating. But due to their higher fat content they are not zero Points foods, so be sure to calculate SmartPoints when you eat them.

FUN FACT

Tryptophan, an amino acid, is often blamed for making us sleepy after a turkey feast. But the truth is that turkey contains no more tryptophan than chicken or other meats, and less than foods like nuts, seeds, and soy products.

Buying & storing

Turkey breast is now available year-round in most larger supermarkets and at most butchers. **Ground turkey breast** is probably the most common turkey product available; check labels, however, to make sure what you buy is pure skinless breast meat if you want a zero Points meat. **Whole turkey breasts** for roasting are also usually available (check the freezer aisle if you don't find it fresh), as are **boneless breast cuts,** either whole or as cutlets.

Most of the same terminology used for chicken also applies to turkey; see page xiv for a rundown of the most common terms, like free-range, organic, etc. You may also see the term **heirloom** or **heritage.** This refers to birds belonging to breeds that were almost completely phased out as turkeys became bred for mass production. Some heritage names you may see include Bourbon Red, Narragansett, and Standard Bronze. These turkeys grow more slowly and typically have less white meat than commercial breeds, so you're more likely to see them in connection with whole turkeys rather than breast meat.

When it comes to storing turkey, the rules for all raw poultry apply: **Keep it cold, avoid cross contamination** by keeping the meat and its juices from touching other foods, and **freeze it after 2 days** if you haven't cooked it. See page xiv for more details.

FUN FACT

The "gobble, gobble" noise associated with turkeys is made only by male (tom) turkeys; females (hens) communicate with clucks and chirps.

No-recipe skinless turkey breast dishes

Simple roast turkey breast

Preheat oven to 400°F. Sprinkle a 6- to 7-pound whole turkey breast with salt, pepper, and chopped fresh herbs, rubbing some of the seasoning under the skin. Place breast in a roasting pan and roast until an instant-read thermometer inserted into the thickest part of the breast registers 165°F or until the juices run clear (not red or pink) when the thickest part is pierced with the tip of a paring knife, about 2 hours. Discard skin before eating.

Grilled turkey cutlets

Slice skinless boneless turkey breast into portions about ¾-inch thick. (Pound them between two sheets of wax paper with a rolling pin if they're very uneven in thickness.) Season the cutlets generously with salt and pepper and spray with nonstick spray. Grill the cutlets over medium-high heat just until cooked through, 3 to 4 minutes per side.

Turkey breakfast sausage patties

Combine about a pound of ground skinless turkey with 1 egg and salt, pepper, and dried sage. Spray a skillet with nonstick spray and cook about a teaspoon of the filling until cooked through; cool and taste the filling, adding more salt, pepper, or sage if needed. Form turkey mixture into patties about 3 inches in diameter and ½-inch thick. Spray skillet again with nonstick spray and cook patties over medium heat until just cooked through, 2 to 3 minutes per side.

Spicy turkey burgers

Season about a pound of ground skinless turkey breast with salt, pepper, and chili powder. Mix in a few tablespoons each of finely chopped onion and finely chopped cilantro. Form into 4 patties, each about ¾-inch thick, and cook on a hot ridged grill pan just until cooked through in the center, about 4 minutes per side. Serve topped with fat-free salsa or pico de gallo.

Turkey taco filling

Heat a nonstick skillet over medium heat. Add about 1 pound ground skinless turkey breast, a handful of chopped onion, a few minced garlic cloves, and a diced tomato. Cook, stirring and breaking turkey apart with wooden spoon, until turkey is cooked through and most liquid has evaporated, about 8 minutes. Stir in salt and chili powder to taste. Use the mixture to fill tortillas (a medium flour tortilla has a SmartPoints value of 3) or spoon over greens and top with chopped cilantro and a drizzle of ime juice for a taco salad.

Fish and seafood

Most of us know it's healthier to include fish in our diets, and here's a fact that may revolutionize how often we eat it: All types of fresh fish and shellfish are now zero Points on the WW Freestyle program. That means you can indulge in everything from salmon, mahimahi, and flounder to shrimp, clams, and lobster without tracking. And even some kinds of processed fish fit the bill: Tuna or salmon canned in water, for instance, and smoked trout and smoked salmon cured without sugar are also zero Points.

Nutrition

Fish has one of the lowest fat contents of any animal protein. And even "fatty" varieties like salmon and mackerel have a benefit: They're great sources of omega-3 fatty acids—the ones that play an important role in heart health.

Seafood is also packed with protein. Although exact amounts vary, most finfish contain around 25 grams per 4-ounce raw portion, and most shellfish contain about 23 grams per 4-ounce portion. Fish and shellfish are natural sources of B vitamins, vitamin D, selenium, zinc, and iodine. And all varieties of finfish and shellfish are 0 SmartPoints as long as they're skinless and cooked or prepared with only zero Points ingredients (that means no sugar or oil in canned, cured, or pickled fish products).

FUN FACT

The World Health Organization recommends a diet that includes two servings of fatty fish (such as salmon or mackerel) a week.

Buying & storing

Choosing good fish is just as important as cooking it well, so take care when shopping for it and store it correctly when you get it home. The better and fresher your seafood, the simpler it will be to cook deliciously!

Freshness at the market Only buy seafood that is properly stored, preferably on a thick bed of ice or in a cold case with a sell-by date on the package. Fish should smell fresh and mild, like the ocean, not fishy or like ammonia. Fillets should be shiny and plump, with no discolored or drying around the edges. Whole fish should have shiny skin, bright-red gills, and clear, rounded (not shrunken) eyes. Some shellfish spoils so quickly it should only be bought live: Crabs and lobsters should move when touched, and clams, mussels, and oysters should be firmly closed with unbroken shells.

Storing seafood at home Always use fresh seafood within 2 days of purchase. Store it in the coldest part of the refrigerator (usually the far back corner). Keep it freshest by storing it over a pan of ice covered with a kitchen towel.

Frozen seafood Keeping a bag of shrimp or some fish fillets in the freezer makes healthy meals super-convenient. And don't think these frozen choices are necessarily less "fresh" than what you buy at the fish counter: Most shrimp and some fish sold at markets are actually previously frozen, so thawing seafood yourself only when you need it may mean you're cooking a higher-quality product. Just make sure the package is completely sealed with no signs of frost or ice crystals, which may indicate that it's been stored improperly or for too long.

Sustainable choices Choosing seafood from sustainable fisheries or reputable fish farmers is a vital step in protecting our planet. For more information about the best choices, go to the Environmental Defense Fund at seafood.edf.org, the Monterey Bay Aquarium at seafoodwatch.org, or the Safina Center at safinacenter.org.

FUN FACT

Shrimp is the most popular seafood consumed in the United States, followed by canned tuna.

No-recipe seafood dishes

Poached salmon

Place skin-on salmon fillet in a deep skillet in a single layer (one single piece is best, but cut portions are okay). Pour in cold water to cover by 1 inch and season the water generously with salt. Bring to boil over medium heat. Turn off heat, cover the skillet, and let sit until the flesh is cooked through and flakes easily with a fork, about 30 minutes. Lift fish from water and remove skin. Use immediately or refrigerate up to 2 days.

Seafood brochettes

Cut thick skinless fillets like salmon, tuna, halibut, sea bass, or swordfish into 1-inch chunks, or use peeled deveined large shrimp. Thread seafood on metal skewers, alternating with cherry tomatoes, chunks of vegetables, or small mushrooms. Brush generously with low-fat vinaigrette (calculate 1 SmartPoints value per tablespoon used), sprinkle with salt and pepper, and grill or broil, turning occasionally and brushing once or twice more with vinaigrette, until fish is just cooked through and vegetables are browned, 6–8 minutes.

Easy ceviche

Dice very fresh firm skinless fish fillets and place in a large glass bowl. Pour in lime juice to just cover fish; stir gently, cover the bowl, and refrigerate until fish is no longer opaque, 30 minutes to 1 hour. Drain and toss with diced onion, diced bell pepper, chopped cilantro, and a sprinkling of salt. Add finely diced jalapeño if you like. This technique is also great with very fresh "dry" scallops (those not treated with phosphates); you can use small bay scallops or dice larger sea scallops.

Shrimp marinara

Heat a heavy skillet over medium-high heat. Add a thin layer of olive oil (calculate 1 SmartPoints value per teaspoon) to just cover the bottom of the pan. Pat peeled deveined medium or large shrimp dry with a paper towel and add to pan in a single layer. Sprinkle with salt and red pepper flakes and cook, stirring frequently, just until pink on the outside. Add homemade or store-bought marinara sauce (3 SmartPoints value per ½ cup) and simmer until shrimp are cooked through. Garnish with chopped basil.

Garlicky mussels

Pour white wine into a large pot to a depth of ½ inch (calculate 4 SmartPoints per ½ cup wine). Add a generous amount of chopped garlic and fresh thyme sprigs. Cover and bring to a boil over high heat; boil 3 minutes. Add scrubbed mussels, cover the pan, and boil until the mussels open, stirring once or twice, about 6 minutes. (Discard any that do not open.) Divide mussels and liquid between bowls and sprinkle with coarse sea salt, freshly ground pepper, and chopped parsley.

FUN FACT

Wild salmon has fewer calories and less saturated fat than farmed salmon, so choose wild when you can.

Tofu

For years tofu was associated almost solely with Asian cooking. Stir-fries, ma-pao tofu, and soups like sweet-and-sour and miso seemed to be about the limit of its range in our kitchens. Then something happened: The food's mild flavor and creamy texture, plus a new interest in plant-based dining, made it a prime ingredient to experiment with. Pretty soon it was going undercover in everything from smoothies and burgers to puddings and cheesecake. And now that it's a zero Points food, there's more reason to cook with it than ever before.

Nutrition

It's no wonder that vegans and vegetarians have been eating tofu for years: It's high in protein, contains calcium and iron, and is rich in a number of vitamins and minerals. Tofu boasts all 8 essential amino acids and so is referred to as a "complete" protein, like eggs and meat. All forms of tofu—firm, extrafirm, silken, and baked or smoked—are zero Points foods, but remember that any added seasonings or oils used to cook it may add SmartPoints.

FUN FACT

The art of tofu making dates back at least 2,000 years to China. The word "tofu," however, is Japanese, and was widely adopted in the United State in the 1970s, pushing out the term "bean curd."

Buying & storing

Tofu is made from skimming the solids from soy milk and pressing them to remove liquid. It's most often sold refrigerated in water-filled, heat-sealed packages or in aseptic (shelf-stable) cartons. You may find it sold in bulk in Asian markets or health-food stores.

Firm and **extra firm** varieties, sometimes called Chinese tofu, are made from pressed curds, resulting in a dense, cakey texture. These types are best for stir-frying, baking, and grilling. **Silken tofu** is made from uncurdled soy milk for a very smooth, moist texture. It makes a wonderfully creamy base when pureed for soups, sauces, puddings, and more.

Baked tofu and **smoked tofu** are newly popular and now widely available in most supermarkets. These varieties have had most of tofu's characteristic moisture removed and are often flavored, so they're a very tasty addition to dishes right out of the package. Smoked tofu has a particularly rich, meaty flavor that makes it a favorite meat substitute.

A package of tofu can keep unopened for up to 2 months in the fridge; however, you should pay attention to the "use by" date for best freshness. Once opened, tofu will keep refrigerated for 3 to 4 days. Drain off any water and store it in an airtight container. Always discard tofu if it smells sour.

How to press tofu

Although you can almost always use tofu straight out of the package, removing excess moisture from firm or extra firm tofu helps it retain its shape and increase its flavor in some dishes. There are several ways to do this, but here's one of the easiest: Remove tofu from its packaging and drain if it is packed in water. Place the entire block on a plate and top with another plate. Let stand for 30 minutes; liquid should pool in the bottom plate. Remove the block from the plates and pat dry. You can now cut or dice it as needed.

FUN FACT

Tofu turns yellow when frozen but reverts to its original ivory color as it thaws. The texture, however, will be chewier and spongier once thawed, a quality some people prefer.

No-recipe tofu dishes

Tofu breakfast scramble

Heat a thin layer of oil in nonstick skillet (1 teaspoon canola oil or olive oil is 1 SmartPoints value) and sauté onion and garlic until softened. Add more veggies if you like (mushrooms, zucchini, tomatoes, etc.) and cook until softened. Add diced tofu (firm, extra firm, or silken) and cook, breaking up large chunks. Sprinkle with a little turmeric, salt, and pepper and cook until heated through.

Home-baked tofu

Place a block of firm or extra firm tofu between plates and let sit 30 minutes. Preheat oven to 400°F and line a baking sheet with parchment paper. Pour off liquid and pat tofu dry. Cut tofu into 1-inch cubes and place on baking sheet. Spray with nonstick spray and bake until firm and just browned, about 30 minutes. Sprinkle with soy sauce or seasoning blend.

Tofu caprese salad

Place a block of firm or extra firm tofu between plates and let sit 30 minutes. Pour off liquid and pat tofu dry, cut in half, and slice again. Sprinkle tofu slices with 1 tablespoon cider vinegar and ¾ teaspoon kosher salt; place on a wire rack set over plate and refrigerate, uncovered, so tofu dries out, for at least 8 hours or up to 1 day. Layer tofu on platter with sliced tomato and basil leaves; drizzle with balsamic vinegar (1 tablespoon has 1 SmartPoints value) and sprinkle with black pepper and a little more salt.

Tofu "fries"

Place a block of firm or extra firm tofu between plates and let sit 30 minutes. Preheat oven to 400°F. Pour off liquid and pat tofu dry. Cut into sticks that resemble fries and brush with olive oil on all sides (1 teaspoon olive oil will add 1 SmartPoints value). Lay "fries" in single layer on baking sheet covered with parchment paper, sprinkle with salt and chili powder or other spice mix, and bake until browned, about 30 minutes, turning the pieces once halfway through baking.

Miso-tofu dip

Whirl silken tofu in a food processor or blender until smooth. Blend again with miso paste to taste (1 tablespoon miso paste is 1 SmartPoints value; try about 2 tablespoons per 14-ounce block of tofu). Stir in salt, pepper, and cider vinegar to taste. Flavor with your choice of fresh herbs, citrus zest, garlic, or scallions. Serve with raw veggies like carrot sticks, cucumber slices, and radishes for dipping.

Beans, peas, and lentils

Love beans? You're not alone: This inexpensive, heart-healthy source of protein is one of the most popular staples worldwide. You'll find beans and lentils starring in dishes from around the United States as well as in Italian, Mexican, Caribbean, African, and South and Central American cuisines. That the WW Freestyle program now designates all beans, lentils, and peas (dried and fresh) as zero Points foods is worth celebrating. Simmering up a batch from dried is ideal (see our easy instructions at right), but beans also taste great canned, too.

Nutrition

Nutritionists love to tout beans and lentils. A diet incorporating a significant amount of beans is associated with longevity in many areas of the world, and it's not hard to see why. They're a great source of protein and fiber and high in a number of important vitamins and minerals, including folate, iron, and potassium. Exact nutritional qualities differ slightly by variety: A half cup of cooked, drained beans or lentils contains 6–9 grams of protein, 6–10 grams of fiber, and 105–125 calories. And all are 0 SmartPoints.

Like beans and lentils, green peas are also a member of the legume family. We eat them fresh, of course, as spring peas or English peas, but also dried as split peas for soup and other dishes. Peas are slightly lower in protein than beans but have the added benefit of a good amount of vitamins A and C. Both fresh and dried peas are 0 SmartPoints, so we encourage you to enjoy them in soups, salads, and more.

FUN FACT
Although beans are eaten in many cultures on January 1 for good luck (think of black-eyed peas in the American South), National Bean Day is actually January 6.

Buying & storing

Canned beans are convenient for impromptu cooking, so we recommend you keep some on hand. Many cooks, however, prefer the taste and texture of **dried beans** cooked from scratch. They're generally more buttery and toothsome.

An added benefit? Beans cooked from scratch are about half the price of canned beans and freeze exceptionally well.

Which beans are the best to stock up on? The comfort-food recipes in this book most often call for white beans (cannellini and navy beans), black beans, pinto beans, and chickpeas. But the good news is that substituting one kind of bean for another can pretty much be done with abandon. Red beans, cranberry beans, fava beans, black-eyed peas, and adzuki beans are colorful ways to add variety to your dishes. **Edamame** (green soy beans) are popular in salads and Asian dishes; they're available frozen, either shelled or in the pod.

In addition to beans, **lentils** are an excellent quick-cooking staple to keep on hand, as are **dried split peas,** the standard for split pea soup.

Canned beans will keep in a cool cabinet indefinitely. Dried beans and lentils also have a long shelf life but will take longer to soften the older they are; store them in a cool dark place and plan to use them within 6 months of purchase. You can refrigerate cooked beans for up to 3 days or freeze them in airtight containers or freezer-safe zip-close plastic bags for up to 4 months.

FUN FACT
Digestive discomfort from beans is caused by complex carbohydrates called oligosaccharides. Eating them more often, however, reduces these effects.

Cooking dried beans
Makes about 6 cups

1 Spread 1 pound of dried beans out on a tray; sort through them, picking out any small stones or debris. Pour beans into a strainer and rinse well.

2 Transfer beans to a large pot and cover by 5 inches with water. Add 1 teaspoon salt, a few garlic cloves, and 1–2 bay leaves. Place beans on the stovetop and bring to boil. Lower heat and simmer, partially covered, until the beans are tender, 45 minutes–2 hours, depending on variety.

3 Drain and cool beans. Discard bay leaves; discard garlic cloves or leave them in. Refrigerate beans for up to 3 days or freeze for up to 4 months.

No-recipe bean and lentil dishes

Italian shrimp and white bean salad
Place baby arugula in a bowl and top with rinsed and drained cannellini beans, medium cooked and peeled shrimp, thinly sliced red onion, halved cherry tomatoes, and sliced basil. Drizzle with olive oil (count 1 SmartPoints value per teaspoon) and red-wine vinegar and sprinkle with salt and pepper.

Easy refried beans
Pour olive oil or canola oil into a medium skillet until it just covers the bottom (count 1 SmartPoints per teaspoon) and heat over medium heat. Sauté a few garlic cloves and a handful of finely diced onion in the oil until onion is translucent, 2–3 minutes. Add kidney, pinto, or black beans and cook, mashing with a large fork, until fairly smooth and bubbling (add a little water if necessary). Season with salt, cumin, and cayenne to taste.

Spicy edamame snack
Boil frozen edamame (green soy beans) in the pod until tender, about 8 minutes. Drain and pat dry. Toss with coarse sea salt and shichimi togarashi (Japanese chile powder) to taste; you can also use a combination of chili powder and red pepper flakes instead of shichimi togarashi. Serve the edamame warm. To eat, bite the beans out of the pods with your teeth, and then discard the pods.

Lentil soup
Combine rinsed lentils with twice their volume of chicken or vegetable broth. Add diced onion and a little garlic, plus other diced vegetables like carrot, celery, or bell pepper. Simmer, partially covered, until lentils are very tender, 20–30 minutes depending on variety. Season with salt and pepper to taste.

Lentil salad
Combine cooked and cooled lentils, sliced scallions, diced red bell pepper, and shredded carrot in a bowl. Drizzle with olive oil (count 1 SmartPoints value per teaspoon) and white-wine vinegar and sprinkle with salt and pepper to taste. Toss with lots of chopped fresh parsley or dill.

FUN FACT
Rwanda has the highest per-capita bean consumption based on a 2013 survey of 133 countries, followed by Nicaragua and Brazil.

Fat-free yogurt

If you think yogurt is just something that comes in a cup and is eaten with a spoon, think again. There are a few culinary superstars that are also a zero Points ingredient, and plain fat-free yogurt is one of them. Its winning combination of creaminess, acidity, and milky flavor finds favor in everything from soups and sauces to desserts and snacks. Our members have taken to it with gusto, finding ways to use it in delicious breakfasts, fancy baking, and dinner favorites. We're impressed!

Nutrition

Plain unsweetened fat-free yogurt has 137 calories, 14 grams of protein, and 0 of grams fat in an 8-ounce serving. Greek yogurt is a little different, with slightly more calories and fat but a big boost of protein: An 8-ounce serving has 142 calories, 1 gram of fat, and a whopping 24 grams of protein. Want a dairy-free alternative? Plain unsweetened soy yogurt is also a zero Points food, with 150 calories, 6 grams of protein, and 4 grams of fat.

Read labels carefully; only unsweetened fat-free dairy or soy yogurts are zero Points foods. Products like fruit-flavored yogurt and yogurt flavored with artificial sweeteners should be measured and tracked. And although many recipes in this book call for low-fat rather than fat-free yogurt, low-fat yogurt is not a zero Points food.

And yogurt's health benefits aren't just about numbers; the presence of probiotics in yogurt is a nutritional bonus that shouldn't be overlooked. Probiotics are live bacteria (sometimes called "good bacteria") that have been shown to improve digestion and gut health and may have wider-ranging health benefits.

FUN FACT

The active cultures in yogurt produce lactase, the enzyme that helps us to digest the lactose in milk. This makes yogurt tolerable for many people who are lactose-intolerant.

Buying & storing

Check the "best before" date on yogurt cartons and try to buy the product with the latest date. Yogurt keeps well refrigerated (1 to 3 weeks, and sometimes more), but you should plan to use it within a few days of the suggested date. Once a carton is open, try to use it within 3 days. Always store yogurt on the coldest shelf of the refrigerator, never on the door. You can freeze yogurt, but its texture will be affected when it thaws, so only freeze it if you plan to eat it frozen (which can be delicious!).

And remember, always read the labels on yogurt. If you're looking for a zero Points food, it must be made with fat-free milk and contain no fruit or sweetener of any kind. Soy yogurt will always contain a certain amount of fat but should not contain sweeteners or fruit to be considered a zero Points food. And if probiotics are important to you, look for yogurts labeled as containing live and active cultures.

FUN FACT

The first commercial production of yogurt dates to Isaac Carasso's Barcelona factory, founded in 1919. Isaac's son, Daniel, emigrated to the United States and founded Dannon, the country's first large-scale yogurt company.

No-recipe yogurt dishes

Peanut butter–yogurt breakfast bowl

Blend 2 tablespoons powdered peanut butter (1 SmartPoints) into ½ cup plain fat-free Greek yogurt. Place in small bowl and top with banana slices. Sprinkle on chopped almonds, green pumpkin seeds, or ground flaxseed (all 1 SmartPoints value per tablespoon).

Yogurt-marinated chicken

Whisk together ⅓ cup plain fat-free yogurt (not Greek), 1 tablespoon olive oil (4 SmartPoints), 1 tablespoon lime juice, 1 large garlic clove, minced, 1 teaspoon minced peeled fresh ginger, 1 teaspoon garam masala, ¾ teaspoon salt, ¼ teaspoon ground turmeric, and pinch cayenne in bowl. Add boneless skinless chicken breast cutlets (1 to 2 pounds total), turn to coat, cover, and refrigerate for at least 1 hour or up to 1 day. Remove chicken from marinade, discard excess marinade, and grill until cooked through, 3 to 5 minutes per side depending on the thickness of the cutlets.

Creamy cucumber-yogurt soup with dill

Remove about half the peel from an English (seedless) cucumber and combine in a blender or food processor with about half as much plain fat-free Greek yogurt. Add a small amount of fresh dill and blend, adding a little fat-free chicken or vegetable stock until you have a thick soup. Season with salt, a tiny bit of cayenne, and a squeeze of lemon juice and chill for at least an hour. Serve sprinkled with dill.

Yogurt dip with pita and veggies

Drizzle 1 teaspoon olive oil (1 SmartPoints value) over ⅓ cup plain fat-free Greek yogurt and sprinkle with a generous amount of coarse sea salt and a little black pepper. Surround with a small pita cut into wedges (2 SmartPoints) and vegetable dippers like carrot and celery sticks, strips of bell pepper and fennel, cherry tomatoes, and snap peas.

Frozen berry yogurt

Cook berries (fresh or frozen unsweetened) with a splash of water over medium-low heat, stirring often, until very soft. Strain through a sieve to remove seeds. Stir berries into plain fat-free Greek yogurt (about 1 cup per every ½ cup of berry mixture). Stir in sweetener of choice (each tablespoon of sugar will add 3 SmartPoints). Transfer to individual containers and freeze. Thaw 15 minutes before eating.

FUN FACT

Plain fat-free Greek yogurt is Chef Eric's favorite zero Points ingredient.

Veggies

Encouragement to eat a rainbow of gorgeous, delicious vegetables is one of the highlights of the WW Freestyle program. WW has always championed filling your plate with veggies, but now almost all of them (including sweet corn and all types of peas!) are zero Points foods. You could eat a different variety of vegetable almost every day of the year and still never run out of new options. There's no reason to ever say you're tired of vegetables!

Nutrition

The range of nutrients vegetables offer is as diverse as their looks, although you can count on an abundance of fiber and antioxidants from just about all of them. Leafy vegetables like lettuces, kale, and spinach are rich in iron and vitamins A and K. Orange veggies like winter squash, carrots, and sweet potatoes are high in vitamins A and C, while tomatoes pack vitamin C and the antioxidant lycopene. Mushrooms, artichokes, asparagus, green peas, and green beans are a few popular vegetables that also contain a dose of protein.

Although almost all vegetables are 0 SmartPoints on the WW Freestyle program, there are a few exceptions: Avocados, potatoes, sweet potatoes, and parsnips all contain a modest amount of SmartPoints; consult your program materials or the online app for specific information on these.

FUN FACT

A number of produce items we think of culinarily as vegetables are actually fruits, including tomatoes, eggplants, avocados, bell peppers, and cucumbers.

Buying & storing

Purchasing vegetables at their freshest pays off in taste and nutrition. Many nutrients begin to break down soon after harvest, and flavors and textures can also change rapidly. When possible, keep in mind what's local and in season so you can maximize freshness when you're meal planning.

Here's advice for getting the most out of vegetable shopping so you can get the best flavor and value from your produce and bring meals to the table quickly:

- Stocking a mix of perishable vegetables like asparagus, lettuce, and tomatoes as well as long-keeping vegetables like carrots, cabbage, and potatoes is ideal for ensuring you always have something fresh on hand.

- A trip to your area farmers' market will give you an overview of what's local and in season. Most of the veggies will have been harvested only a day or two earlier, offering peak freshness and nutrition.

- Look into a farm-to-door subscription like a CSA (community-supported agriculture) or "farm share" to get a load of fresh produce on a weekly or monthly schedule. These group-buying programs reserve an assortment of local seasonal produce that you pick up at a neighborhood delivery point.

- Most vegetables keep best when wrapped loosely in plastic and refrigerated. If your fridge has one, use your crisper drawer—it controls temperature and moisture to keep your veggies fresher longer.

- A few vegetables store well in a cool place rather than in the refrigerator: potatoes, sweet potatoes, tomatoes, onions, shallots, avocados, and pumpkins and winter squash are among them.

- Supplement vegetables in season with frozen ones to make sure you always have variety.

No-recipe vegetable dishes

Anything slaw

Shred just about any mix of firm vegetables on a box grater or with the shredding disk of a food processor: carrots, cabbage, beets, broccoli stems, jicama, zucchini, winter squash—go wild, but taste the shredded vegetable first to make sure you like the flavor! Add finely diced apple for sweetness and an accent or two like sliced scallions, chopped herbs, or finely diced onion or shallot. Dress the mix with vinegar, salt, and pepper.

Make-ahead crudité

Prepare an assortment of veggie dippers to keep on hand: favorites like carrots, celery, and sweet bell pepper sticks; crunchy trimmed green beans, sugar snap peas, and snow peas; broccoli, cauliflower, or Romanesco florets; and Belgian endive leaves. Wrap them in barely moist paper towels and seal in zip-close plastic bags and they'll keep totally fresh for several days. Snack on them plain or pair them with a no-count or low-count dip like spiced-up Greek yogurt or hummus.

Asparagus breakfast plate

Lay freshly steamed asparagus spears (large or jumbo spears are best) on a plate and sprinkle generously with lemon juice and fresh parsley or chives. Top with a poached or soft-cooked egg and sprinkle with salt and pepper.

Chopped salad bowl with feta

Place chopped romaine in the bottom of a bowl and top with diced cucumber, tomato, red onion, bell pepper, and chopped parsley or oregano. Dress with a drizzle of extra-virgin olive oil (1 teaspoon has a SmartPoints value of 1), red-wine vinegar, and salt and pepper. Sprinkle crumbled feta over the top (2 tablespoons have a SmartPoints value of 2).

Steamed vegetables with tahini sauce

Steam some of your favorite vegetables and arrange them with some freshly poached or boiled and peeled eggs in bowls or on a platter. Whisk ¼ cup tahini paste with 1 tablespoon lemon juice, 1 tablespoon water, 1 small garlic clove, and salt and cayenne pepper to taste together and serve alongside vegetables (each tablespoon of sauce has a SmartPoints value of 2).

FUN FACT

Artichoke hearts, Brussels sprouts, asparagus, and beets are surprisingly delicious raw; shave them thinly and dress them with a generous amount of an acidic ingredient like citrus juice or vinegar for best taste and mouthfeel.

Fruits

Just the variety and beauty of fruit could make us swoon. Add in their enticing sweetness, and we understand why fruits are some of the world's most celebrated foods. It's easy to gauge the seasons by the changing fruits that flood our markets: strawberries in spring, cherries and peaches in summer, apples in fall, and juicy citrus through the winter months. Most of us are so fond of fruit that we need little coaxing to eat it daily. But knowing that it's a zero Points food is reason to reach for it a little more often.

Nutrition

Fruits are packed with a range of nutrients, and many like blueberries, cherries, and watermelon are so full of great stuff that they're considered "superfoods," foods that are particularly beneficial to health. The nutritional profiles of fruits vary greatly, but most are high in fiber, vitamins, minerals, and antioxidants.

Although all fresh fruits are zero Points, there is one technical exception: avocadoes. While they're treated culinarily as a vegetable, they're botanically a fruit and contain a modest amount of SmartPoints. And remember that dried fruits or fruits processed with added sugar are not zero Points foods. Consult your program materials or the online app for specific information on these.

FUN FACT

Ever accidentally eat one of those small stickers affixed to grocery store fruits? Don't worry; the stickers are made from food-grade "edible paper"— even the glue is edible.

Buying & storing

Common sense is your best guide when buying fruit: Look for pieces with smooth, plump skins without wrinkles or signs of bruising or decay. Most fruits should smell, well, fruity, not sour or musty, although some varieties may have little aroma. Ripeness is vitally important in fruits, and that's where it can get tricky. Some fruits continue to ripen after harvest, while others don't. Here are a few general guidelines:

- Apricots, bananas, melons, kiwifruit, mangoes, nectarines, papaya, peaches, pears, pineapples, and plums will continue to ripen after picking, so you can buy these ahead and leave them on the counter until they reach peak.

- Fruits such as berries, cherries, citrus, figs, grapes, and pomegranates will not ripen after picking, so it's important to make sure you buy them in good shape and eat them fairly quickly. Apples ripen a bit after picking, but generally you'll want apples that are completely tree-ripened for best flavor.

- How to consistently get the tastiest, freshest fruit? Buy fruits locally in season for best flavor and nutrition. Farmers' markets will often have fruit harvested just that morning or the day before. Also look into subscribing to a CSA (community-supported agriculture) program to get a regular delivery of local produce. These group-buying services deliver boxes of peak-season fruits and veggies to a central point where you can pick them up.

- Most fruit stores well at room temperature, although a few perishable fruits like berries, cherries, and grapes should be refrigerated loosely wrapped. Always refrigerate cut fruit.

- Citrus fruits, apples, and pears will keep longer if refrigerated; store them in the crisper drawer and they'll stay fairly fresh for weeks.

- Got a glut of fresh fruit? Most will freeze well. Peel and cut up fruits like mangoes, papaya, kiwifruit, peaches, and bananas; small berries can be frozen whole, as can stemmed grapes.

No-recipe fruit dishes

Crunchy grape turkey salad

Toss grapes, diced cooked skinless boneless turkey breast, chopped celery, and halved seedless grapes with plain fat-free Greek yogurt, chopped fresh tarragon, and salt and pepper to taste. Mound on lettuce or radicchio leaves.

Berry, corn, and crab salad

Combine raspberries, blueberries, or sliced strawberries with sweet corn kernels (cooked or raw) and picked-over lump crabmeat. Toss gently with fat-free balsamic vinaigrette (2 tablespoons has a SmartPoints value of 1), and sprinkle with sliced fresh basil leaves and freshly ground black pepper.

Fruit salsa

Dice just about any fruit (mangoes, papaya, peaches, and pineapples are good choices). Toss the fruit with chopped cilantro, finely diced jalapeño, finely chopped red onion, a drizzle of lime juice, and a sprinkle of salt. Serve over grilled meat, poultry, or chops; in tacos; or with shrimp cocktail.

Spice-roasted pears

Peel, halve, and core pears. Sprinkle with lemon juice, cinnamon, a little ground allspice, and a few grains of flaky sea salt. Place on a parchment-lined sheet pan and roast in an oven at 450°F until browned and tender, 15 to 20 minutes. Transfer to plates and top with plain fat-free Greek yogurt.

Grilled pineapple

Peel pineapple and cut into slices, about 1-inch thick. Remove the central core with a small round cutter so you have nice rings. Brush rings with melted butter (calculate 1 SmartPoints value per teaspoon) and sprinkle with cinnamon, a little nutmeg, and a few pinches of sea salt. Grill over medium heat, turning rings once, until soft and browned, about 3 minutes per side.

Fruit kebabs

Thread an assortment of fruits on bamboo skewers, alternating colors: Strawberries, pineapple cubes, melon balls, grapes, and chunks of kiwifruit are all good choices. Serve plain or with a sweet dip or yogurt-based dip, if you like (remember to calculate SmartPoints for the dip as necessary).

Fruit vinegar

Mash some berries, pear slices, red or black currants, figs, or other fruit in a bowl and transfer to a glass jar. Add a sprig or two of herbs like rosemary or thyme and pour in champagne vinegar or white-wine vinegar. Cover the bottle and shake. Refrigerate at least 8 hours or up to a week for a sweet, fruity vinegar for salads, sauces, or drinks.

FUN FACT

The jackfruit is one of the world's largest fruits, growing up to 2 feet long and weighing as much as 40 pounds. The flesh of the fruit is newly popular as a vegan meat substitute for dishes like curried jackfruit, jackfruit teriyaki, and pulled jackfruit.

cense
Sauvignon
Blanc

Salmon pasta
salad with
sugar snaps and
dill, page 40

Get to know Cense wines

What pours best with good food and good friends? For many of us it's a great glass of wine. That's why WW has partnered with Cense wines to craft high-quality offerings that delight the palate while being particularly SmartPoints value–friendly. A special process removes some of the alcohol created during fermentation, making the wines lower in carbohydrates and calories without compromising taste. A 5-ounce pour of either Cense Sauvignon Blanc or Rosé is just 3 SmartPoints values, with only 85 calories and 3 grams of carbohydrates. You can find out more and order wines at www.censewines.com.

Wine pairings for comfort food

Which wines go best with which dishes? Following your own taste and inclination is always the best bet, but to start you off we matched the Cense offerings to some of the most wine-friendly recipes in this book.

Sauvignon Blanc

Cense New Zealand Sauvignon Blanc is fresh and bright, with aromas of lemon and lime, crisp acidity, and juicy grapefruit flavors. Try it with:

- "Umami bomb" stuffed mushrooms, page 231
- Figs with honey and goat cheese, page 237
- Bouillabaisse, page 89
- Cauliflower-crust pizza with feta, peppers, and olives, page 110
- Cioppino, page 91
- Cobb salad with smoked chicken, page 36
- Fish tacos with mango salsa, page 73
- Flash-cooked peppered tuna with Mediterranean salad, page 199
- Haddock-and-potato stew with saffron, page 176
- Mussels with leeks and white wine, page 180
- Salmon pasta salad with sugar snaps and dill, page 40
- Saturday night chicken and pasta, page 111
- Shrimp burgers with jalapeño tartar sauce, page 65
- Shrimp scampi "zoodles" with garlic crumbs, page 133
- Vegetable pad thai, page 131

Rosé

Cense California Rosé exudes floral aromas followed by flavors of strawberry and cherry, and it finishes crisp and elegant. It's versatile enough to be enjoyed year-round. Try it with:

- Crispy jalapeño poppers, page 229
- Hot spinach-artichoke dip, page 228
- Blueberry-corn salad with spicy lobster, page 43
- Coconut-curry salmon stir-fry, page 196
- Crunchy pan-fried fish fillets, page 201
- Farfalle with sausage, broccoli rabe, and white beans, page 113
- Food truck souvlaki salad, page 30
- Garlic-herb roasted pork loin with pears, page 148
- Maryland-style crab salad, page 44
- Ramen noodle soup with jammy eggs, page 94
- Sweet-and-smoky Sunday chicken, page 143
- Thai coconut soup with shrimp, page 92
- Turkey mole, page 165
- Vietnamese beef and broccoli with jasmine rice, page 195
- Vietnamese beef pho, page 84
- Warm udon salad with spicy pork, page 127

And look for Cense Sparkling Wine

The brand new Cense California Sparkling Wine is due out for the 2018 holiday season. It's made in the *méthode traditionnelle* style, requiring a secondary fermentation in the bottle to create fantastic bubbles. This graceful, balanced wine has floral and fruity notes, making it excellent for cocktail hour as well as with celebratory meals and desserts.

Sunday morning
fruit-and-
cinnamon bread
pudding, page 20

Better breakfasts

In this chapter

🥕 Vegetarian   🌱 Vegan   🌾 Gluten free   🥛 Dairy free   🥜 Nut free

Bacon-and-Swiss quiche with phyllo crust

Serves 8

Lining the pan with phyllo leaves rather than a bottom crust makes this quiche particularly low in SmartPoints.

2 **sheets phyllo, each cut into 3 strips**

4 **large eggs**

1 **cup evaporated fat-free milk**

½ **teaspoon salt**

¼ **teaspoon black pepper**

¼ **teaspoon ground nutmeg**

Pinch cayenne

½ **cup shredded reduced-fat Swiss cheese**

4 **ounces turkey bacon, crisp cooked and crumbled**

1 Preheat oven to 350°F. Spray 9-inch pie plate with nonstick spray.

2 Lay phyllo in pie plate, one piece at a time, spraying each layer with nonstick spray (dough should cover bottom and sides of plate in overlapping layers). Fold in any overhanging corners.

3 Whisk together eggs, milk, salt, pepper, nutmeg, and cayenne in small bowl.

4 Sprinkle Swiss cheese and bacon over phyllo. Pour in egg mixture and place on rimmed baking sheet. Bake until firm, 30–35 minutes. Cool at least 5 minutes before cutting into 8 wedges.

3 **SmartPoints value per serving** (1 wedge): 140 Cal, 7 g Total Fat, 2 g Sat Fat, 533 mg Sod, 7 g Total Carb, 5 g Sugar, 0 g Fib, 12 g Prot.

Note from Chef Eric

At the core I'm a breakfast guy, and when I trained in France and longed for a comfort food breakfast, I would turn to quiche. This recipe captures the essence of that French egg staple, but in a balanced way.

Egg-and-prosciutto breakfast bowls with tender greens

Serves 2

2 teaspoons olive oil

8 cherry tomatoes

2 slices (about 1 ounce) prosciutto, cut into thin strips

1 whole garlic clove, peeled and smashed

4 cups (about 4 ounces) very thinly sliced kale leaves (remove tough ribs and stems before slicing)

⅛ teaspoon salt

¼ teaspoon freshly ground black pepper, plus more for serving

2 large eggs

½ avocado, peeled, pitted, and sliced

2 lemon wedges

Flaky sea salt for serving

1 Heat 1 teaspoon oil in large nonstick skillet over medium heat. Add tomatoes and cook, shaking pan occasionally, until beginning to soften, about 4 minutes. Push tomatoes to one side of skillet; add prosciutto to other side. Cook until prosciutto is crisp and tomatoes are very soft, about 3 minutes longer. Remove and set aside.

2 Pour remaining 1 teaspoon oil into skillet and return to medium heat. Add garlic and cook 30 seconds. Stir in kale, salt, pepper, and 1 tablespoon water. Cook, stirring occasionally, until kale is wilted and tender but still bright green, about 4 minutes. Remove garlic. Set kale aside.

3 While kale is cooking, fill small skillet two-thirds full of water and bring to boil over high heat. Reduce heat so water just simmers. Crack each egg separately into cup, then gently slip each egg into water and cook until whites are set and yolk is barely firm, 3–4 minutes. Remove eggs with slotted spoon and drain on paper towel.

4 Reheat prosciutto, tomatoes, and kale if necessary and divide evenly between 2 bowls. Arrange avocado evenly on top and squeeze lemon wedge over each. Place poached egg on each serving and sprinkle with flaky sea salt and more pepper.

6 **SmartPoints value per serving** (1 cup kale and prosciutto mix, ¼ avocado, and 1 egg): 280 Cal, 21 g Total Fat, 5 g Sat Fat, 832 mg Sod, 12 g Total Carb, 3 g Sugar, 7 g Fib, 15 g Prot.

Egg-and-prosciutto breakfast bowls with tender greens

Easy egg chilaquiles with avocado

Serves 2

These quick chilaquiles (eggs scrambled with tortilla strips) are perfect for a cozy breakfast for two, although you can also scale the recipe up or down to suit your household. We suggest using the classic Mexican cheese queso fresco, but you can also substitute crumbled goat cheese for no change in SmartPoints.

2	**(6-inch) corn tortillas, halved and cut into thin strips**
4	**large eggs**
⅛	**teaspoon salt, or to taste**
⅛	**teaspoon black pepper, or to taste**
4	**tablespoons fat-free salsa**
½	**small avocado, pitted, peeled, and thinly sliced**
3	**tablespoons crumbled queso fresco cheese**
2	**tablespoons torn or chopped fresh cilantro**

1 Spray medium skillet with nonstick spray. Add tortilla strips and cook over medium-high heat, tossing and stirring, until edges of tortillas begin to brown. Transfer to plate.

2 Beat eggs, salt, and pepper in medium bowl. Spray skillet again with nonstick spray and set over medium heat. Pour eggs into skillet and cook until they begin to set, about 2 minutes, pushing eggs toward center of skillet to form large, soft curds. Add tortilla strips and continue cooking until eggs are just set, about 2 minutes longer.

3 Divide egg mixture evenly between 2 plates; top each with 2 tablespoons salsa, half of avocado, and 1½ tablespoons queso fresco. Sprinkle with cilantro.

 SmartPoints value per serving (1 plate): 300 Cal, 18 g Total Fat, 5 g Sat Fat, 531 mg Sod, 18 g Total Carb, 2 g Sugar, 4 g Fib, 17 g Prot.

Freestyle it

Want to try scrambled tofu chilaquiles? Just substitute 1 cup drained silken tofu for the eggs and cook, breaking up chunks with your spatula, until heated through, about 6 minutes. You can add a pinch of turmeric for yellow color if you like. The SmartPoints total for the recipe will remain the same.

Curried breakfast oats with salmon and soft-cooked eggs

Serves 2

This savory oat dish takes inspiration from kedgeree, the spiced fish-and-rice breakfast that traveled to Britain via colonial India. We use smoked salmon to give it more Stateside breakfast appeal, but you could also use smoked trout, mackerel, or whitefish—all are zero Points foods on the WW Freestyle program.

2	large eggs
⅔	cup uncooked old-fashioned oats
½	cup light (low-fat) coconut milk
1¼	cups water
½	teaspoon curry powder
¼	teaspoon salt
1	teaspoon canola oil
1	large shallot, sliced
2	ounces thin-sliced smoked salmon
2	teaspoons finely chopped fresh mint or parsley

1 Put eggs in medium saucepan and cover by ½ inch with water; bring to boil. Cover pan, remove from heat, and let sit for 7 minutes; drain and cool in cold water. Crack shells against side of pan and peel eggs.

2 Meanwhile, put oats in medium saucepan with coconut milk, water, curry powder, and salt. Bring to simmer over high heat; adjust heat and simmer until thick and soft, about 4 minutes, stirring often. Keep warm if necessary.

3 While oats and eggs are cooking, heat oil in medium nonstick skillet over medium heat. Add shallot and cook, stirring, until soft and golden, about 4 minutes. Push shallot to one side of skillet, remove skillet from heat, and lay salmon on the other side of skillet. Let salmon sit just until warmed, about 1 minute, turning once.

4 Halve eggs. Spoon spiced oats evenly onto 2 plates and top each evenly with salmon, shallot, eggs, and parsley.

6 **SmartPoints value per serving** (1 plate): 279 Cal, 14 g Total Fat, 6 g Sat Fat, 936 mg Sod, 23 g Total Carb, 2 g Sugar, 3 g Fib, 15 g Prot.

Note from Chef Eric
A great way to change how you eat is to find inspiration from other cultures. This Indian-influenced dish is a shift from the standard Western breakfast in a spicy, flavorful way. To make it even more authentic, try adding golden raisins (2 SmartPoints value per tablespoon) for welcome bursts of sweetness.

Lox, eggs,
and onions

Lox, eggs, and onions

Serves 6

1   **tablespoon whipped butter**

½   **large red onion, thinly sliced**

12 **large eggs, beaten**

⅛   **teaspoon salt**

¼   **teaspoon pepper**

¼   **pound chopped lox or smoked salmon**

2   **scallions, finely chopped**

Melt butter in large nonstick skillet over medium-low heat. Add onion and cook, stirring frequently, until translucent, about 7 minutes. Pour in eggs and add salt and pepper; cook, stirring occasionally, until soft curds form. Add salmon and stir well with wooden spoon or spatula. Reduce heat to low and cook until eggs are set. Transfer to serving bowl and sprinkle with scallion.

SmartPoints value per serving (½ cup): 184 Cal, 12 g Total Fat, 4 g Sat Fat, 579 mg Sod, 2 g Total Carb, 1 g Sugar, 0 g Fib, 16 g Prot.

Note from Chef Eric

Comfort food is meant to remind you of family and childhood, and this one does it for me. It's also a great low-SmartPoints way to enjoy lox (brined salmon) without the bagel and cream cheese. Choose some regular or gluten-free bagel chips to eat along with the eggs instead—½ ounce of fat-free bagel chips has 2 SmartPoints.

Red flannel hash with sunnyside-up eggs

Serves 4

Beets give this tasty potato hash a rosy hue New Englanders liken to red flannel. Our recipe calls for diced cooked potatoes, a great way to use leftovers, but definitely reach for a package of frozen potatoes if you prefer.

3	**teaspoons canola oil**
2	**cups finely chopped red cabbage**
1	**pound diced boiled potatoes or 1 (16-ounce) package thawed diced frozen potatoes**
1½	**cups packaged precooked beets, diced**
1	**small sweet onion, diced**
1	**teaspoon salt**
¼	**teaspoon black pepper**
¼	**cup chopped fresh parsley**
4	**large eggs**
2	**tablespoons snipped fresh chives**

1 To make hash, heat 2 teaspoons oil in large nonstick skillet over medium heat. Add cabbage and cook, stirring frequently, until wilted, about 5 minutes. Stir in potatoes, beets, onion, ¾ teaspoon salt, and pepper. Cook, stirring, until onion is tender, about 5 minutes. Stir in parsley. Transfer to plate and keep warm.

2 Wipe out skillet. Heat remaining 1 teaspoon oil in skillet over medium heat. Crack eggs into skillet. Sprinkle with remaining ¼ teaspoon salt. Cover skillet and cook until whites are set and yolks are how you like them, 3–4 minutes.

3 Divide hash evenly among 4 plates. Top each with an egg and sprinkle evenly with chives.

4   **SmartPoints value per serving** (1 plate): 242 Cal, 9 g Total Fat, 2 g Sat Fat, 795 mg Sod, 33 g Total Carb, 7 g Sugar, 5 g Fib, 10 g Prot.

Note from Chef Eric

My sons love to eat beets simply because of their bright, cheerful color. Here's a healthy, hearty way to start your day with brilliant beets.

**Red flannel hash with
sunnyside-up eggs**

**Egg-and-veggie
mini-casseroles**

Egg-and-veggie mini-casseroles

Serves 4

One-serving casseroles make a great go-to breakfast or an easy brunch dish for company: Dress them up with chopped fresh herbs like parsley, basil, or chives sprinkled on top and serve them alongside a colorful fruit salad.

4	slices whole wheat bread
½	teaspoon canola oil
½	cup diced red onion
½	cup diced red bell pepper
½	cup diced zucchini
½	teaspoon salt
4	large eggs
4	large egg whites
¼	teaspoon black pepper
½	cup reduced-fat Mexican cheese blend

1 Preheat oven to 400°F. Lightly coat 4 (8-ounce) ramekins or oven-safe bakers with nonstick spray. Cut 4-inch circle from each slice of bread and firmly press 1 into bottom of each ramekin; set aside. Discard scraps or save for another use.

2 Heat oil in medium skillet over medium-high heat. Add onion, bell pepper, zucchini, and ¼ teaspoon salt; cook, stirring occasionally, until vegetables soften and onion is translucent, 3–5 minutes. Remove from heat and set aside.

3 In medium bowl, whisk eggs, egg whites, remaining ¼ teaspoon salt, and the black pepper together until frothy; stir in cooked vegetables and ¼ cup cheese blend. Divide mixture evenly among ramekins. Sprinkle each with 1 tablespoon remaining cheese.

4 Place ramekins on small baking sheet and bake until knife inserted into center of each casserole comes out clean, about 20 minutes. Remove from oven and cool 5–10 minutes before serving.

3 **SmartPoints value per serving** (1 casserole): 192 Cal, 8 g Total Fat, 3 g Sat Fat, 578 mg Sod, 13 g Total Carb, 3 g Sugar, 2 g Fib, 16 g Prot.

Note from Chef Eric
These mini-casseroles are convenient to make ahead and refrigerate—perfect for a healthy breakfast on the run.

Spinach-garlic grits with poached eggs

Serves 4

2½ cups water
¼ teaspoon salt
½ cup quick-cooking grits
2 teaspoons olive oil
2 garlic cloves, minced
3 cups coarsely chopped fresh spinach
¾ cup fresh or frozen corn kernels, thawed
2 tablespoons fat-free cream cheese
2 tablespoons plain nonfat Greek yogurt
⅛ teaspoon black pepper
2 teaspoons cider vinegar
4 large eggs

1 Combine water and salt in large saucepan; bring to boil over medium-high heat. Slowly pour in grits in thin, steady stream, stirring constantly. Reduce heat and cook, covered, stirring often, until grits are softened and creamy, about 15 minutes.

2 Meanwhile, heat oil in large nonstick skillet over medium heat. Add garlic; cook, stirring constantly, until fragrant, 30 seconds. Add spinach and corn and cook, stirring frequently, until spinach is wilted, 1–2 minutes.

3 Add spinach mixture, cream cheese, yogurt, and pepper to grits; stir until well blended. Cover and keep warm.

4 Fill another large skillet halfway with water and bring to boil over high heat. Add vinegar and reduce heat until water is simmering. Crack each egg separately into cup, then gently slip each egg into water and cook until whites are set and yolk is barely firm, 3–4 minutes. Remove eggs with slotted spoon and drain on paper towels.

5 Divide grits mixture evenly among 4 shallow serving bowls. Using slotted spoon, top each serving with a poached egg. Sprinkle with more salt and pepper, if desired, and serve at once.

 SmartPoints value per serving (¾ cup grits and 1 egg): 210 Cal, 8 g Total Fat, 2 g Sat Fat, 298 mg Sod, 24 g Total Carb, 2 g Sugar, 2 g Fib, 11 g Prot.

Note from Chef Eric

I love using nonfat Greek yogurt to "cream out" my grits. It's a great low-SmartPoints way to get a creamy result with just a bit of cheese, and the acidity balances the richness of the egg.

**Spinach-garlic grits
with poached eggs**

Strawberry-lemon pancakes

Strawberry-lemon pancakes

Serves 8

These brightly flavored pancakes are a perfect reason to sit down to breakfast. If strawberries aren't in season, you can use frozen thawed unsweetened berries or another seasonal fruit, like diced mango or diced peaches.

1½ **cups whole wheat flour**

1 **teaspoon baking powder**

½ **teaspoon baking soda**

½ **teaspoon salt**

3 **large eggs**

¾ **cup low-fat (1%) milk**

⅔ **cup fat-free Greek yogurt**

3 **tablespoons honey**

2 **tablespoons + 2 teaspoons canola oil**

½ **teaspoon vanilla extract**

1½ **teaspoons grated lemon zest, plus additional for garnish**

2 **cups finely chopped fresh strawberries, plus additional for garnish**

1 Whisk together flour, baking powder, baking soda, and salt in large bowl.

2 Whisk together eggs, milk, yogurt, honey, 2 tablespoons oil, vanilla, and 1½ teaspoons lemon zest in medium bowl. Add egg mixture to flour mixture and stir just until blended. Fold in 2 cups chopped strawberries.

3 Heat 1 teaspoon oil in nonstick griddle or large nonstick skillet over medium heat. Pour batter by ¼ cupfuls onto griddle and cook just until bubbles begin to appear at edges of pancakes, about 3 minutes. Turn and cook about 2 minutes longer. Repeat with remaining oil and batter to make 16 pancakes. Serve pancakes topped with strawberries and grated lemon zest.

6 **SmartPoints value per serving** (2 pancakes): 204 Cal, 7 g Total Fat, 1 g Sat Fat, 332 mg Sod, 30 g Total Carb, 11 g Sugar, 3 g Fib, 7 g Prot.

Note from Chef Eric

I love a bright, fluffy ricotta pancake, and using plain nonfat Greek yogurt to replace the cheese here adds acidity and creaminess for 0 SmartPoints. Top pancakes with maple syrup or honey; each has 1 SmartPoints value per teaspoon.

Multigrain waffles with maple-berry sauce

Serves 8

⅓   **cup old-fashioned oats**

⅓   **cup all-purpose flour**

⅓   **cup whole wheat flour**

⅓   **cup yellow cornmeal**

1   **teaspoon baking powder**

½   **teaspoon baking soda**

¼   **teaspoon salt**

1   **small very ripe banana, mashed**

1   **large egg**

¾   **cup low-fat (1%) milk**

½   **cup plain low-fat yogurt**

2   **teaspoons canola oil**

½   **teaspoon vanilla extract**

3   **large egg whites**

1   **(1-pound container) fresh strawberries, hulled**

1   **tablespoon maple syrup**

1   **pint fresh blueberries or blackberries**

½   **teaspoon grated lemon zest**

1 Preheat waffle maker according to manufacturer's directions.

2 Put oats in food processor and process until finely ground. Whisk together ground oats, all-purpose flour, whole wheat flour, cornmeal, baking powder, baking soda, and salt in large bowl.

3 Whisk together banana, egg, milk, yogurt, oil, and vanilla in medium bowl. Add banana mixture to flour mixture, stirring just until blended.

4 With electric mixer on high speed, beat egg whites in another medium bowl until stiff peaks form when beaters are lifted. With rubber spatula, gently fold beaten egg whites, one third at a time, into batter, stirring just until blended.

5 When waffle maker is ready, spray with nonstick spray. Pour batter for 1 waffle onto center and quickly spread to within 1 inch of edges. Close waffle maker and bake as manufacturer directs. Repeat, reheating and spraying waffle maker with nonstick spray, to make 8 waffles.

6 Meanwhile, to make sauce, place 1 cup strawberries in large bowl. Add maple syrup and crush berries with potato masher or fork. Slice remaining strawberries and add to bowl. Stir in blueberries and lemon zest. To serve, top each waffle with about ½ cup berry sauce. (Sauce can be stored refrigerated in airtight container overnight; freeze leftovers in a zip-close plastic freezer bag.)

(4)   **SmartPoints value per serving** (1 waffle and ½ cup sauce): 172 Cal, 3 g Total Fat, 1 g Sat Fat, 264 mg Sod, 31 g Total Carb, 12 g Sugar, 4 g Fib, 7 g Prot.

Note from Chef Eric

Adding maple syrup to this berry sauce is a great way to "stretch" a small amount of sweetener. The maple flavor is pronounced, so you don't need too much, and the berries help carry the flavor along to every bite.

Creamy banana
French toast casserole

Serves 12

Adding just a little lemon juice not only keeps the bananas from turning dark but also adds bright flavor to this creamy casserole. Use the rum if you'd like a hint of bananas Foster in your French toast.

12 **slices whole wheat or oatmeal bread, cut into quarters**

1 **cup reduced-fat (2%) milk**

½ **cup maple syrup**

6 **large eggs**

4 **ounces Neufchâtel (light cream cheese), softened**

4 **ripe bananas**

1 **tablespoon rum (optional)**

2 **teaspoons lemon juice**

1 **teaspoon vanilla extract**

½ **teaspoon ground nutmeg**

½ **teaspoon cinnamon**

¼ **teaspoon salt**

3 **tablespoons confectioners' sugar**

1 Spray 9x13-inch baking dish with nonstick spray.

2 Overlap bread in prepared dish so it lines sides and bottom in single layer.

3 Combine milk, maple syrup, eggs, Neufchâtel, 2 bananas, rum (if using), lemon juice, vanilla, nutmeg, cinnamon, and salt in blender; process until smooth. Slowly pour mixture over bread; gently press down on bread to make sure bread is completely submerged. Cover dish with foil; refrigerate for at least 30 minutes or up to overnight.

4 Preheat oven to 350°F. Thinly slice remaining 2 bananas; tuck in between pieces of bread. Cover dish with foil and bake 25 minutes. Remove foil and bake until casserole is golden brown and knife inserted into center comes out clean, about 10 minutes longer. Dust with confectioners' sugar and cut into 12 portions.

6 · **SmartPoints value per serving** (¹⁄₁₂ of casserole): 234 Cal, 6 g Total Fat, 3 g Sat Fat, 273 mg Sod, 35 g Total Carb, 18 g Sugar, 3 g Fib, 9 g Prot.

Note from Chef Eric
A serving of this decadent casserole is ideal to grab for a quick and satisfying breakfast. I also love it as a dessert.

Sunday morning fruit-and-cinnamon bread pudding

Serves 6

(icons)

Talk about comfort: A delicious not-too-sweet bread pudding loaded with fruit as a luxurious breakfast. If fresh summer fruits are not available, use thawed, unsweetened frozen fruit instead. Top the pudding with 1 teaspoon powdered sugar just before serving for no change in SmartPoints.

½   **cup dried apricots, diced**

2   **tablespoons orange juice**

6   **(½-inch-thick) slices white sandwich bread (about 7 ounces total), crusts removed**

3   **large eggs**

2¾   **cups reduced-fat (2%) milk**

1¼   **teaspoons cinnamon**

1¼   **teaspoons vanilla extract**

1½   **tablespoons turbinado sugar or granulated sugar**

1   **teaspoon finely grated orange zest**

2   **nectarines or peaches, halved, pitted, and thinly sliced**

1½   **cups mixed berries**

1   Put apricots and orange juice in small bowl and let soak. Meanwhile, spray 4- to 6-cup gratin dish or baking dish with nonstick spray. Cut each bread slice into 4 triangles. Lay bread in dish, overlapping pieces to cover dish evenly.

2   In medium bowl, whisk eggs until frothy. Whisk in milk, cinnamon, vanilla, sugar, and orange zest. Scatter apricots over bread in dish. Pour egg mixture over bread so each piece is coated. Let soak for 15–20 minutes.

3   Meanwhile preheat oven to 350°F. Bake pudding until top is crisp and browned and egg mixture puffs and is set, 40–45 minutes. Remove and let pudding sit for 5 minutes, then top with one half of the nectarines and berries; serve remaining fruit on side. Best eaten warm and freshly baked!

7   **SmartPoints value per serving** (1 cup pudding and about ½ cup fruit): 246 Cal, 6 g Total Fat, 2 g Sat Fat, 262 mg Sod, 40 g Total Carb, 23 g Sugar, 4 g Fib, 10 g Prot.

Note from Chef Eric

The spice in this bread pudding is a terrific way to liven up a healthy breakfast. You can experiment with nutmeg, ground ginger, clove, and allspice, too.

Sunday morning
fruit-and-cinnamon
bread pudding

Creamy quinoa and
apple breakfast cereal

Creamy quinoa and apple breakfast cereal

Serves 6

Quinoa has become a breakfast-bowl favorite, and for good reason: This flavorful whole grain is rich in fiber and protein and cooks in just 20 minutes. Here it's prepared for big-time comfort with caramelized apples, brown sugar, and butter.

1   **cup quinoa**

1   **tablespoon salted butter**

2   **apples, cored and chopped**

2   **cups water**

½   **cup fat-free milk**

3   **tablespoons packed brown sugar**

½   **teaspoon cinnamon**

1 Rinse quinoa well under cold running water. Set aside.

2 Coat large skillet with nonstick spray; set over medium heat. When skillet is hot, add ½ tablespoon butter and cook until melted and beginning to sizzle. Add apples and cook, turning occasionally, until apples are soft and begin to caramelize, 5–10 minutes depending on variety; set aside.

3 Add quinoa and water to medium saucepan and bring to boil over medium-high heat; boil 1 minute. Reduce heat to low, cover tightly, and simmer for 20 minutes. When quinoa is cooked (a white spiral will appear on each grain), remove from heat and fluff with fork. Add remaining ½ tablespoon butter, the milk, brown sugar, and cinnamon; stir to combine and fold in apples. Divide among 6 bowls.

 6 **SmartPoints value per serving** (about ⅔ cup): 186 Cal, 4 g Total Fat, 1 g Sat Fat, 30 mg Sod, 34 g Total Carb, 14 g Sugar, 4 g Fib, 5 g Prot.

Note from Chef Eric

Explore your color options for this easy breakfast by using red quinoa, or mix it up with different apples: Tart, glossy green Granny Smith or sweet Red Delicious varietes will give you different looks, flavors, and textures.

Triple-grain cereal with fruit and brown sugar

Serves 4

Tiny flaxseeds are powerfully good. They're loaded with omega-3 fatty acids, antioxidant-rich lignans, and a healthful dose of fiber—both soluble and insoluble. Keep in mind that flaxseeds need to be ground to work their magic.

3½ **cups fat-free milk**

¼ **teaspoon salt**

½ **cup quick-cooking barley**

½ **cup bulgur**

½ **cup old-fashioned oats**

2 **tablespoons flaxseed meal**

¼ **teaspoon cinnamon**

1 **large peach, cut into 12 wedges**

1 **cup fresh raspberries or blueberries**

4 **teaspoons packed light brown sugar**

1 Combine milk and salt in medium saucepan and cook over medium-high heat until bubbles form around edge of pan. Stir in barley, bulgur, and oats. Reduce heat and simmer, stirring frequently, until milk is absorbed and grains are tender but still chewy, about 10 minutes.

2 Remove saucepan from heat; stir in flaxseed meal and cinnamon. Divide cereal evenly among 4 bowls. Top each serving with 3 peach wedges, ¼ cup raspberries, and 1 teaspoon brown sugar.

8 **SmartPoints value per serving** (1 bowl): 260 Cal, 3 g Total Fat, 0 g Sat Fat, 240 mg Sod, 50 g Total Carb, 20 g Sugar, 8 g Fib, 13 g Prot.

Note from Chef Eric

I love folding soft poached eggs into oatmeal and other warm breakfast cereals like this. The dish becomes luxuriously creamy and even more satisfying for no additional SmartPoints.

Breakfast parfaits with chia seeds

Serves 4

(icons)

These easy parfaits get a kick from chia seeds, loaded with protein and fiber. They're great for no-cook puddings like this one, or try them sprinkled over yogurt or cereal. Be aware that they develop a thick, viscus quality when soaked, somewhat like the texture of cooked tapioca.

2   **cups plain fat-free Greek yogurt**

2   **tablespoons chia seeds**

1   **cup diced mango or papaya**

1   **cup strawberries, hulled and sliced, plus 4 whole strawberries**

4   **teaspoons maple syrup**

¼   **cup low-fat granola**

1   Stir together yogurt and chia seeds in small bowl. Let stand 5 minutes.

2   Spoon ¼ cup yogurt mixture into each of 4 parfait glasses or wineglasses. Layer each with ¼ cup of the mango, another ¼ cup yogurt mixture, and ¼ cup sliced strawberries. Drizzle each parfait with 1 teaspoon maple syrup, sprinkle each with 1 tablespoon granola, and garnish tops with 1 whole strawberry.

(3)   **SmartPoints value per serving** (1 parfait): 170 Cal, 3 g Total Fat, 0 g Sat Fat, 56 mg Sod, 25 g Total Carb, 17 g Sugar, 4 g Fib, 14 g Prot.

Freestyle it

Want to replace the yogurt in this delicious parfait with a nondairy ingredient? Whirl 16 ounces of silken tofu in a food processor and use it instead of yogurt. Tofu is a zero Points food just like fat-free yogurt, so you don't have to track it.

Cobb salad with
smoked chicken,
page 36

Chapter 2
Main-course salads and veggie bowls

In this chapter

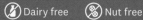

Vegetarian   Vegan   Gluten free   Dairy free   Nut free

Crispy chicken Waldorf salad

Serves 4

This riff on the classic Waldorf salad makes for terrific eating on the WW Freestyle program: Lots of crunchy veggies, sweet apple and grapes, and chicken breast are all zero Points ingredients that come together quickly and deliciously.

CRISPY CHICKEN

- 4   **(3-ounce) thin-sliced chicken cutlets**
- ½   **teaspoon salt**
- ¼   **teaspoon black pepper**
- 1   **large egg, beaten**
- 1½   **teaspoons Dijon mustard**
- ½   **cup panko (Japanese bread crumbs)**
- 2   **teaspoons canola oil**

SALAD

- 2   **tablespoons reduced-fat mayonnaise**
- 1   **tablespoon plain fat-free yogurt**
- 1   **tablespoon red-wine vinegar**
- 1½   **teaspoons Dijon mustard**
- ¼   **teaspoon salt**
- ¼   **teaspoon black pepper**
- 1   **Granny Smith or other tart apple, cored and thinly sliced or diced**
- 1   **cup seedless red grapes, halved**
- 1   **celery stalk, thinly sliced**
- ¼   **small red onion, chopped**
- ¼   **cup walnut halves, chopped**
- 4   **cups baby spinach**

1 To make crispy chicken, sprinkle cutlets with salt and pepper. Whisk egg and mustard in shallow bowl until blended. Spread panko on sheet of wax paper. Dip chicken cutlets, one at a time, into egg mixture. Coat cutlets with panko, pressing lightly so it adheres. Spray evenly with nonstick spray.

2 Heat oil in large nonstick skillet over medium heat. Add cutlets and cook until lightly browned and cooked through, 3–4 minutes per side. Transfer to cutting board.

3 To make salad, whisk together mayonnaise, yogurt, vinegar, mustard, salt, and pepper in large bowl. Add apple, grapes, celery, onion, and walnuts to dressing and toss to combine. Cut chicken into thin strips. Place 1 cup spinach on each of 4 plates and top evenly with salad and chicken strips.

5 **SmartPoints value per serving** (1 plate): 323 Cal, 13 g Total Fat, 2 g Sat Fat, 765 mg Sod, 25 g Total Carb, 12 g Sugar, 3 g Fib, 24 g Prot.

Food truck souvlaki salad

Serves 4

DRESSING

½	**cup plain low-fat Greek yogurt**
½	**cup shredded English (seedless) cucumber**
2	**tablespoons chopped fresh mint**
1	**tablespoon lemon juice**
1	**small garlic clove, minced**
¼	**teaspoon salt**

PORK AND SALAD

¾	**pound lean pork tenderloin, trimmed, cut on diagonal into 1-inch-thick slices and then into strips**
1	**teaspoon dried oregano**
¼	**teaspoon salt**
¼	**teaspoon red pepper flakes**
1	**tablespoon olive oil**
6	**cups lightly packed baby salad greens**
1	**cup chickpeas**
1	**cup halved cherry tomatoes**
¼	**cup diced red onion**
10	**black olives, halved**

Fresh oregano leaves for serving (optional)

1 To make dressing, stir all ingredients together in small bowl until blended; cover and refrigerate.

2 To make pork and salad, spray pork with nonstick spray; sprinkle with oregano, salt, and pepper flakes and toss. Heat oil in large cast-iron or other heavy skillet over medium-high heat. Add pork and cook, without stirring, until pork is browned and just cooked through, about 3 minutes.

3 Toss together salad greens, chickpeas, tomatoes, onion, and ½ cup dressing in large bowl until coated. Put 1½ cups salad onto each of 4 plates or bowls. Top each serving evenly with pork and drizzle each with 2 tablespoons dressing. Sprinkle evenly with olives and fresh oregano (if using).

3 **SmartPoints value per serving** (1 salad): 270 Cal, 9 g Total Fat, 2 g Sat Fat, 576 mg Sod, 23 g Total Carb, 5 g Sugar, 6 g Fib, 27 g Prot.

Note from Chef Eric

If you can find it, try using lean trimmed lamb loin instead of pork in this recipe for no change in the SmartPoints. Lamb has a subtle gaminess that's great in a Greek-influenced salad like this one.

Food truck
souvlaki salad

**Warm turkey
taco salad**

Warm turkey taco salad

Serves 4

1 teaspoon olive oil

¾ pound ground skinless turkey breast

1 small onion, finely chopped

2 garlic cloves, minced

1 tablespoon chili powder

1 teaspoon ground cumin

½ teaspoon salt

1 canned chipotle en adobo, seeded and minced (leave seeds if you want more heat)

1 (14½-ounce) can crushed tomatoes

1½ teaspoons brown sugar

1½ tablespoons lime juice

1 cup cooked white rice, prepared according to package directions if frozen

2 teaspoons chopped fresh cilantro, plus more for garnish

½ teaspoon grated lime zest

16 iceberg lettuce leaves

1 cup chopped fresh tomatoes

¼ cup prepared salsa

2 scallions, thinly sliced

1 Heat oil in large nonstick skillet over medium heat. Add turkey, onion, and garlic. Cook, breaking turkey apart with wooden spoon, until turkey is no longer pink and onion begins to soften, 3–5 minutes. Add chili powder, cumin, salt, chipotle, and canned tomatoes; simmer, stirring occasionally, until turkey is fully cooked and sauce thickens, 8–10 minutes. Stir in brown sugar and 1 tablespoon lime juice; remove from heat.

2 Meanwhile, combine cooked rice, 2 teaspoons cilantro, lime zest, and remaining ½ tablespoon lime juice in small bowl.

3 To serve, make 4 lettuce cups by layering 4 lettuce leaves in each of 4 bowls or on 4 plates and top with ¾ cup turkey mixture, ¼ cup rice, ¼ cup fresh tomatoes, and 1 tablespoon salsa; garnish with scallions and cilantro.

5 **SmartPoints value per serving** (1 salad): 256 Cal, 9 g Total Fat, 2 g Sat Fat, 704 mg Sod, 25 g Total Carb, 8 g Sugar, 5 g Fib, 20 g Prot.

Note from Chef Eric

Instead of serving this salad over the lettuce, you can fold the ingredients inside large leaves to make lettuce wraps. Change it up more by adding sliced radish, red cabbage, or lime wedges as well for 0 SmartPoints.

Turkey club salad with peppercorn dressing

Serves 4

Here's a protein-packed salad based on the flavors and textures of the classic turkey club sandwich. We use a judicious amount of croutons to replace the sandwich's traditional 3 slices of bread, then make smart substitutions for a satisfying bowl that fits easily into a healthy eating plan.

6	slices turkey bacon, cut into ½-inch pieces
½	cup reduced-fat mayonnaise
3	tablespoons half-and-half
1	tablespoon lemon juice
1	teaspoon Dijon mustard
¼	teaspoon cracked black pepper
8	cups lightly packed salad greens
2	cups cubed cooked skinless turkey breast
10	cherry tomatoes, halved
1	cup plain fat-free croutons

1 Cook bacon in nonstick skillet over medium heat until crisp, about 3 minutes. Transfer to paper towels to drain.

2 To make dressing, whisk together mayonnaise, half-and-half, lemon juice, mustard, and pepper in mixing bowl. Add salad greens and toss. Divide among 4 plates or bowls. Top evenly with turkey, tomatoes, and croutons; sprinkle with bacon.

7   **SmartPoints value per serving** (2 cups): 359 Cal, 17 g Total Fat, 4 g Sat Fat, 772 mg Sod, 18 g Total Carb, 3 g Sugar, 3 g Fib, 30 g Prot.

Note from Chef Eric
Cracked pink peppercorns are a fun addition to this dressing. They add crunch, unexpected fruitiness, and a burst of color.

Steak house salad with chipotle-balsamic dressing

Serves 4

Ⓥ Ⓖ Ⓢ

Skirt steak is one of the best lean cuts for slicing: It's rich and flavorful and doesn't require a lot of trimming, and it cooks up browned and juicy in minutes. It stars in this hearty salad along with a sweet-and-smoky dressing and a host of colorful veggies. We like raw, in-season sweet corn in the salad, but you can also use 1 cup frozen, grilled, or boiled corn kernels.

1 **(1-pound) lean boneless skirt steak, trimmed**

¾ **teaspoon salt**

¼ **teaspoon black pepper**

3 **tablespoons balsamic vinegar**

2 **teaspoons minced chipotle en adobo**

1 **shallot, minced**

4 **teaspoons extra-virgin olive oil**

1 **(½-pound) head escarole, chopped**

1 **red bell pepper, diced**

1 **large ear of corn, husk and silk removed and kernels cut off**

4 **radishes, thinly sliced**

1 Prepare outdoor grill for medium-high-heat cooking or place ridged grill pan over medium-high heat.

2 Sprinkle steak with ½ teaspoon salt and black pepper and spray with nonstick spray. Place steak on grill rack or in grill pan and cook until instant-read thermometer inserted into side of steak registers 145°F for medium, 4–5 minutes per side. Transfer to cutting board.

3 To make dressing, whisk together vinegar, chipotle, shallot, oil, and remaining ¼ teaspoon salt in small bowl. Combine escarole, bell pepper, corn, and radishes in mixing bowl; divide mixture among 4 plates or bowls. Cut steak into 16 slices and arrange evenly over greens. Drizzle with one half of dressing; serve remaining dressing on the side.

5 **SmartPoints value per serving** (4 slices steak, 2 cups salad, and 2 tablespoons dressing): 262 Cal, 11 g Total Fat, 3 g Sat Fat, 541 mg Sod, 13 g Total Carb, 5 g Sugar, 4 g Fib, 27 g Prot.

Note from Chef Eric

I love skirt steak! The marbling means it's moist and juicy, and it holds up great to a marinade. For extra savoriness, marinate the steak in soy sauce and balsamic vinegar for up to a day before cooking.

Cobb salad with smoked chicken

Serves 4

The chicken in the classic Cobb salad is usually just plain chicken breast; kind of boring, right? We've given it much more of a starring role in this classic comfort salad by using smoked chicken breast, available at most deli counters.

¼ **cup chicken broth**

2 **tablespoons minced shallot**

4 **teaspoons extra-virgin olive oil**

4 **teaspoons red-wine vinegar**

1 **teaspoon Dijon mustard**

¼ **teaspoon salt**

⅛ **teaspoon freshly ground black pepper**

4 **cups thinly sliced romaine lettuce**

4 **cups lightly packed baby arugula**

1 **pound sliced smoked chicken breast, cut into strips**

1½ **cups grape tomatoes, halved**

4 **hard-cooked eggs, halved**

1 **small avocado, peeled, pitted, and diced**

2 **mini (Persian) cucumbers, chopped**

½ **cup crumbled reduced-fat blue cheese**

1 To make dressing, whisk broth, shallot, oil, vinegar, mustard, salt, and pepper in medium bowl.

2 Place 1 cup each lettuce and arugula in 4 large salad bowls. Drizzle each with 1½ tablespoons dressing. Evenly divide chicken, tomatoes, eggs, avocado, cucumbers, and blue cheese among bowls. Drizzle evenly with remaining dressing.

 5

SmartPoints value per serving (1 bowl with 3 tablespoons dressing): 432 Cal, 22 g Total Fat, 6 g Sat Fat, 578 mg Sod, 10 g Total Carb, 4 g Sugar, 4 g Fib, 48 g Prot.

Note from Chef Eric

I used to think it couldn't be a Cobb salad without bacon, but using smoked chicken here gives me all the smoky goodness of bacon without the SmartPoints. It's a win-win.

Cobb salad with
smoked chicken

BLT salad with green
goddess dressing

BLT salad with green goddess dressing

Serves 4

½ **avocado, pitted and peeled**

¼ **cup reduced-fat mayonnaise**

¼ **cup low-fat buttermilk**

2 **tablespoons lemon juice**

2 **tablespoons chopped fresh parsley**

1 **tablespoon chopped fresh tarragon**

1 **teaspoon anchovy paste**

¼ **teaspoon salt**

1 **small head iceberg lettuce**

2 **heirloom or beefsteak tomatoes, cut into thin wedges**

4 **slices turkey bacon, crisp-cooked and crumbled**

½ **small red onion, finely diced**

1 To make dressing, combine avocado, mayonnaise, buttermilk, lemon juice, parsley, tarragon, anchovy paste, and salt in blender and puree.

2 Core lettuce and cut into 4 equal wedges. Place 1 wedge on each of 4 plates. Top evenly with tomatoes and drizzle with dressing. Sprinkle evenly with bacon and onion.

4 **SmartPoints value per serving** (1 salad with ¼ cup dressing): 143 Cal, 10 g Total Fat, 2 g Sat Fat, 528 mg Sod, 11 g Total Carb, 5 g Sugar, 4 g Fib, 5 g Prot.

Note from Chef Eric

Anchovies are so misunderstood. Part of my WW Freestyle journey has been about maximizing flavor—intense flavors make for delicious, satisfying dishes. The briny, ocean-like savoriness anchovies bring to the dressing for this salad is irreplaceable.

Salmon pasta salad with sugar snaps and dill

Serves 4

This salad is packed with bright flavors from dill, lemon, scallions, and tomatoes. Using poached salmon is ideal, but you can also use water-packed canned salmon in a pinch.

4	**ounces whole wheat rotini**
1	**cup sugar snap peas, strings removed**
1	**pound skinless poached salmon (see page xix), or 1 (14¾-ounce) can water-packed wild salmon, drained**
¼	**cup plain fat-free Greek yogurt**
3	**tablespoons fat-free mayonnaise**
2	**tablespoons chopped fresh dill, plus more for garnish**
1	**teaspoon grated lemon zest**
2	**tablespoons lemon juice**
¼	**teaspoon salt**
¼	**teaspoon black pepper**
1	**cup grape tomatoes, halved**
2	**scallions, thinly sliced**
4	**lemon wedges for serving**

1 Cook pasta according to package directions, adding sugar snap peas during last minute of cooking; drain in colander. Cool under cold running water; drain again.

2 Place salmon in large bowl. Flake with fork and pick out and discard any large pieces of bone or skin. Set aside.

3 Whisk together yogurt, mayonnaise, dill, lemon zest and juice, salt, and pepper in large bowl. Add pasta, sugar snap peas, tomatoes, and scallions; toss to combine. Stir salmon gently into pasta mixture. Divide among 4 plates. Garnish with more dill and serve with lemon wedges.

3 **SmartPoints value per serving** (generous 1½ cups): 377 Cal, 15 g Total Fat, 3 g Sat Fat, 323 mg Sod, 30 g Total Carb, 5 g Sugar, 5 g Fib, 32 g Prot.

Note from Chef Eric

I sometimes poach a large piece of salmon at the beginning of the week and use it as a go-to protein in tons of dishes like this. Toss pea tendrils into this salad to freshen it up even more.

Salmon pasta
salad with sugar
snaps and dill

Kale Caesar salad with grilled shrimp

Serves 4

It seems like kale salads are everywhere, but here's one of the most delicious ones around: curly kale tossed with a zesty anchovy-spiked Caesar dressing and topped with luscious grilled shrimp. We love this with kale, but you can always substitute sliced romaine if your crowd prefers.

1½ pounds large shrimp, peeled and deveined

1 teaspoon grated lemon zest

1 garlic clove, crushed through garlic press

¼ teaspoon salt, or to taste

2 tablespoons plain fat-free Greek yogurt

2 tablespoons low-fat mayonnaise

2 tablespoons lemon juice

2 teaspoons extra-virgin olive oil

2 anchovies, rinsed and well mashed, or 1 teaspoon anchovy paste

½ teaspoon Dijon mustard

⅛ teaspoon black pepper

¼ cup freshly grated Parmesan

1 (¾-pound) bunch curly kale, stems and tough ribs removed and discarded, leaves thinly sliced (about 12 cups)

½ ounce Parmesan shaved with vegetable peeler

1 Toss shrimp, lemon zest, ¼ teaspoon garlic, and ⅛ teaspoon salt in medium bowl; set aside.

2 To make dressing, whisk yogurt, mayonnaise, lemon juice, oil, anchovies, mustard, pepper, remaining garlic, and remaining ⅛ teaspoon salt together in large bowl. Whisk in grated Parmesan. Add kale and toss with hands thoroughly so kale softens slightly. Cover and refrigerate for 20 minutes.

3 Spray large grill pan with nonstick spray and place over medium-high heat. Place shrimp on pan in single layer (work in batches if necessary) and grill just until opaque in center, 2–3 minutes per side.

4 Place kale in large bowl or platter. Top with shrimp and sprinkle with shaved Parmesan.

3 **SmartPoints value per serving** (1¼ cups salad, about 9 shrimp, and about 3 Parmesan shavings): 245 Cal, 10 g Total Fat, 3 g Sat Fat, 1,451 mg Sod, 8 g Total Carb, 2 g Sugar, 4 g Fib, 30 g Prot.

Note from Chef Eric

When I first started my journey with WW Freestyle, I pored through my existing menus to find ways to eat well at work. At the time, we served a kale Caesar at The Roof on Wilshire. I topped it with grilled shrimp and ate it almost daily until I got used to preparing more WW friendly dishes at home and at the restaurant.

Blueberry-corn salad with spicy lobster

Serves 4

½ teaspoon finely grated
lemon zest

2 tablespoons lemon juice

1 teaspoon honey

½ teaspoon salt

¼ teaspoon black pepper

2 teaspoons extra-virgin olive oil

2 cups fresh corn kernels (from
about 3 ears)

1 cup fresh blueberries

¾ cup coarsely chopped
fresh parsley

½ small red onion, very
thinly sliced

¾ pound cooked lobster meat, cut
into ¾-inch chunks

2 tablespoons reduced-fat
mayonnaise

1 small jalapeño pepper, seeded
and minced, or to taste

Small bunch watercress, separated
into sprigs (optional)

1 To make dressing, whisk together lemon zest and juice, honey, salt, black pepper, and 1 teaspoon oil in large bowl until blended. Add corn, blueberries, parsley, and onion; toss until mixed well.

2 Toss together lobster, mayonnaise, jalapeño, and remaining 1 teaspoon oil in medium bowl.

3 Divide corn mixture evenly among 4 plates or bowls; top evenly with lobster and surround with watercress, if using.

2 **SmartPoints value per serving** (1½ cups): 230 Cal, 6 g Total Fat, 1 g Sat Fat, 774 mg Sod, 29 g Total Carb, 9 g Sugar, 4 g Fib, 19 g Prot.

Freestyle it

Lobster meat is a sweet, luxurious shellfish to use in this salad and matches nicely with corn and blueberries. But you can also substitute another zero Points protein for it instead: Try peeled cooked shrimp, flaked cooked salmon, or baked diced tofu.

Maryland-style crab salad

Serves 4

Here's the classic Chesapeake combo of blue crabs and Old Bay Seasoning reimagined as a bright, light salad. We've turned to the creamy blend of mayonnaise and Greek yogurt to make the dressing; it's both wonderfully comforting and low in SmartPoints, and it's a combination you can turn to again and again in dishes like shrimp salad, tuna salad, and even egg salad.

3	**tablespoons reduced-fat mayonnaise**
2	**tablespoons plain fat-free Greek yogurt**
2	**teaspoons Old Bay Seasoning, plus more for sprinkling**
1½	**teaspoons finely grated lemon zest**
2	**teaspoons lemon juice**
¼	**teaspoon black pepper**
1	**pound crabmeat, picked over**
1	**cup diced English (seedless) cucumber**
1	**celery stalk, finely diced**
4	**large red leaf lettuce leaves**
2	**hard-cooked large eggs, coarsely chopped**
2	**scallions, thinly sliced**

1 To make dressing, stir together mayonnaise, yogurt, Old Bay, lemon zest and juice, and pepper in large bowl.

2 Add crabmeat, cucumber, and celery and toss. Line each of 4 plates with a lettuce leaf. Top each leaf evenly with crab salad, egg, and scallion and sprinkle each serving with a dusting of Old Bay.

 SmartPoints value per serving (1 plate): 181 Cal, 7 g Total Fat, 1 g Sat Fat, 795 mg Sod, 4 g Total Carb, 2 g Sugar, 1 g Fib, 25 g Prot.

Note from Chef Eric

I sometimes stir in a spoonful of chili sauce to crab salad to make it a play on a classic crab Louis (a tablespoon of tomato chili sauce per serving adds just 1 SmartPoints value). I serve a similar dish at The Roof on Wilshire. It's a crowd-pleaser, and diners don't even realize how WW Freestyle-friendly it is!

Frisée salad with poached egg and warm bacon dressing

Serves 4

Ⓥ Ⓐ Ⓢ

If there's a must-try bacon salad it's this one! Crispy bacon and seared mushrooms give it lots of umami, the savory flavor that awakens our taste buds, while sherry vinegar adds balancing acid.

1	**tablespoon white vinegar or white-wine vinegar**
4	**large eggs**
6	**slices reduced-fat center-cut bacon**
½	**pound sliced wild mushrooms (such as cremini, oyster, and shiitake)**
1	**large shallot, minced**
½	**cup chicken broth**
1½	**tablespoons sherry vinegar**
½	**teaspoon salt**
¼	**teaspoon freshly ground black pepper**
4	**ounces (about 8 cups) tender frisée sprigs**

1 Fill large skillet two-thirds full of water and add white vinegar. Bring to boil over high heat, then lower heat so water just simmers. Crack 1 egg into small cup and slip egg into skillet; repeat with remaining eggs. Simmer until whites are set but yolks are still runny, about 3 minutes. Remove eggs using a slotted spoon and transfer to plate lined with paper towel to drain. Keep warm.

2 Cook bacon in large skillet over medium heat until crisp, about 10 minutes. Remove bacon to paper towel to cool. Coarsely crumble.

3 Pour off all but 1 teaspoon bacon fat from skillet. (Reserve remaining bacon fat.) Add mushrooms to skillet and cook over medium-high heat, stirring occasionally, until mushrooms release their juices and become golden, about 7 minutes. Remove mushrooms and set aside.

4 Add 2 tablespoons bacon fat and shallot to skillet and cook over medium heat, stirring occasionally, until shallot is tender, about 2 minutes. Add broth, sherry vinegar, salt, and pepper to skillet; scrape bottom of skillet with wooden spoon and bring to simmer over medium-high heat. Put frisée in large bowl and drizzle with hot dressing. Toss until well coated. Divide frisée among 4 plates or bowls. Top each with poached egg, ¼ cup mushrooms, and 2 tablespoons crumbled bacon.

1 **SmartPoints value per serving** (1 salad): 133 Cal, 7 g Total Fat, 2 g Sat Fat, 596 mg Sod, 5 g Total Carb, 2 g Sugar, 2 g Fib, 12 g Prot.

Note from Chef Eric

Since I'm a French-trained chef, comfort food often harks back to my time in Paris. This salad is a version of *frisée lardon,* a bistro mainstay that's a favorite of mine. The liquid yolk of the egg coats the greens and tames their bitterness, while the smokiness of the bacon pulls the flavors together.

Tricolore salad
with white beans

Tricolore salad with white beans

Serves 6

½ **pound arugula (about 1 large bunch), trimmed**

2 **heads Belgian endive, core removed, leaves sliced if large**

1 **head Treviso or radicchio, leaves torn**

1 **(15½-ounce) can white beans, drained and rinsed**

¼ **cup dried currants**

2 **tablespoons toasted pine nuts**

2 **tablespoons fresh lemon juice**

1 **tablespoon extra-virgin olive oil**

½ **teaspoon salt**

¼ **teaspoon black pepper**

3 **tablespoons grated Parmesan or ¼ cup shaved Parmesan**

Toss arugula, endive, radicchio, beans, currants, and pine nuts together in large bowl. Drizzle with lemon juice and oil and sprinkle with salt and pepper. Transfer to platter or 6 plates or bowls and sprinkle with Parmesan.

3 **SmartPoints value per serving** (1½ cups salad and ½ tablespoon Parmesan): 194 Cal, 5 g Total Fat, 1 g Sat Fat, 552 mg Sod, 30 g Total Carb, 5 g Sugar, 10 g Fib, 10 g Prot.

Note from Chef Eric
This is my take on a classic *insalata tricolore,* the "three-color salad" of Italy. I love the intense bitterness of the greens, endive, and radicchio and how they play off the sweetness of the currants and the nuttiness of the pine nuts. The beans are a great zero Points way to add protein, texture, and flavor.

Edamame and chickpea Buddha bowls with miso dressing

Serves 4

Colorful, plant-based Buddha bowls have been popular for decades as a healthy, delicious meal that's quick to put together and great for taking on the road. We've packed our version with edamame (green soybeans) and chickpeas and tossed it with a tasty miso-based dressing for big flavor.

1	**(10-ounce) package frozen shelled edamame**
2	**tablespoons white miso paste**
1	**teaspoon grated lemon zest**
2	**tablespoons lemon juice**
1	**tablespoon extra-virgin olive oil**
½	**teaspoon grated peeled fresh ginger**
¼	**teaspoon salt**
1	**(15½-ounce) can chickpeas, rinsed and drained**
½	**English (seedless) cucumber, halved lengthwise and sliced**
1	**carrot, shredded**
½	**cup shredded daikon radish**
3	**tablespoons chopped red onion**

1 Bring medium saucepan filled two-thirds with water to boil. Add edamame and cook 5 minutes; drain and rinse under cold running water.

2 Whisk miso, lemon zest and juice, oil, ginger, and salt together in large bowl until smooth. Add edamame, chickpeas, cucumber, carrot, daikon, and onion and stir to combine. Let stand at room temperature a few minutes before serving, or cover and refrigerate for up to 2 hours. Divide evenly among 4 bowls.

2 **SmartPoints value per serving** (1 cup): 322 Cal, 12 g Total Fat, 1 g Sat Fat, 749 mg Sod, 39 g Total Carb, 10 g Sugar, 11 g Fib, 18 g Prot.

Freestyle it
Topping each bowl with a quartered hard-cooked egg is a protein-packed addition that adds 0 SmartPoints.

Tex-Mex barley bowls with smoked tofu and veggies

Serves 4

We love nutty, toothsome barley, and it makes a fantastic base for grain bowls. Here we pair it with the bright flavors of Tex-Mex cuisine. Barley is also a great addition to soups, stews, and salads, so consider making a double batch and using what's left over later in the week.

1¾ cups water

⅛ teaspoon + ½ teaspoon salt

½ cup uncooked pearl barley

¼ cup chopped fresh
 cilantro leaves

4 teaspoons extra-virgin olive oil

¼ cup lime juice

1 teaspoon ground cumin

1 garlic clove, minced

¼ teaspoon black pepper

3 cups shredded red cabbage

3 cups very thinly sliced
 romaine lettuce

1 (15½-ounce) can black beans,
 rinsed and drained

1 pint grape tomatoes, halved

1 cup diced peeled jicama

2 (8-ounce) packages smoked tofu

½ avocado, peeled, pitted,
 and sliced

1 Bring water and ⅛ teaspoon salt to boil in small saucepan; stir in barley. Cover and simmer until tender, about 45 minutes. Drain any excess liquid.

2 Meanwhile, whisk together cilantro, 3 teaspoons oil, the lime juice, cumin, garlic, pepper, and remaining ½ teaspoon salt in large bowl. Add cabbage, lettuce, beans, tomatoes, and jicama and toss.

3 Cut tofu into strips. Heat remaining 1 teaspoon oil in large nonstick skillet over medium heat. Add tofu and cook until golden brown on both sides, about 5 minutes.

4 Divide barley evenly among 4 bowls. Top evenly with vegetable mixture, tofu, and avocado.

5 **SmartPoints value per serving** (1 bowl): 508 Cal, 19 g Total Fat, 3 g Sat Fat, 1,310 mg Sod, 58 g Total Carb, 8 g Sugar, 19 g Fib, 17 g Prot.

Freestyle it

Sweet corn is a terrific bowl ingredient, and with the WW Freestyle program it's now a zero Points food. Add it to this recipe in place of the jicama if you like.

**Brown rice–veggie bowls
with ginger-lime dressing**

Brown rice–veggie bowls with ginger-lime dressing

Serves 4

Ⓥ Ⓖ Ⓕ Ⓢ

- **2 tablespoons lime juice**
- **4 tablespoons fresh cilantro leaves**
- **4 teaspoons Asian (dark) sesame oil**
- **2 teaspoons honey**
- **2 teaspoons grated peeled fresh ginger**
- **¼ teaspoon salt**
- **1 tablespoon water**
- **1½ cups cooked brown rice, at room temperature**
- **1 (15-ounce) can black beans, rinsed and drained**
- **½ avocado, peeled, pitted, and diced**
- **1 small red onion, finely chopped**
- **1 carrot, cut into matchstick strips**
- **1 red bell pepper, chopped**
- **1 cup grape tomatoes, halved or quartered**
- **1 cup diced mango**

1 Combine lime juice, 2 tablespoons cilantro, the oil, honey, ginger, salt, and water in a blender and puree. Set aside.

2 Combine rice, beans, avocado, onion, carrot, bell pepper, tomatoes, and mango in large bowl and toss to combine. Add dressing and toss to coat. Divide evenly among 4 bowls and sprinkle with remaining 2 tablespoons cilantro.

6 **SmartPoints value per serving** (1 bowl): 333 Cal, 10 g Total Fat, 2 g Sat Fat, 568 mg Sod, 55 g Total Carb, 12 g Sugar, 13 g Fib, 10 g Prot.

Freestyle it

We love the bright Asian-inspired flavors and mix of textures in these colorful bowls. If you want to add a zero Points ingredient for more protein, you can't go wrong with smoked tofu, an excellent match for the lime-and-ginger dressing and the mango.

Fish tacos with
mango salsa,
page 73

Sandwiches, burgers, and tacos

In this chapter

Vegetarian Vegan Gluten free Dairy free Nut free

Turkey joes

Serves 8

2	**teaspoons canola oil**
1	**small onion, chopped**
1	**small green bell pepper, chopped**
1	**celery stalk, chopped**
2	**garlic cloves, minced**
1	**tablespoon chili powder**
1	**teaspoon dried oregano**
⅛	**teaspoon cayenne**
1¼	**pounds ground skinless turkey breast**
¾	**teaspoon salt**
1	**(14½-ounce) can diced tomatoes**
¼	**cup barbecue sauce**
1	**tablespoon Dijon mustard**
1	**cup frozen corn kernels, thawed**
8	**reduced-calorie hamburger rolls, split**
3	**tablespoons finely diced white onion**

1 Heat oil in Dutch oven over medium-high heat. Add onion, bell pepper, and celery; cook, stirring occasionally, until softened, about 5 minutes. Add garlic, chili powder, oregano, and cayenne; cook, stirring frequently, about 1 minute. Transfer to bowl.

2 Spray Dutch oven with nonstick spray. Add turkey and ½ teaspoon salt; cook, breaking turkey apart with wooden spoon, until turkey is no longer pink, about 5 minutes.

3 Stir in cooked vegetables, tomatoes, barbecue sauce, and mustard; bring to boil. Reduce heat and simmer, covered, stirring occasionally, until flavors are blended, about 15 minutes. Stir in corn and remaining ¼ teaspoon salt. Spoon into buns and top meat with about a teaspoon of white onion.

SmartPoints value per serving (1 bun with ¾ cup filling): 243 Cal, 5 g Total Fat, 1 g Sat Fat, 671 mg Sod, 31 g Total Carb, 8 g Sugar, 5 g Fib, 21 g Prot.

Note from Chef Eric
Who says *sloppy* and *comfort* can't live with healthy? These WW Freestyle–friendly sandwiches are packed with flavor and easy to make. For me, you can't have a sloppy joe without raw onions on top. They bring bite and freshness to balance out the richness of the sandwich.

Cornmeal-crusted catfish po' boys

Serves 4

Catfish is a classic filling for New Orleans' famous po' boy sandwiches. Add your choice of shredded lettuce, sliced tomato, and sliced red onion to each sandwich for full po' boy flavor.

1	**large egg**
1	**teaspoon water**
⅓	**cup cornmeal**
½	**teaspoon salt**
¼	**teaspoon black pepper**
	Pinch cayenne
4	**(5-ounce) skinless catfish fillets**
2	**teaspoons canola oil**
4	**small (3-ounce) sub rolls, split**
2	**tablespoons fat-free tartar sauce**
	Small sprigs dill
	Lettuce (optional)
	Thinly sliced tomato (optional)
	Thinly sliced red onion (optional)
	Lemon wedges

1 Lightly beat egg and water in shallow bowl. Mix together cornmeal, salt, pepper, and cayenne on sheet of wax paper. Dip catfish fillets, one at a time, into egg until coated; then coat fillets on both sides with seasoned cornmeal, pressing so it adheres. Discard any remaining egg.

2 Heat 1 teaspoon oil in large heavy nonstick skillet over medium-high heat. Add fillets and cook until golden on bottom, about 4 minutes. Carefully turn fish over with wide spatula; add remaining 1 teaspoon oil to skillet, tilting pan so oil flows underneath fillets. Cook until fillets are just opaque in center, about 3 minutes longer.

3 Pull out and discard soft centers from rolls. Spread inside of rolls with tartar sauce and fill with fish, dill, lettuce, tomato, and onion (if using). Serve with lemon wedges.

 SmartPoints value per serving (1 sandwich): 430 Cal, 14 g Total Fat, 3 g Sat Fat, 932 mg Sod, 43 g Total Carb, 4 g Sugar, 2 g Fib, 30 g Prot.

Note from Chef Eric

The cornmeal coating on this fish gives you a crispy golden crust with only 2 teaspoons oil. You may never deep-fry fish again.

Cornmeal-crusted
catfish po' boys

Pulled pork and cabbage sandwiches

Serves 4

Use your slow cooker to make lean, perfectly flavorful pulled pork for great sandwiches. We garnish ours with crunchy sliced cabbage and a little red onion, but you can also use dill pickle chips or sliced pickled jalapeño as well.

1½	**cups thinly sliced green cabbage**
1½	**red onions, thinly sliced**
¼	**cup cider vinegar**
¼	**cup ketchup**
¼	**cup packed light brown sugar**
2	**tablespoons water**
1	**tablespoon tomato paste**
1	**teaspoon hot paprika, preferably smoked**
½	**teaspoon chili powder**
½	**teaspoon kosher salt**
¼	**teaspoon ground cumin**
1	**(1-pound) lean pork tenderloin, trimmed**
4	**hamburger rolls, split and warmed**

1 Combine 1 cup cabbage, 1 onion, the vinegar, ketchup, brown sugar, water, and tomato paste in 5- or 6-quart slow cooker.

2 Mix together paprika, chili powder, salt, and cumin in cup. Spread on sheet of wax paper. Roll pork in spice mixture until coated on all sides, pressing lightly so it adheres. Place pork in slow cooker and sprinkle with any remaining spice mixture. Cover and cook until pork is fork-tender, 6–8 hours on Low. Transfer to cutting board.

3 When cool enough to handle, using two forks, shred pork; return to slow cooker, stirring well. Spoon ¾ cup pork mixture onto bottom of each roll. Top each serving with one quarter of the remaining ½ cup cabbage and remaining ½ onion. Cover with tops of rolls.

 SmartPoints value per serving (1 sandwich): 359 Cal, 6 g Total Fat, 2 g Sat Fat, 708 mg Sod, 47 g Total Carb, 23 g Sugar, 3 g Fib, 29 g Prot.

Toasted Cuban-style sandwiches with pickle

Serves 4

¼   **cup Neufchâtel (light cream cheese), softened**

3   **tablespoons minced shallot**

4   **teaspoons country-style Dijon mustard**

8   **slices reduced-calorie bread**

¾   **cup shredded reduced-fat Swiss cheese (about 3 ounces)**

4   **(½-ounce) slices lean ham**

12   **bread-and-butter pickle chips**

1 Mix together Neufchâtel, shallot, and mustard in small bowl. Spread about 1 tablespoon of mixture on one side of each slice of bread. Sprinkle 3 tablespoons cheese over each of 4 slices of bread and top each with a slice of ham and 3 pickle chips. Cover with remaining slices of bread, Neufchâtel side down.

2 Spray large skillet with nonstick spray and set over medium heat. Add sandwiches and cook until bread is lightly toasted and cheese is melted, about 2 minutes per side. Cut in half and serve warm.

6   **SmartPoints value per serving** (1 sandwich): 194 Cal, 6 g Total Fat, 3 g Sat Fat, 693 mg Sod, 23 g Total Carb, 4 g Sugar, 5 g Fib, 13 g Prot.

Note from Chef Eric

The Cuban sandwich is one of my all-time favorites, and so much of the flavor of this version comes from low SmartPoints ingredients like pickles, mustard, and sliced ham. I like using a panini press to "grill" the bread. It compacts the sandwich perfectly, melts the cheese, and forms a nice crust on the bread without a ton of fat.

Vegetable tartines

Vegetable tartines

Serves 4

8   **thick spears asparagus, halved crosswise**

1   **small eggplant, cut in half and then sliced into 12 half-moons**

1   **zucchini, cut into 16 slices**

3   **teaspoons olive oil**

1   **teaspoon salt**

1   **cup fat-free ricotta**

4   **(1½-ounce) slices toasted whole-grain country bread or boule**

4   **teaspoons aged balsamic vinegar or balsamic glaze**

1   **carrot, cut into thin ribbons with a vegetable peeler**

1   **radish, thinly sliced**

1   **cup lightly packed baby arugula (use fronds from carrot greens instead if you have them)**

Coarsely ground black pepper

1   Preheat oven to 375°F. Toss asparagus, eggplant, and zucchini individually in 1 teaspoon oil each. Place vegetables in single layer on baking sheet, keeping them separate. Sprinkle vegetables with ¾ teaspoon salt. Roast until browned and tender, about 15 minutes for asparagus and 25 minutes for zucchini and eggplant, turning vegetables once halfway through roasting.

2   Meanwhile, combine ricotta and remaining ¼ teaspoon salt.

3   Spread ¼ cup ricotta on each piece of toast. Drizzle each with 1 teaspoon balsamic and top with a mix of roasted vegetables. Garnish tartines evenly with carrot, radish, and arugula. Sprinkle with pepper.

5   **SmartPoints value per serving** (1 tartine): 227 Cal, 6 g Total Fat, 1 g Sat Fat, 913 mg Sod, 30 g Carb, 10 g Sugar, 7 g Fib, 16 g Prot.

Note from Chef Eric

Tartines are a great way to enjoy a sandwich while cutting SmartPoints: Because they're open-face, you use just one slice of bread, not two. Feel free to substitute any grilled vegetables for the ones called for here, or top with canned tuna packed in water for a zero Points addition.

Ultimate bacon cheeseburgers

Serves 4

Is this the best burger ever? It just might be, and for only 8 SmartPoints it's a must-try for bacon lovers. The addition of mushrooms to the burger patties add great flavor and moisture to lean ground beef, and cheese and garden fixins' round out the package.

1	**ounce dried porcini mushrooms, sliced**
8	**slices center-cut bacon**
1	**pound ground lean beef (5% fat)**
6	**ounces cremini mushrooms, finely chopped**
½	**small red onion, grated**
1	**teaspoon kosher salt**
¼	**teaspoon black pepper**
1	**cup shredded reduced-fat sharp Cheddar**
8	**thin slices tomato**
4	**light hamburger rolls, split and toasted**
¼	**cup diced red onion**
4	**Boston lettuce leaves**
Mustard (optional)	

1 Combine porcini mushrooms and enough hot water to cover in small bowl; let stand until mushrooms soften, about 15 minutes. Transfer mushrooms to sieve; rinse under cool running water to remove any grit; pat dry with paper towel and chop.

2 Meanwhile, arrange 4 slices bacon in single layer between paper towels; microwave on High until partially cooked but still flexible, about 30 seconds. Drain on paper towels. Repeat with remaining 4 slices bacon; let cool.

3 Mix together beef, porcini and cremini mushrooms, grated onion, and ½ teaspoon salt in large bowl until combined well but not overmixed; shape into 4 (3½-inch) patties and sprinkle with ¼ teaspoon salt and pepper. Place 2 bacon slices crisscross style on each patty, tucking ends of bacon underneath.

4 Spray grill rack or large grill pan with nonstick spray. Preheat to medium-high or prepare medium-high fire or heat grill pan over medium-high heat. Place patties on grill rack or in pan and cook until instant-read thermometer inserted into middle of each patty registers 160°F, about 6 minutes per side. Sprinkle ¼ cup Cheddar over each patty; grill, covered, until cheese is melted, about 30 seconds.

5 Sprinkle tomato slices with remaining ¼ teaspoon salt. Place 1 patty on bottom of each burger roll; top with tomato slices, diced onion, lettuce leaves, and tops of rolls. Serve with mustard (if using).

8 **SmartPoints value per serving** (1 garnished burger): 384 Cal, 11 g Total Fat, 5 g Sat Fat, 1,141 mg Sod, 28 g Total Carb, 5 g Sugar, 6 g Fib, 42 g Prot.

Ultimate bacon
cheeseburgers

Blue cheese–chicken burgers

Serves 4

These spicy burgers pack the flavors of Buffalo chicken wings with a fraction of the fat. Serve the burgers with a simple carrot-celery slaw for more Buffalo goodness.

¼ cup Buffalo wing sauce

1 teaspoon hot pepper sauce, or to taste

1 pound ground skinless chicken breast

3 scallions, chopped

¼ cup chopped celery

¼ cup plain dried bread crumbs

1 small garlic clove, minced

½ teaspoon salt

4 light hamburger rolls, split

2 cups lightly packed thinly sliced romaine lettuce

1 large tomato, cut into 8 slices

2 tablespoons crumbled blue cheese

1 Stir together wing sauce and pepper sauce in small bowl.

2 Transfer 1 tablespoon of sauce mixture to large bowl. Add chicken, scallions, celery, bread crumbs, garlic, and salt, stirring just until mixed well. With wet hands, shape mixture into 4 (½-inch-thick) patties; brush tops of patties with some of remaining sauce mixture. Discard any remaining sauce mixture.

3 Spray grill pan with nonstick spray and set over medium-high heat. Add patties and cook until instant-read thermometer inserted into center of each registers 165°F, about 5 minutes per side. Set aside.

4 Place rolls, cut side down, in grill pan and cook until toasted. Place bottoms of rolls on 4 plates. Top each with ½ cup lettuce, 2 tomato slices, 1 patty, and ½ tablespoon blue cheese; cover with tops of rolls.

5 **SmartPoints value per serving** (1 garnished burger): 304 Cal, 7 g Total Fat, 2 g Sat Fat, 1,062 mg Sod, 27 g Total Carb, 4 g Sugar, 5 g Fib, 32 g Prot.

Freestyle it

Prefer turkey burgers? You can replace the ground chicken with the same amount of skinless ground turkey breast for no change in SmartPoints.

Shrimp burgers with jalapeño tartar sauce

Serves 4

Here's a delicious and absolutely comforting seafood burger. The patty itself is full of sweet shrimp flavor, while the tartar sauce adds a bit of kick from pickled jalapeño.

1	**pound large shrimp, peeled and deveined**
1	**large egg white**
1	**scallion, sliced**
¼	**teaspoon salt**
1	**tablespoon + 2 teaspoons chopped fresh dill**
2	**tablespoons sliced pickled jalapeño pepper, drained and chopped**
⅓	**cup panko (Japanese bread crumbs)**
⅓	**cup prepared tartar sauce**
2	**teaspoons olive oil**
4	**reduced-fat hamburger rolls**
4	**thin slices tomato**
1	**cup shredded romaine lettuce**

1 Combine shrimp, egg white, scallion, salt, 1 tablespoon dill, and 1 tablespoon jalapeño in food processor; pulse until shrimp is coarsely chopped. Add panko and 1 tablespoon tartar sauce and pulse until mixed. Measure out ½-cupfuls of shrimp mixture and shape into 4 (½-inch-thick) patties.

2 To make sauce, stir together remaining tartar sauce, remaining 2 teaspoons dill, and remaining 1 tablespoon jalapeño in cup.

3 Heat oil in large nonstick skillet over medium heat. Add shrimp patties and cook until golden and cooked through, about 4 minutes per side. Brush rolls with spicy tartar sauce. Fill each roll with 1 shrimp patty, a tomato slice, and shredded lettuce.

6 **SmartPoints value per serving** (1 garnished burger): 274 Cal,8 g Total Fat, 1 g Sat Fat, 1,225 mg Sod, 29 g Total Carb, 4 g Sugar, 4 g Fib, 21 g Prot.

Beet-and-pea
veggie burgers

Beet-and-pea veggie burgers

Serves 4

3 **portobello mushroom caps, cut into thin strips**

2½ **teaspoons olive oil**

1 **medium beet**

½ **cup frozen green peas, thawed**

½ **cup cooked green lentils**

½ **cup cooked farro**

1 **cup lightly packed fresh parsley leaves**

½ **cup plain dried bread crumbs**

1 **large egg**

3 **garlic cloves, finely chopped**

1 **teaspoon salt**

2 **tablespoons Dijon mustard**

2 **tablespoons reduced-fat mayonnaise**

4 **reduced-fat whole wheat hamburger rolls**

4 **thin slices (rounds) red onion**

12 **dill pickle chips**

Baby greens (optional)

1 Preheat oven to 400°F. Place mushrooms on one side of baking sheet, drizzle with 1½ teaspoons oil, and toss. Wrap beet in foil and place on other side of baking sheet. Roast until mushrooms are dried and beet is fork-tender, about 45 minutes. Let beet cool and rub off skin.

2 Place beet and mushrooms in food processor with peas, lentils, farro, parsley, bread crumbs, egg, garlic, and salt and pulse until chunky and mixture just holds together (do not over-process). Shape mixture into 4 patties, using about ½ cup mixture each and making patties about ¾-inch thick. Place on large plate or platter lined with parchment paper, cover with another sheet of parchment, and refrigerate 1 hour.

3 Heat remaining 1 teaspoon oil in large nonstick skillet over medium heat. Add the patties and cook until browned on both sides, approximately 5 minutes per side.

4 To serve burgers, spread mustard on one side of rolls and mayonnaise on the other side. Place 1 veggie patty inside each along with 1 slice red onion, 3 dill pickle chips, and baby greens (if using).

 6 **SmartPoints value per serving** (1 garnished burger): 316 Cal, 8 g Total Fat, 1 g Sat Fat, 1,595 mg Sod, 49 g Total Carb, 9 g Sugar, 13 g Fib, 15 g Prot.

Note from Chef Eric

To me, a good veggie burger is not meant to be a substitute for a beef burger, but a great dish on its own. This burger is not only low in SmartPoints, it's also super-tasty and meaty. The beets bring earthiness, the roasted mushrooms have savory umami flavor, and farro is a great way to add toothsome bite.

Grilled flank steak and avocado tacos

Serves 12

Ever try grilled avocado? It's delicious and makes a great filling for these wonderfully spiced steak tacos.

12   (6-inch) corn tortillas

1½   teaspoons kosher salt

1½   teaspoons granulated garlic

¾   teaspoon chipotle chile powder

¾   teaspoon ground cumin

1   firm-ripe Hass avocado

1½   teaspoons olive oil

2   large red bell peppers, each cut into 6 thick rings, seeds removed

12   scallions

1   (1-pound) lean flank steak, trimmed

⅓   cup diced red onion thinly sliced

½   cup crumbled cotija or feta cheese

½   cup coarsely chopped fresh cilantro

2   limes, each cut into 6 wedges

1   tablespoon hot pepper sauce, or to taste

1 Preheat grill to high or prepare hot fire.

2 Stack tortillas and wrap in foil. Mix together salt, garlic, chile powder, and cumin in cup.

3 Cut avocado in half and remove pit and peel. Brush cut sides of avocado with ½ teaspoon oil; sprinkle with ¼ teaspoon spice mixture.

4 Drizzle bell peppers and scallions with remaining 1 teaspoon oil and toss with 1 teaspoon spice mixture. Rub remaining spice mixture over flank steak.

5 Place tortilla packet, flank steak, bell peppers, scallions, and avocado on grill rack. Grill vegetables and avocado until charred, about 2 minutes per side; grill steak about 4 minutes per side for medium-rare or to desired degree of doneness. Transfer steak to cutting board and let stand 5 minutes. Cut across grain into about 24 very thin slices.

6 To serve, cut each avocado half into 6 pieces. Place 1 piece in middle of each tortilla and mash with fork. Layer with 1 bell pepper ring, 1 scallion, and 2 slices steak (about 1 ounce). Top with onion, cotija, and cilantro. Serve with lime wedges and pepper sauce.

 SmartPoints value per serving (1 taco): 174 Cal, 7 g Total Fat, 2 g Sat Fat, 397 mg Sod, 18 g Total Carb, 2 g Sugar, 4 g Fib, 12 g Prot.

Note from Chef Eric
To me, tacos exemplify the balance between comfort and healthy living.
Use them as a vessel for any of your favorite meat-and-veggie combos.

Grilled flank steak
and avocado tacos

Korean-style brisket in lettuce-leaf "tacos"

Serves 8

Flavorful brisket is cooked with aromatic Korean-style ingredients until meltingly tender, then wrapped taco-style in crisp lettuce leaves.

½ **cup reduced-sodium soy sauce**

1 **tablespoon honey**

1 **teaspoon Asian (dark) sesame oil**

4 **garlic cloves, minced**

1 **tablespoon grated peeled fresh ginger**

1 **(3½-pound) lean flat-cut brisket, trimmed**

¼ **small head cabbage, thinly sliced (about 5 ounces)**

2 **carrots, grated**

2 **scallions, thinly sliced**

1 **small sweet onion, very thinly sliced**

2 **tablespoons black sesame seeds**

2 **tablespoons seasoned rice vinegar**

24 **large Bibb lettuce leaves**

1 **cup lightly packed fresh cilantro leaves**

1 **tablespoon gochujang or hot pepper sauce (optional)**

1 **large lime, cut into 8 wedges**

1 Combine soy sauce, honey, oil, garlic, and ginger in large zip-close plastic bag; add brisket and turn to coat. Squeeze out air and seal bag. Refrigerate brisket for at least 8 hours or up to overnight, turning bag occasionally.

2 Transfer brisket and marinade to 6-quart slow cooker. Cover and cook, turning occasionally, until beef is very tender and falling apart, 7–8 hours on Low. Transfer beef to cutting board. Using two forks, shred beef and transfer to serving bowl or platter. Spoon pan drippings into small bowl.

3 To make slaw, toss together cabbage, carrots, scallions, onion, sesame seeds, and vinegar in medium bowl.

4 To serve, spoon ¼ cup brisket onto a lettuce leaf; drizzle with some drippings. Top with ¼ cup slaw and ½ tablespoon cilantro. Repeat with remaining brisket, lettuce, drippings, slaw, and cilantro to make 24 tacos. Arrange on platter and serve with gochujang (if using), and lime wedges.

SmartPoints value per serving (3 lettuce "tacos"): 326 Cal, 10 g Total Fat, 3 g Sat Fat, 838 mg Sod, 11 g Total Carb, 6 g Sugar, 2 g Fib, 46 g Prot.

Note from Chef Eric

Gochujang is optional in this recipe but strongly recommended. The combination of sweetness and heat is common in lots of my favorite WW Freestyle program meals.

Chicken picadillo tacos

Serves 4

A classic picadillo, studded with raisins and olives, makes a flavorful filling for tortillas.
Like planning ahead? You can make the picadillo up to 3 days in advance and refrigerate it;
reheat it just before filling the tacos.

1	**teaspoon olive oil**
1	**pound ground lean chicken**
¼	**teaspoon salt**
1	**small onion, chopped**
1	**celery stalk, halved lengthwise and sliced**
1	**large garlic clove, finely chopped**
2	**teaspoons ground cumin**
½	**teaspoon cinnamon**
¼	**teaspoon black pepper**
1	**cup fat-free salsa**
¼	**cup raisins, coarsely chopped**
¼	**cup pimiento-stuffed olives, sliced**
8	**(6-inch) corn tortillas, warmed**
2	**cups lightly packed thinly sliced iceberg lettuce**
⅓	**cup plain low-fat Greek yogurt**
1	**cup lightly packed fresh cilantro sprigs**

Lime wedges

1 Heat oil in large skillet over medium-high heat. Add chicken and salt and cook, breaking apart with wooden spoon, until chicken is no longer pink, about 3 minutes.

2 Add onion and celery to skillet. Cook, stirring occasionally, until vegetables are golden and tender, about 4 minutes. Add garlic, cumin, cinnamon, and pepper; cook, stirring constantly, until fragrant, about 30 seconds longer.

3 Stir salsa, raisins, and olives into chicken mixture; cook, stirring occasionally, until heated through, about 3 minutes.

4 Fill each tortilla with scant ⅓ cup chicken mixture and ¼ cup lettuce. Top evenly with yogurt and cilantro sprigs. Serve with lime wedges.

10 **SmartPoints value per serving** (2 tacos): 387 Cal, 14 g Total Fat, 4 g Sat Fat, 776 mg Sod, 41 g Total Carb, 10 g Sugar, 6 g Fib, 27 g Prot.

Note from Chef Eric

The pairing of sweet and salty makes this taco a standout. Try substituting
other dried fruits, like cherries or cranberries, for the raisins and use capers
instead of olives for a different kind of briny taste.

Fish tacos with
mango salsa

Fish tacos with mango salsa

Serves 4

These tacos feature meaty, flavorful mahimahi oven-baked in a sweet lime sauce and rolled in corn tortillas with tangy fruit salsa. Serve Sriracha or other hot sauce on the side.

4   **(6-ounce) mahimahi fillets**

½   **teaspoon salt**

⅓   **cup lime juice**

2   **tablespoons minced scallion**

1½   **tablespoons minced peeled fresh ginger**

1½   **teaspoons dark brown sugar**

8   **(6-inch) corn tortillas, warmed**

2   **cups lightly packed thinly sliced green leaf lettuce**

¼   **cup chopped fresh cilantro**

½   **cup prepared mango or peach salsa**

2   **tablespoons crema or reduced-fat sour cream**

Lime wedges

1 Preheat oven to 450°F. Spray large baking dish with nonstick spray.

2 Sprinkle fish with salt and arrange in single layer in prepared dish.

3 Stir together lime juice, scallion, ginger, and brown sugar in small bowl; pour over fish. Cover dish and bake until fish is just opaque in center, about 15 minutes.

4 Transfer fish to cutting board and cut into small pieces. Top each tortilla evenly with fish, lettuce, cilantro, and salsa. Drizzle with crema. Fold each taco in half; serve with lime wedges.

 6 **SmartPoints value per serving** (2 tacos): 309 Cal, 3 g Total Fat, 1 g Sat Fat, 605 mg Sod, 34 g Total Carb, 7 g Sugar, 4 g Fib, 35 g Prot.

Ramen noodle soup with jammy eggs, page 94

Big-bowl soups

In this chapter

Vegetarian   Vegan   Gluten free   Dairy free   Nut free

Classic chicken soup with egg noodles

Serves 6

Chicken soup may be the most comforting of all dishes, a delicious fix anytime you feel you need something particularly sustaining. This version is made wonderfully rich by cooking bone-in chicken thighs and vegetables right in the broth.

6 **cups chicken broth**

3 **carrots, halved lengthwise and cut into 1-inch pieces**

2 **parsnips, halved lengthwise and cut into 1-inch pieces**

2 **celery stalks, cut into 1-inch pieces**

1 **leek (white and light green parts only), thinly sliced and rinsed well**

3 **parsley sprigs**

1 **bay leaf**

1 **large garlic clove, smashed with side of knife**

4 **skinless bone-in chicken thighs (about 1½ pounds)**

2 **cups (4 ounces) uncooked medium home-style egg noodles**

1 **teaspoon kosher salt, or to taste**

¼ **teaspoon black pepper**

¼ **cup chopped fresh parsley**

1 Bring broth, carrots, parsnips, celery, leek, parsley sprigs, bay leaf, and garlic clove to boil in Dutch oven. Add chicken; reduce heat and simmer, covered, until chicken is cooked through and very tender, about 40 minutes. Transfer chicken to cutting board to cool. Discard parsley sprigs, bay leaf, and garlic clove.

2 Return soup to a boil and stir in noodles. Simmer, uncovered, until noodles are tender, about 8 minutes.

3 When cool enough to handle, pull chicken meat from bones. Discard bones; tear meat into large shreds and stir into soup. Stir in salt, pepper, and chopped parsley. Ladle evenly into 6 bowls.

 SmartPoints value per serving (1½ cups): 260 Cal, 6 g Total Fat, 1 g Sat Fat, 1,319 mg Sod, 26 g Total Carb, 6 g Sugar, 5 g Fib, 26 g Prot.

Freestyle it
Want more veggies in this recipe? Add a cup of fresh or frozen green peas (they're now a zero Points food) to the soup after the noodles are cooked. And if they're in season, garnish each bowl with a handful of fresh pea shoots for super freshness.

Matzo ball soup

Serves 6

MATZO BALLS

4	large eggs
2	tablespoons canola oil
1	teaspoon salt
¼	teaspoon freshly grated nutmeg
¼	teaspoon black pepper
⅛	teaspoon baking powder
¼	cup seltzer
2	tablespoons snipped fresh chives
2	teaspoons grated peeled fresh ginger (optional)
1	cup matzo meal

SOUP

8	cups chicken broth
2	large bone-in skinless chicken breasts (about 1¾ pounds total)
2	garlic cloves, smashed
2	large carrots, cut into large dice
2	inner celery stalks, cut into large dice
2	tablespoons small fresh dill sprigs
¼	teaspoon salt, or to taste

1 To make matzo balls, whisk eggs, oil, salt, nutmeg, pepper, and baking powder in medium bowl until blended. Stir in seltzer, chives, and ginger (if using). Stir in matzo meal until blended. Cover and refrigerate for at least 30 minutes.

2 Bring large pot of lightly salted water to boil. With wet hands, form matzo mixture into 12 balls, each slightly larger than a ping-pong ball. Carefully drop balls into pot. Return water to boil, then reduce heat and simmer, covered, until matzo balls are very tender and cooked through, 35–40 minutes.

3 Meanwhile, to make soup, combine broth, chicken, and garlic in large saucepan. Bring to boil over medium-high heat. Reduce heat and simmer, covered, skimming off and discarding foam from top of broth occasionally, until chicken is cooked through, about 15 minutes.

4 Transfer chicken to cutting board. Remove and discard garlic. Return broth to boil and add carrots and celery. Reduce heat and simmer, covered, until vegetables are tender, about 15 minutes.

5 Transfer cooked matzo balls with slotted spoon to soup. Simmer 5 minutes for matzo balls to absorb flavor. Meanwhile, when chicken is cool enough to handle, shred meat with fork or your fingers and discard bones. Stir chicken into soup. Remove from heat and stir in dill and salt. Ladle evenly into 6 bowls.

(4) **SmartPoints value per serving** (1½ cups soup and 2 matzo balls): 357 Cal, 12 g Total Fat, 2 g Sat Fat, 1,770 mg Sod, 23 g Total Carb, 3 g Sugar, 2 g Fib, 39 g Prot.

Note from Chef Eric

I was raised in a Jewish home, so I know my way around matzo ball soup. I always felt bad for the solo carrot that floated sadly in my bubbe's broth, and now I add a ton of other vegetables to keep the carrot company: Celery root, rutabagas, turnips, and leeks all make the broth come alive, so feel free to use your favorites.

**Matzo ball
soup**

Hearty lemon-chicken soup with whole wheat orzo

Hearty lemon-chicken soup with whole wheat orzo

Serves 4

Here's an excellent version of *avgolemono*, the traditional Greek soup thickened with egg and brightened with lemon and dill. The result is totally transporting, as delicious as an intro to a larger meal as it is to comfort anyone feeling under the weather. We make ours with whole wheat orzo, but you can use regular orzo or pastina for no change in SmartPoints.

2	**(10-ounce) bone-in skinless chicken breasts**
1	**carrot, finely chopped**
1	**small celery stalk, finely chopped**
½	**onion, finely chopped**
¾	**teaspoon salt, or to taste**
¼	**teaspoon black pepper**
4	**cups reduced-sodium chicken broth**
½	**cup whole wheat orzo**
2	**large eggs**
3	**tablespoons lemon juice**
2	**tablespoons chopped fresh dill**

1 Place chicken, carrot, celery, onion, ¼ teaspoon salt, and the pepper in large saucepan. Add broth and bring to boil over high heat. Reduce heat; skim and discard any foam that rises to top. Lower heat and simmer, covered, until chicken is cooked through and vegetables are tender, about 20 minutes.

2 Transfer chicken to plate with slotted spoon to cool slightly. Add orzo to saucepan, adjust heat, and cook at bare simmer until tender, 6–8 minutes. Meanwhile, when chicken is cool enough to handle, shred meat with fork or your fingers and discard bones.

3 Whisk eggs, lemon juice, and remaining ½ teaspoon salt together in medium bowl until frothy. Stirring constantly, gradually add ½ cup hot liquid from soup into egg mixture. Stir egg mixture back into soup. Add chicken and cook, stirring constantly, just until heated through, about 1 minute (do not simmer). Ladle evenly into 4 bowls and top with dill.

 SmartPoints value per serving (about 1¼ cups): 239 Cal, 6 g Total Fat, 1 g Sat Fat, 1,082 mg Sod, 16 g Total Carb, 2 g Sugar, 2 g Fib, 31 g Prot.

Note from Chef Eric

The lemon really brings this soup to life, and using eggs (a zero Points food) as a thickener makes it *so* satisfying.

Old-world mushroom-barley soup with turkey

Serves 6

Here's a hands-down favorite that gets heft from nutty barley, one of our favorite ingredients for soups as well as for grain bowls. Quick-cooking barley is tender in 10 to 15 minutes, making it a particularly convenient whole grain.

1   **tablespoon olive oil**

2   **carrots, sliced**

2   **celery stalks with leaves, chopped**

1   **onion, chopped**

½   **pound cremini mushrooms, thickly sliced**

2   **garlic cloves, minced**

6   **cups chicken broth**

½   **cup quick-cooking barley**

½   **teaspoon salt**

¼   **teaspoon black pepper**

Pinch cayenne

3   **cups diced cooked skinless turkey breast**

¼   **cup chopped fresh dill**

1   **tablespoon lemon juice**

1 Heat oil in Dutch oven over medium heat. Add carrots, celery, and onion; cook, stirring frequently, until onion is softened, about 5 minutes. Add mushrooms and cook until softened, about 4 minutes. Stir in garlic and cook, stirring, until fragrant, about 30 seconds longer.

2 Add broth, barley, salt, pepper, and cayenne to pot; bring to boil. Reduce heat and simmer, covered, until barley is tender, about 15 minutes. Stir in turkey and simmer just until heated through, about 2 minutes longer. Stir in dill and lemon juice; ladle soup evenly into 6 bowls.

 SmartPoints value per serving (2 cups): 158 Cal, 4 g Total Fat, 1 g Sat Fat, 1,124 mg Sod, 11 g Total Carb, 4 g Sugar, 2 g Fib, 20 g Prot.

Freestyle it

This is a great recipe to make if you have leftover turkey from a holiday meal, or you can use chicken breast from an any-day rotisserie chicken—both are zero Points foods so you can substitute them interchangeably.

Beefy borscht

Serves 6

The beet-red hue of borscht makes it as glorious to look at as it is to spoon into. We've made this borscht particularly rich with chunks of beef round, a flavorful cut that turns wonderfully tender with slow cooking.

4   **beets (about 1⅓ pounds total), peeled**

3   **teaspoons olive oil**

¾   **pound lean beef round, trimmed and cut into ½-inch cubes**

¾   **teaspoon salt**

1   **onion, chopped**

1   **large (10-ounce) russet potato, peeled and cut into ¾-inch dice**

1   **carrot, cut into ½-inch dice**

2   **tomatoes, seeded and diced**

4   **cups beef broth**

2   **cups lightly packed finely sliced red cabbage**

1   **tablespoon red-wine vinegar**

6   **tablespoons plain low-fat yogurt**

2   **tablespoons chopped fresh dill or chives**

¼   **teaspoon freshly ground black pepper**

1 Cut 3 beets into ½-inch dice. Shred the remaining beet. Set aside.

2 Heat 2 teaspoons oil in Dutch oven or large heavy saucepan over medium-high heat. Add beef and ½ teaspoon salt and cook, stirring occasionally, until browned, about 5 minutes. Transfer with slotted spoon to plate. Heat remaining 1 teaspoon oil in same pan; add onion and cook until golden, about 5 minutes.

3 Return beef and any juices to pan. Stir in diced beets, potato, carrot, tomatoes, and broth. Bring to simmer; cover, adjust heat, and simmer 50 minutes. Stir in cabbage, vinegar, and remaining ¼ teaspoon salt and simmer until meat and vegetables are very tender, about 30 more minutes.

4 Add the grated beet to soup and simmer 3 minutes. Ladle evenly into 6 bowls and top each with 1 tablespoon yogurt and sprinkling of dill and pepper.

(4)   **SmartPoints value per serving** (1⅓ cups soup and 1 tablespoon yogurt): 203 Cal, 6 g Total Fat, 2 g Sat Fat, 901 mg Sod, 22 g Total Carb, 9 g Sugar, 4 g Fib, 17 g Prot.

Note from Chef Eric

Add some freshly grated horseradish to the borscht for a bit of heat; it plays magically off both the beets and the beef.

Vietnamese beef pho

Serves 4

¾ **pound lean sirloin beef, trimmed**

¼ **teaspoon salt, or to taste**

¼ **teaspoon black pepper**

2 **teaspoons canola oil**

1 **cup chopped onion**

2 **cinnamon sticks**

2 **star anise pods**

10 **black peppercorns**

4 **cups low-sodium beef broth**

1½ **tablespoons Asian fish sauce**

4 **ounces dried flat rice noodles**

3 **scallions, thinly sliced**

4 **radishes, thinly sliced**

¼ **cup fresh cilantro leaves**

4 **lime wedges**

1 Heat ridged grill pan over medium-high heat. Sprinkle beef with ⅛ teaspoon salt and the pepper. Place steak on grill pan and cook until browned and instant-read thermometer inserted into center of steak registers 145°F for medium, 6–8 minutes per side. Transfer steak to cutting board and let stand 5 minutes.

2 Meanwhile, heat oil in large saucepan over medium heat. Add onion and cook, covered, stirring occasionally, until golden, about 8 minutes. Bundle cinnamon sticks, star anise, and peppercorns in cheesecloth and add to pan along with broth and remaining ⅛ teaspoon salt. Bring to boil; reduce heat to low, cover, and simmer 5 minutes. Stir in fish sauce.

3 Cook rice noodles according to package directions. Drain and divide evenly among 4 shallow bowls.

4 Remove and discard cheesecloth bundle from broth. Slice beef against grain into about 20 thin slices. Layer beef evenly over noodles. Top beef with scallions, radishes, and cilantro. Ladle remaining broth and onions over bowls and serve with lime wedges.

 6 **SmartPoints value per serving** (1 bowl): 277 Cal, 6 g Total Fat, 1 g Sat Fat, 1,138 mg Sod, 33 g Total Carb, 3 g Sugar, 3 g Fib, 23 g Prot.

Freestyle it

Add a sliced hard-cooked egg to each bowl for a boost of protein and no additional SmartPoints. You can also add more herbs for flavor: Mint and basil are classic additions.

**Vietnamese
beef pho**

Homestyle split pea soup with Canadian bacon

Serves 6

Classic pea soup: rich, thick, and satisfying, and on the WW Freestyle program it's remarkably low in SmartPoints. You can use your choice of either green or yellow dried split peas in this since both are zero Points foods.

1	**tablespoon olive oil**
3	**celery stalks, chopped**
3	**carrots, chopped**
2	**leeks (white and light green parts only), chopped and rinsed well**
1	**onion, chopped**
¼	**teaspoon salt**
2	**garlic cloves, finely chopped**
6	**ounces Canadian bacon, diced**
8	**cups reduced-sodium chicken broth**
1	**pound dried split peas, picked over and rinsed**
1	**bay leaf**
1	**teaspoon chopped fresh rosemary leaves**
¼	**teaspoon black pepper**

1 In large pot, heat oil over medium-high heat. Add celery, carrots, leeks, onion, and salt; cook, stirring occasionally, until vegetables soften, about 10 minutes.

2 Stir in garlic and bacon; cook, stirring frequently, 1 minute. Add broth, split peas, bay leaf, rosemary, and pepper; bring to boil over high heat. Reduce heat to low and simmer, uncovered, stirring occasionally, until peas soften and soup has thickened, about 1 hour. Discard bay leaf and ladle soup evenly into 6 bowls.

 SmartPoints value per serving (about 1¼ cups): 380 Cal, 6 g Total Fat, 1 g Sat Fat, 1,042 mg Sod, 58 g Total Carb, 7 g Sugar, 19 g Fib, 26 g Prot.

Robust black bean soup with onion and cilantro

Serves 6

Immigrants from Cuba brought recipes for black bean soup along with them, and this hearty soup is now an American favorite.

2 **teaspoons olive oil**

½ **pound (about 2 large links) hot Italian turkey sausage**

1 **yellow onion, chopped**

2 **teaspoons ground cumin**

1 **teaspoon dried oregano**

1 **jalapeño pepper, seeded and minced**

2 **large garlic cloves, minced**

3 **(15½-ounce) cans black beans, rinsed and drained**

4 **cups chicken broth**

¼ **teaspoon salt, or to taste**

1 **bay leaf**

½ **small red onion, thinly sliced**

½ **cup coarsely chopped fresh cilantro**

Lime wedges for serving

1 Heat 1 teaspoon oil in large nonstick saucepan over medium heat. Add sausage and cook until browned on all sides and cooked through, about 15 minutes. Transfer sausage to plate. When cool enough to handle, cut into ½-inch slices.

2 Heat remaining 1 teaspoon oil in same saucepan over medium heat. Add yellow onion and cook, stirring occasionally, until softened, about 5 minutes; stir in cumin and oregano. Add jalapeño and garlic; cook, stirring, until fragrant, about 30 seconds. Stir in beans, broth, salt, and bay leaf; bring to boil. Reduce heat and simmer, covered, until flavors are blended, about 15 minutes longer. Remove saucepan from heat and let soup cool 5 minutes. Discard bay leaf.

3 Transfer 2 cups of bean mixture to blender or food processor and puree. Stir puree and sausage into soup. Cook until soup is heated through, about 5 minutes. Ladle soup evenly into 6 bowls; sprinkle with red onion and cilantro and serve with lime wedges.

2 **SmartPoints value per serving** (generous 1 cup): 292 Cal, 5 g Total Fat, 1 g Sat Fat, 1,718 mg Sod, 41 g Total Carb, 3 g Sugar, 16 g Fib, 21 g Prot.

Freestyle it

For a creamy, tangy garnish, top each serving of soup with a spoonful of plain fat-free Greek yogurt or plain unsweetened soy yogurt—both zero Points foods.

Bouillabaisse

Bouillabaisse

Serves 6

Every bustling Mediterranean seaport has a favorite soup or stew. Bouillabaisse is the world-celebrated fish soup of Provence, with numerous variations up and down the coast. It's beloved by residents and visitors alike and not hard to make at home.

1	**tablespoon olive oil**
4	**cups thinly sliced leeks (white and light green parts only), rinsed well and patted dry**
4	**garlic cloves, minced**
½	**fennel bulb, chopped (reserve fronds for garnish)**
2	**bell peppers (preferably 1 red and 1 green), cut into very thin strips**
4	**cups chicken broth**
1	**(14½-ounce) can diced tomatoes**
½	**cup dry white wine**
2	**tablespoons Pernod liqueur**
1	**tablespoon chopped fresh thyme**
2	**strips orange zest, removed with vegetable peeler**
½	**teaspoon saffron threads, crushed**
⅛	**teaspoon cayenne**
¾	**teaspoon salt**
6	**small red potatoes, scrubbed and cut into ½-inch dice**
1	**pound skinless halibut fillet, cut into 1-inch chunks**
½	**pound large shrimp, peeled and deveined**
½	**pound mussels, scrubbed and debearded**
¼	**pound scallops or shucked oysters**

1 Heat oil in large Dutch oven over medium-high heat. Add leeks and garlic and cook, stirring, until golden, 7–10 minutes. Add fennel and bell peppers and cook, stirring, 3 minutes. Add broth, tomatoes, wine, Pernod, thyme, orange zest, saffron, cayenne, and salt; bring to boil. Reduce heat and simmer until flavors are blended, about 10 minutes.

2 Add potatoes to Dutch oven and bring to boil. Reduce heat and simmer, partially covered, until potatoes are tender, about 15 minutes.

3 Add halibut, shrimp, mussels, and scallops and bring to boil. Reduce heat and simmer, covered, until fish and shellfish are just opaque in center and mussels open, about 5 minutes. Discard any mussels that do not open. Ladle into bowls and sprinkle with fennel fronds.

 6 **SmartPoints value per serving** (2 cups): 388 Cal, 5 g Total Fat, 1 g Sat Fat, 1,323 mg Sod, 49 g Total Carbs, 11 g Sugar, 6 g Fib, 33 g Prot.

Salmon chowder with fennel and dill

Serves 6

This comforting chowder is rich and creamy without the addition of any cream. Adding lemon zest, mustard, and dill to the soup at the end of cooking brightens the flavor.

1	**tablespoon unsalted butter**
1	**large leek (white and light green parts only), halved lengthwise, sliced, and rinsed well**
½	**large fennel bulb, diced**
2	**carrots, diced**
4	**cups chicken broth**
2	**medium Yukon Gold potatoes (5 ounces total), scrubbed and diced**
1¼	**cups low-fat (1%) milk**
3	**tablespoons all-purpose flour**
1	**pound skinless salmon fillet, cut into 1-inch chunks**
¾	**teaspoon salt**
½	**teaspoon black pepper**
¼	**cup chopped fresh dill**
2	**teaspoons Dijon mustard**
1	**teaspoon grated lemon zest**
2	**teaspoons lemon juice**

1 Melt butter in Dutch oven or large saucepan over medium heat. Add leek, fennel, and carrots; cook, stirring occasionally, until almost tender, about 10 minutes.

2 Stir in broth, potatoes, and 1 cup milk and bring to boil over medium-high heat. Reduce heat and simmer 5 minutes.

3 Stir together remaining ¼ cup milk and the flour in cup until blended. Stir into soup and simmer, stirring occasionally, until soup is slightly thickened, 3–5 minutes. Stir in salmon, salt, and pepper;.simmer until salmon is just cooked through, about 4 minutes longer.

4 Remove from heat and stir in dill, mustard, and lemon zest and juice. Ladle evenly into 6 bowls.

3 **SmartPoints value per serving** (1½ cups): 282 Cal, 13 g Total Fat, 4 g Sat Fat, 997 mg Sod, 21 g Total Carb, 6 g Sugar, 3 g Fib, 20 g Prot.

Freestyle it

Get creative! All fresh fish and shellfish are 0 SmartPoints on the WW Freestyle program. That means you could use any (or any combination) you like in this soup without adjusting the SmartPoints value. Need some inspiration? Cod and halibut also make excellent chowder, or try a mix of shrimp and scallops.

Cioppino

Serves 4

Although cioppino means "fish stew" in Italy's Genovese dialect, this classic rendition of seafood soup has been associated with San Francisco since the 1930s. Recipes vary, but cioppino invariably contains a mix of fish and seafood, tomatoes, wine, and a delicious dose of herbs and spice.

2	**teaspoons olive oil**
1	**onion, chopped**
1	**fennel bulb, diced**
3	**large garlic cloves, minced**
⅔	**cup dry white wine**
1	**small green bell pepper, cut into ½-inch dice**
2	**tablespoons tomato paste**
1	**(28-ounce) can whole peeled tomatoes with juice, broken up**
2	**cups chicken broth**
½	**teaspoon salt, or to taste**
½	**teaspoon black pepper**
¼	**teaspoon red pepper flakes**
1	**dozen littleneck clams, scrubbed**
½	**pound (about 18) mussels, scrubbed and debearded**
¾	**pound skinless halibut fillet, cut into 1-inch chunks**
2	**tablespoons chopped fresh basil leaves**

1 Heat oil in large pot over medium heat. Add onion and fennel; cook, stirring frequently, until softened, about 5 minutes. Add garlic and cook, stirring, until fragrant, about 30 seconds. Add wine and cook until almost evaporated, about 5 minutes.

2 Add bell pepper and tomato paste to pot, stirring until tomato paste is mixed well with vegetables. Add tomatoes with juice, broth, salt, black pepper, and pepper flakes; bring to boil. Reduce heat and simmer, covered, stirring occasionally, 10 minutes.

3 Add clams and cook just until shells start to open, about 3 minutes. Add mussels and halibut; cook until clams and mussels open and fish is just opaque in center, about 5 minutes longer. Discard any clams or mussels that do not open. Ladle soup evenly into 4 large soup bowls and sprinkle with basil.

 SmartPoints value per serving (3 cups): 286 Cal, 6 g Total Fat, 1 g Sat Fat, 1,476 mg Sod, 23 g Total Carb, 10 g Sugar, 5 g Fib, 31 g Prot.

Thai coconut soup with shrimp

Serves 4

Ⓥ Ⓖ

A combination of rich coconut milk and warming red curry are the comforting base of this soup, while lemongrass, lime, and cilantro add brightness.

2	**teaspoons peanut or canola oil**
2	**teaspoons grated peeled fresh ginger**
2	**garlic cloves, minced**
1	**lemongrass stalk, cut into 3 pieces and smashed to release oils**
1	**red Thai chile pepper, seeded, ½ finely chopped, ½ cut in thin strips**
1½	**tablespoons Thai red curry paste**
3	**cups chicken broth or vegetable broth**
5	**ounces (2 cups) sugar snap peas, sliced diagonally into thirds**
1	**(15-ounce) can baby corn, drained and cut into 1-inch pieces**
¾	**pound medium shrimp, peeled and deveined**
1	**(13½-ounce) can light (low-fat) coconut milk**
¼	**cup Asian fish sauce**

Zest and juice of ½ lime

2	**tablespoons fresh cilantro leaves**
1	**tablespoon sliced fresh basil leaves**
4	**lime wedges for serving**

1 Heat oil in medium saucepan over medium heat. Add ginger, garlic, lemongrass, and chopped chile pepper and cook, stirring, 2 minutes. Stir in curry paste and cook 30 seconds. Pour in broth and bring to simmer; lower heat and cook at bare simmer for 5 minutes to infuse flavors.

2 Add sugar snap peas and baby corn; simmer 2 minutes. Add shrimp; simmer until shrimp are just cooked through and sugar snap peas are crisp-tender, about 3 minutes. Pour in coconut milk and fish sauce and heat through. Remove from heat and stir in lime zest and juice. Discard lemongrass pieces.

3 Ladle soup evenly into 4 bowls. Top with cilantro, basil, and chile pepper strips. Serve with lime wedges on the side.

(6) **SmartPoints value per serving** (1¾ cups): 239 Cal, 12 g Total Fat, 7 g Sat Fat, 2,845 mg Sod, 19 g Total Carb, 5 g Sugar, 5 g Fib, 18 g Prot.

Note from Chef Eric

Want to make this soup even more exciting? Sprinkling in chopped peanuts is a great low SmartPoints way to keep the flavors authentic and make the textures sing! A tablespoon of chopped roasted salted peanuts adds 2 SmartPoints.

New England clam chowder

Serves 4

1   teaspoon safflower oil or
    canola oil

3   slices turkey bacon, diced

1   small onion, finely diced

1   small rib celery, finely chopped

3   tablespoons all-purpose flour

1   cup reduced-fat (2%) milk

3½ cups chicken broth

2   potatoes (about 12 ounces),
    peeled and diced

2   (6½-ounce) cans chopped clams

1   teaspoon chopped fresh
    thyme leaves

⅛   teaspoon salt, or to taste

⅛   teaspoon cayenne, or to taste

1   tablespoon chopped
    fresh parsley

1 Heat oil in large nonstick saucepan over medium heat. Add bacon, onion, and celery; cook, stirring frequently, until bacon has rendered fat and onion is soft, about 6 minutes. Stir in flour; cook, stirring, 1 minute. Very gradually whisk in milk and broth. Bring to simmer, add potatoes, and cook, covered, until potatoes are tender, 10–15 minutes.

2 Stir in clams with their juice and thyme. Bring to simmer. Stir in salt and cayenne. Ladle evenly into 4 bowls and garnish with parsley.

5 **SmartPoints value per serving** (2 cups): 295 Cal, 6 g Total Fat, 2 g Sat Fat, 1,095 mg Sod, 29 g Total Carb, 6 g Sugar, 3 g Fib, 29 g Prot.

Freestyle it

Want to give your chowder a summery feel? Add a cup of fresh sweet corn kernels (corn is now a zero Points food!) along with the potatoes and garnish the soup with sliced fresh basil instead of parsley.

Ramen noodle soup with jammy eggs

Serves 4

Ramen noodles are in, and most well-stocked supermarkets will have a number of authentic types to choose from. We've packed this recipe with veggies and give you instructions for simmering up a super-flavorful vegetable broth spiked with ginger, garlic, and chili paste.

4	**large eggs, at room temperature**
1½	**teaspoons canola oil**
6	**ounces shiitake mushrooms, stems removed, caps sliced (about 3 cups)**
1	**onion, thinly sliced**
2	**large garlic cloves, minced**
1	**tablespoon + 2 teaspoons minced peeled fresh ginger**
7	**cups vegetable broth**
¼	**cup soy sauce, or to taste**
2	**heads baby bok choy (12 ounces), stalks halved lengthwise and sliced**
4	**ounces ramen noodles**
½	**cup snow peas, halved crosswise diagonally**
1	**carrot, halved lengthwise and thinly sliced or cut into strips**
2	**scallions, sliced lengthwise**
½	**cup chopped fresh cilantro leaves**
2	**teaspoons garlic-chili paste or sambal oelek**

1 Fill medium saucepan half full of water and bring to boil over high heat. Add eggs to water and boil gently 6½ minutes. Fill medium bowl with ice water. Add eggs and let cool 3 minutes. Carefully peel eggs and set aside.

2 Heat oil in large Dutch oven or deep skillet over medium heat. Add mushrooms and onion and cook, stirring occasionally, until golden, about 6 minutes.

3 Reduce heat, add garlic and 1 tablespoon ginger and cook, stirring, until fragrant, about 30 seconds. Stir in broth and soy sauce and bring to boil over medium-high heat.

4 Add bok choy, noodles, snow peas, and carrot. Reduce heat and simmer, stirring occasionally, until vegetables and noodles are tender, about 5 minutes.

5 Remove from heat and stir in remaining 2 teaspoons ginger, the scallions, and cilantro. Season with more soy sauce, if desired. Ladle soup evenly into 4 bowls. Halve eggs and put 2 halves into each bowl. Top each serving with ½ teaspoon garlic-chili paste.

 6 **SmartPoints value per serving** (2 cups soup and 1 egg): 305 Cal, 17 g Total Fat, 3 g Sat Fat, 2,002 mg Sod, 24 g Total Carb, 7 g Sugar, 5 g Fib, 13 g Prot.

Freestyle it

Ramen soup is a fabulous dish to change up with zero Points foods. Feel free to substitute a few ounces of diced firm tofu for the eggs if you'd prefer a vegan soup.

Ramen noodle soup
with jammy eggs

Miso soup with mushrooms

Miso soup with mushrooms

Serves 4

4 teaspoons canola oil

2 garlic cloves, chopped

1 tablespoon grated peeled fresh ginger

3 ounces sliced shiitake mushroom caps

3 ounces cremini mushrooms

3 ounces thinly sliced portobello mushrooms

6 cups water

2 teaspoons sesame oil

¼ cup mirin

1 tablespoon soy sauce

½ teaspoon salt, or to taste

3 tablespoons miso paste

14 ounces firm tofu, diced

2 scallions, cut into thin strips

1 Heat canola oil in large saucepan over medium heat. Add garlic and ginger and cook, stirring, 1 minute. Add shiitake, cremini, and portobello mushrooms and cook, stirring frequently, until tender, about 5 minutes. Add water, sesame oil, mirin, soy sauce, and salt; reduce heat and simmer 10 minutes longer.

2 Place miso in cup. Whisk in ¼ cup hot broth from saucepan until miso is dissolved. Remove soup from heat and whisk in miso mixture until fully incorporated. (Once miso is added, do not bring soup back to a boil.)

3 Divide diced tofu evenly among 4 bowls. Ladle soup into bowls. Sprinkle with scallion.

 SmartPoints value per serving (2 cups soup and ¼ of tofu): 196 Cal, 12 g Total Fat, 2 g Sat Fat, 1,014 mg Sod, 11 g Total Carb, 3 g Sugar, 3 g Fib, 13 g Prot.

Note from Chef Eric

For me, miso soup is the epitome of nourishing soups. The addition of mushrooms and tofu makes this soup a satisfying and low SmartPoints meal, and aromatic ginger, garlic, and sesame oil keep it interesting. For additional "wow," top the soup with thin slices of ginger or flaked nori seaweed.

Potato-cheese soup

Serves 6

Craving something rich and creamy? Have it! This soup is great if you're hankering for the flavor of tangy, savory cheese while still keeping your SmartPoints in check. Choose a sharp Cheddar for the deepest cheese flavor.

1 teaspoon canola oil

1 onion, chopped

2 carrots, shredded

¾ teaspoon salt

½ teaspoon black pepper

½ teaspoon paprika

½ teaspoon dry mustard

1 pound small red potatoes, cut into ½-inch cubes

3⅔ cups reduced-sodium chicken broth

½ cup fat-free half-and-half

8 ounces shredded reduced-fat Cheddar or Colby

Fresh thyme or oregano leaves for garnish

1 Heat oil in large nonstick saucepan over medium heat. Add onion and cook, stirring frequently, until browned, about 5 minutes. Stir in carrots, salt, pepper, paprika, and mustard; cook, stirring once or twice, until carrots begin to soften, about 2 minutes.

2 Add potatoes, broth, and half-and-half; increase heat to high and bring to boil. Reduce heat to medium-low and simmer until potatoes are tender, about 20 minutes; add Cheddar and stir until melted. Puree soup in pot with hand-held immersion blender, or cool 5 minutes and blend in small batches in blender. Reheat soup and ladle evenly into 6 bowls.

4 **SmartPoints value per serving** (generous 1 cup): 164 Cal, 4 g Total Fat, 2 g Sat Fat, 992 mg Sod, 20 g Total Carb, 4 g Sugar, 3 g Fib, 13 g Prot.

Freestyle it

This rich puree is simple and delicious, and you can easily ramp it up a bit for no additional SmartPoints: Garnish each bowl with a handful of cooked peeled medium shrimp, shredded crabmeat, or diced grilled chicken breast. All are zero Points ingredients.

**Potato-cheese
soup**

Tomato soup with garlic-Cheddar toasts

Tomato soup with garlic-Cheddar toasts

Serves 4

We gave the classic comfort-food combo of tomato soup and grilled cheese an Italian spin. Flavorful San Marzano tomatoes and a bit of fresh herb make the soup especially delicious.

2	teaspoons unsalted butter
1	onion, chopped
3	minced garlic cloves + 2 halved garlic cloves
1	(28-ounce) can San Marzano peeled tomatoes, tomatoes chopped, juice reserved
1½	cups chicken broth
1	teaspoon brown sugar
¼	teaspoon salt, or to taste
⅛	teaspoon red pepper flakes, or to taste
¼	cup reduced-fat cream cheese (Neufachâtel)
8	small slices ciabatta bread (about 4 ounces)
½	cup shredded reduced-fat sharp Cheddar
¼	cup sliced fresh basil leaves or 1 tablespoon fresh thyme leaves

1 Melt butter in large saucepan over medium heat. Add onion; cover and cook, stirring occasionally, until lightly browned, about 7 minutes.

2 Add minced garlic; cook, stirring, until fragrant, about 30 seconds. Stir in tomatoes and juice, broth, brown sugar, salt, and pepper flakes. Bring to boil; reduce heat to medium-low and simmer 5 minutes, stirring occasionally.

3 Add cream cheese, stirring until melted. Remove from heat. Puree soup in pot with handheld immersion blender, or cool 5 minutes and blend in small batches in blender. Add a little more chicken broth or water if soup is very thick.

4 Preheat broiler. Place ciabatta on baking sheet and broil 6 inches from heat source, turning once, until bread is lightly toasted, about 2 minutes. Remove from oven and rub toasted bread with halved garlic cloves. Sprinkle each slice with 1 tablespoon Cheddar. Broil toasts until cheese melts, about 30 seconds.

5 Ladle soup evenly into 4 bowls. Top each serving with 1 tablespoon basil and serve with toasts on the side, or dice toasts and place on top like croutons.

6 **SmartPoints value per serving** (1¼ cups soup and 2 toasts): 227 Cal, 9 g Total Fat, 5 g Sat Fat, 1,054 mg Sod, 27 g Total Carb, 9 g Sugar, 3 g Fib, 11 g Prot.

Note from Chef Eric

A fun way to garnish this soup is to cut the cheese toasts into a small dice, then float the pieces on top. It's like mini-grilled cheeses instead of croutons for your tomato soup!

Creamy asparagus-leek soup with homemade croutons

Serves 8

Leeks and asparagus are a classic duo, and we give this soup a particularly bright flavor by adding Greek yogurt, lemon juice, and fresh mint.

1	**tablespoon unsalted butter**
4	**large leeks (white and light green parts only), split, cut into 2-inch pieces and rinsed well**
1½	**teaspoons minced garlic**
4	**pounds asparagus, trimmed and cut into 2-inch pieces**
6	**cups reduced-sodium chicken broth**
3	**slices reduced-calorie whole wheat bread, cut into cubes**
1¼	**teaspoons kosher salt, or to taste**
1	**teaspoon finely grated lemon zest**
½	**cup plain low-fat Greek yogurt**
1	**tablespoon lemon juice, or to taste**
2	**tablespoons chopped fresh mint leaves**

1 Preheat oven to 375°F.

2 Melt butter in large pot over medium heat. Add leeks and cook, stirring frequently, until softened, about 5 minutes. Add 1 teaspoon garlic and cook 1 minute. Add asparagus and broth and bring to boil. Reduce heat and simmer until asparagus is soft, 12–15 minutes.

3 Meanwhile, spread bread cubes in single layer on baking sheet. Spray with nonstick spray and sprinkle with ¼ teaspoon salt. Bake, stirring halfway through cooking, until croutons are crisp, about 10 minutes. Remove from oven and toss with lemon zest and remaining ½ teaspoon garlic.

4 Add yogurt, lemon juice, and remaining 1 teaspoon salt to soup. Puree soup in pot with handheld immersion blender, or cool 5 minutes and blend in small batches in blender; reheat (do not let soup boil). Ladle evenly into bowls and serve sprinkled with croutons and mint.

2 **SmartPoints value per serving** (1½ cups soup and ⅓ cup croutons): 127 Cal, 2 g Total Fat, 1 g Sat Fat, 763 mg Sod, 21 g Total Carb, 7 g Sugar, 7 Fib, 10 g Prot.

Note from Chef Eric

I love soups that can be served either hot or cold, and this is one of my favorites. Eat this soup cold and it's like a low SmartPoints alternative to rich vichyssoise, a classic chilled potato soup.

Tuscan pumpkin–white bean soup

Serves 6

This deliciously creamy bisque is a weeknight wonder: With just a handful of pantry staples, you can pull off a fantastic soup worth savoring. For a luxurious touch, drizzle each bowl with white truffle oil or pumpkin-seed oil for big flavor and a heady aroma; ½ teaspoon oil drizzled over each bowl will increase the SmartPoints value by just 1.

1   **onion, coarsely chopped**

1   **(15-ounce) can pumpkin puree**

3½ **cups fat-free chicken broth**

1   **(15½-ounce) can cannellini (white kidney) or navy beans, rinsed and drained**

¼   **teaspoon dried oregano**

⅛   **teaspoon salt, or to taste**

⅛   **teaspoon black pepper, or to taste**

6   **tablespoons shredded Parmesan**

1 Coat large pot with nonstick spray and set over medium-low heat. Add onion; cook, covered, stirring occasionally, until tender, about 6 minutes. Stir in pumpkin puree, broth, beans, and oregano; simmer 8 minutes.

2 Puree soup in pot with handheld immersion blender, or cool 5 minutes and blend in small batches in blender; reheat if necessary. Stir in salt and pepper. Ladle evenly into 6 bowls and top each serving with 1 tablespoon Parmesan.

 SmartPoints value per serving (1 cup soup and 1 tablespoon cheese): 149 Cal, 2 g Total Fat, 1 g Sat Fat, 750 mg Sod, 24 g Total Carb, 3 g Sugar, 6 g Fib, 9 g Prot.

Freestyle it
Want a bigger bowl of soup and a bigger hit of protein? Top each bowl with finely diced lobster meat for decadence, or shredded roast chicken breast for heartiness—both are zero Points foods.

Mac 'n' cheese with
creamy squash sauce,
page 119

Pizza, pasta, and noodle dishes

In this chapter

Ⓥ Vegetarian   Ⓥ Vegan   Ⓖ Gluten free   Ⓓ Dairy free   Ⓝ Nut free

Supereasy BLT pizza for two

Serves 2

Make this speedy pizza any time you need a particularly comforting lunch or casual dinner. We suggest using an Italian cheese blend, but you can use plain reduced-fat shredded mozzarella for no change in SmartPoints.

1	**(8-inch) individual prebaked pizza crust**
1	**large tomato, thinly sliced**
½	**cup shredded reduced-fat Italian cheese blend**
2	**teaspoons reduced-fat mayonnaise**
1½	**teaspoons lemon juice**
⅛	**teaspoon salt**
⅛	**teaspoon black pepper**
1	**cup lightly packed thinly sliced romaine lettuce**
2	**slices crisp-cooked bacon, crumbled**
¼	**cup thinly sliced radishes**
2	**scallions, thinly sliced**

1 Preheat oven to 475°F.

2 Place crust on baking sheet. Arrange tomato slices on crust; sprinkle with cheese blend. Bake until heated through and cheese is melted and bubbly, about 6 minutes.

3 Meanwhile, combine mayonnaise, lemon juice, salt, and pepper in medium bowl. Stir in lettuce. Spoon over pizza; sprinkle with bacon, radishes, and scallions. Cut in half.

11 **SmartPoints value per serving** (½ pizza): 379 Cal, 16 g Total Fat, 7 g Sat Fat, 1,065 mg Sod, 38 g Total Carb, 8 g Sugar, 2 g Fib, 20 g Prot.

Three-cheese pepperoni pizza with garlicky spinach

Serves 6

1   teaspoon olive oil

2   garlic cloves, thinly sliced

1   (5-ounce) package baby spinach

Pinch salt

Pinch red pepper flakes

1   (10-ounce) prebaked thin pizza crust

⅔   cup reduced-fat ricotta

½   cup shredded reduced-fat mozzarella

2   tablespoons grated Parmesan

12 thin slices turkey pepperoni, halved

1 Preheat oven to 450°F. Line large baking sheet with aluminum foil.

2 Heat oil in large nonstick skillet over medium heat. Add garlic and cook, stirring, 1 minute. Add spinach to skillet a few handfuls at a time, stirring constantly and adding more as spinach wilts. Continue cooking until all spinach is wilted. Stir in salt and pepper flakes.

3 Place crust on baking sheet. Spread ricotta evenly over crust. Top with spinach. Sprinkle with mozzarella and Parmesan and dot with pepperoni. Bake until cheeses are melted and just begin to brown in places, about 8 minutes. Cut into 6 slices.

7 **SmartPoints value per serving** (1 slice): 236 Cal, 8 g Total Fat, 3 g Sat Fat, 298 mg Sod, 27 g Total Carb, 2 g Sugar, 1 g Fib, 12 g Prot.

Note from Chef Eric

For me, a white pizza is a canvas for expression. It screams for creative toppings. Maybe some roasted leek? Maybe some nutmeg? Heck, you can even crack an egg on top and bake it in the oven to set!

Three-cheese
pepperoni pizza with
garlicky spinach

Cauliflower-crust pizza with feta, peppers, and olives

Serves 4

Rice-like pieces of cauliflower make a tender pizza crust. If you don't have a food processor, don't worry: Use a box grater or sharp knife to prep the cauliflower. Or save a bit of time by purchasing packaged cauliflower crumbles from a supermarket—many now carry this trendy ingredient both fresh in the produce section or frozen alongside other frozen vegetables.

½   **large head cauliflower, cut into florets (about 2 cups)**

⅔   **cup all-purpose flour**

½   **cup shredded part-skim mozzarella**

2   **large eggs**

1   **teaspoon minced fresh oregano leaves + 1 tablespoon chopped fresh oregano leaves**

½   **teaspoon kosher salt**

½   **teaspoon granulated garlic**

⅛   **teaspoon black pepper**

1   **cup roasted red pepper (not packed in oil), drained well and chopped**

⅔   **cup crumbled feta**

10 **pitted Kalamata olives, sliced**

2   **tablespoons chopped scallion**

1   Preheat oven to 450°F. Line large rimmed baking sheet with parchment paper; spray paper with nonstick spray.

2   Put cauliflower in food processor and pulse until it resembles rice. Transfer to large bowl; add flour, mozzarella, eggs, minced oregano, salt, garlic, and black pepper and stir until well combined. Spoon cauliflower mixture onto parchment forming 2 (8-inch) rounds, pressing to form firm, even layer. Bake until crusts begin to brown on bottom, about 20 minutes. With wide spatula, carefully flip crusts over; bake until browned on second side, about 10 minutes longer.

3   Top crusts evenly with roasted pepper, feta, olives, scallion, and chopped oregano. Bake until heated through, about 5 minutes. Cut each pizza into 4 wedges.

6   **SmartPoints value per serving** (2 wedges): 287 Cal, 12 g Total Fat, 6 g Sat Fat, 926 mg Sod, 34 g Total Carb, 6 g Sugar, 4 g Fib, 15 g Prot.

Note from Chef Eric

Glorious cauliflower! This veggie helps make a superb low SmartPoints alternative to classic pizza dough.

Saturday night chicken and pasta

Serves 4

4   **ounces whole wheat linguine**

1¼   **pounds skinless boneless chicken breasts**

¾   **teaspoon salt**

¼   **teaspoon black pepper**

3   **teaspoons olive oil**

¾   **pound cremini mushrooms, sliced**

2   **shallots, sliced**

3   **garlic cloves, minced**

2   **teaspoons finely chopped thyme leaves**

½   **cup dry white wine or marsala wine**

½   **cup chicken broth**

¼   **cup half-and-half**

4   **tablespoons freshly grated Parmesan**

2   **tablespoons chopped fresh parsley**

1 Cook linguine according to package directions. Drain and keep warm.

2 Meanwhile, sprinkle chicken with ½ teaspoon salt and the pepper. Heat 1½ teaspoons oil in large skillet over medium-high heat. Add chicken and cook until browned and cooked through, about 4 minutes per side. Cut chicken crosswise into slices; keep warm.

3 Add mushrooms, shallots, garlic, thyme, remaining 1½ teaspoons oil and remaining ¼ teaspoon salt to skillet. Cook over medium-high heat, stirring occasionally, until mushrooms are softened and lightly browned, about 5 minutes.

4 Add wine, broth, and half-and-half to skillet; bring to boil. Reduce heat and simmer, stirring occasionally, until sauce is slightly thickened, 3–4 minutes. Return chicken with any accumulated juices to skillet. Add linguine; toss until coated with sauce and heated through, 1–2 minutes longer. Serve sprinkled with Parmesan and parsley.

7   **SmartPoints value per serving** (about 1½ cups): 402 Cal, 11 g Total Fat, 3 g Sat Fat, 738 mg Sod, 30 g Total Carb, 4 g Sugar, 4 g Fib, 41 g Prot.

Freestyle it

If you like, make a quick, colorful (and zero Points!) salad to serve with this dish: Toss together 4 cups chopped escarole, 1 small head sliced radicchio, 3 cups arugula, a splash of fresh lemon juice, and salt and pepper to taste. You can even add some chickpeas if you like.

Farfalle with sausage, broccoli rabe, and white beans

Farfalle with sausage, broccoli rabe, and white beans

Serves 4

This easy pasta combines classic Italian ingredients for a dish bursting with flavor. We like farfalle (aka bowties) because they're fun and easy to eat with just a fork (no cutting or twirling required!), but you can substitute any shape that tickles your fancy.

6   ounces whole wheat farfalle pasta

1   (¾-pound) bunch broccoli rabe, tough stems trimmed, cut into 1½-inch pieces

2   teaspoons olive oil

2   (3½-ounce) links low-fat Italian chicken sausage, casings removed

2   large garlic cloves, minced

¼   teaspoon red pepper flakes

1   cup chicken broth or vegetable broth

1   (15½-ounce) can cannellini (white kidney) beans, rinsed and drained

¼   cup thinly sliced sun-dried tomatoes (not packed in oil)

1   tablespoon chopped fresh oregano leaves

Zest and juice of ½ lemon

2   tablespoons grated Parmesan

1 Cook pasta according to package directions, adding broccoli rabe during final 3 minutes of cooking time. Drain and transfer to large bowl. Cover and keep warm.

2 Heat oil in large skillet over medium-high heat. Add sausage and cook, breaking apart with wooden spoon, until browned and cooked through, about 5 minutes. Stir in garlic and pepper flakes; cook 30 seconds.

3 Stir in broth, beans, sun-dried tomatoes, and oregano. Cook until heated through. Add pasta and broccoli rabe to skillet and toss. Add lemon juice. Divide evenly among 4 plates or bowls and top with Parmesan and lemon zest.

7 **SmartPoints value per serving** (2 cups pasta mixture and ½ tablespoon cheese): 375 Cal, 8 g Total Fat, 2 g Sat Fat, 915 mg Sod, 55 g Total Carb, 2 g Sugar, 11 g Fib, 26 g Prot.

Freestyle it
Replace the chicken sausage with 7 ounces of ground skinless boneless chicken breast, a zero Points food, and save 2 SmartPoints on this dish.

Slow-cooker lasagna

Serves 6

A great meat lasagna right from your slow cooker? Absolutely! The secret is browning the beef before adding it to the cooker for rich flavor, then cooking the dish on Low to give the noodles enough time to become tender.

1	**pound ground lean beef (7% fat or less)**
1	**small onion, chopped**
1	**garlic clove, minced**
1	**(28-ounce) can crushed tomatoes**
1	**(15-ounce) can tomato sauce**
1	**teaspoon dried oregano**
1	**teaspoon kosher salt**
¼	**teaspoon red pepper flakes**
1½	**cups shredded part-skim mozzarella**
1	**cup part-skim ricotta**
6	**lasagna noodles**
½	**cup grated Parmesan**

1 Combine beef, onion, and garlic in large heavy skillet; spray with olive oil nonstick spray, tossing to coat evenly. Set over medium-high heat and cook, breaking beef apart with wooden spoon, until beef is no longer pink, about 6 minutes. Stir in crushed tomatoes, tomato sauce, oregano, salt, and pepper flakes; simmer until flavors are blended, about 5 minutes.

2 Meanwhile, stir together 1 cup of mozzarella and the ricotta in medium bowl.

3 Spoon one third of the beef mixture into 5-quart slow cooker. Break 3 lasagna noodles in half and arrange over beef mixture; top with one half of the mozzarella mixture. Spoon one half of the remaining beef mixture on top; break remaining 3 noodles in half and arrange on top of beef mixture. Spoon remaining beef mixture on top of noodles. Cover and cook 4–6 hours on Low. Uncover and turn slow cooker off.

4 Stir together remaining ½ cup mozzarella and Parmesan in small bowl. Sprinkle over lasagna. Cover and set aside until cheeses are melted and lasagna sets up, about 10 minutes.

10 **SmartPoints value per serving** (⅙ of lasagna): 399 Cal, 16 g Total Fat, 8 g Sat Fat, 1,288 mg Sod, 30 g Total Carb, 8 g Sugar, 4 g Fib, 35 g Prot.

Note from Chef Eric

Lasagna is all about layers. Every layer is another opportunity to bring flavor, texture, and "wow" to the dish. Add greens like chopped sautéed chard or spinach for punch (be mindful of the moisture; squeeze it dry before adding it). Or throw in some roasted veggies like broccoli or squash—or both.

Turkey tetrazzini

Serves 4

Succulent chunks of poultry (chicken or turkey) in a rich, creamy sauce is an all-American pasta dish dating to the early 1900s. We modernized it by lowering the fat and upping the veggies.

6	ounces fettuccine
1	(5-ounce) package baby spinach
2	teaspoons olive oil
2	leeks, white and light green parts only, halved, very thinly sliced, and rinsed well
2	celery stalks, chopped
3	garlic cloves, minced
¼	cup dry sherry or white wine
1	(8-ounce) package button or cremini mushrooms, sliced
1	tablespoon chopped fresh rosemary
½	teaspoon salt
½	cup chicken broth or vegetable broth
3	ounces reduced-fat cream cheese (Neufchâtel)
3	tablespoons grated Parmesan
2	cups cubed or shredded cooked skinless turkey breast

1 Cook pasta according to package directions. Drain and return to pot. Add spinach, stirring until wilted. Cover and keep warm.

2 Heat oil in large skillet over medium heat. Add leeks, celery, and garlic. Cook, covered, stirring frequently, until leeks are tender, about 8 minutes.

3 Stir in sherry, mushrooms, rosemary, and salt. Cook, stirring occasionally, until mushrooms are tender, about 5 minutes.

4 Stir in broth, cream cheese, and 2 tablespoons Parmesan. Cook, stirring frequently, until blended and smooth, about 5 minutes. Stir in turkey, pasta, and spinach; cook until heated through, about 3 minutes. Serve topped with remaining Parmesan.

9 **SmartPoints value per serving** (1½ cups pasta mixture and ¾ teaspoon cheese): 413 Cal, 11 g Total Fat, 4 g Sat Fat, 668 mg Sod, 46 g Total Carb, 5 g Sugar, 4 g Fib, 30 g Prot.

Freestyle it
Add a cup of green peas (fresh shelled or frozen) along with the broth in Step 4. They'll add color and flavor to the dish along with a dose of fiber and protein for 0 SmartPoints.

Spaghetti with mozzarella-stuffed meatballs

Serves 4

Mozzarella cheese is a luscious filling for beefy meatballs in this crowd-pleasing recipe. Be sure to cook the meatballs at a low simmer without allowing the sauce to boil vigorously; this will help keep the meatballs intact and prevent the mozzarella from oozing out.

¼   **pound ground lean beef (7% fat or less)**

¼   **pound ground veal**

¼   **pound ground pork**

6   **tablespoons plain dried whole wheat bread crumbs**

2   **tablespoons fat-free milk**

1   **large egg**

1   **large garlic clove, minced**

¼   **teaspoon salt**

¼   **teaspoon black pepper**

¼   **cup + 2 tablespoons grated Parmesan**

¼   **cup + 2 tablespoons chopped fresh basil or parsley**

16   **(½-inch) cubes part-skim mozzarella (about 1½ ounces)**

2   **cups fat-free marinara sauce**

½   **cup water**

6   **ounces whole wheat spaghetti**

1 Stir together beef, veal, pork, bread crumbs, milk, egg, garlic, salt, pepper, ¼ cup Parmesan, and ¼ cup basil in large bowl. Shape beef mixture around mozzarella cubes to form 16 meatballs.

2 Bring marinara and water to simmer in large skillet. Add meatballs. Cover and simmer, stirring gently a few times, until meatballs are cooked through, about 10 minutes.

3 Meanwhile, cook spaghetti according to package directions. Drain.

4 Divide pasta evenly among 4 plates or bowls. Top each portion evenly with meatballs and sauce, and sprinkle with remaining 2 tablespoons Parmesan and 2 tablespoons basil.

12 **SmartPoints value per serving** (¾ cup pasta, 4 meatballs, ⅔ cup sauce, and ½ tablespoon cheese): 458 Cal, 14 Total Fat, 6 g Sat Fat, 734 mg Sod, 50 g Total Carb, 7 g Sugar, 7 g Fib, 34 g Prot.

Note from Chef Eric

Stuffing these meatballs with mozzarella is a decadent move worth making, but if you want to lower the SmartPoints by using ground turkey or chicken instead of meat, why not? Replace the beef, veal, and pork with ¾ pound of ground skinless poultry breast to reduce each serving by 3 SmartPoints.

Spaghetti with mozzarella-stuffed meatballs

Mac 'n' cheese with creamy squash sauce

Mac 'n' cheese with creamy squash sauce

Serves 6

1	**acorn squash**
1	**teaspoon salt**
¼	**teaspoon black pepper**
⅓	**cup panko (Japanese bread crumbs)**
2	**tablespoons grated pecorino Romano**
1	**teaspoon melted unsalted butter**
1	**teaspoon chopped fresh thyme or ¼ teaspoon dried**
1¼	**cups vegetable broth**
1	**cup shredded reduced-fat Cheddar**
¼	**cup crumbled feta**
¼	**cup plain fat-free yogurt**
1	**teaspoon smoked paprika**
6	**ounces elbow macaroni**
3	**cups small cauliflower florets**

1 Preheat oven to 400°F. Spray rimmed baking sheet and 9-inch square baking dish with nonstick spray.

2 Cut squash in half through stem end; remove seeds. Spray cut sides with nonstick spray and sprinkle with ¼ teaspoon salt and ⅛ teaspoon pepper. Place squash cut side down on prepared baking sheet. Bake until fork-tender, about 40 minutes. Cool 10 minutes.

3 Meanwhile, combine panko, pecorino Romano, butter, and thyme in small bowl.

4 Peel and cut up squash; transfer to blender. Add broth, Cheddar, feta, yogurt, paprika, remaining ¾ teaspoon salt, and remaining ⅛ teaspoon pepper; puree.

5 Bring pot of salted water to boil. Add macaroni and cauliflower; return to boil, stirring occasionally. Cook half the time of package directions for pasta. Drain. Place pasta and cauliflower in large bowl. Stir in sauce. Spread in prepared baking dish; top with panko mixture. Bake until top is golden, about 25 minutes.

6 **SmartPoints value per serving** (1 cup): 250 Cal, 5 g Total Fat, 3 g Sat Fat, 835 mg Sod, 39 g Total Carb, 3 g Sugar, 4 g Fib, 13 g Prot.

Note from Chef Eric

Using strongly flavored feta in the squash-and-yogurt based sauce here helps stretch the cheese flavor while keeping it low in SmartPoints.

Spaghetti carbonara with peas

Serves 4

Creamy carbonara gets its velvety sauce from a mixture of eggs and cheese (either pecorino or Parmesan) that is quickly cooked by the heat of freshly boiled pasta, forming a distinctively rich coating. Make sure you keep the mixture warm, but never hot, to ensure the sauce comes out smooth, not curdled.

2	**teaspoons olive oil**
4	**slices center-cut bacon, chopped**
1	**onion, finely chopped**
3	**garlic cloves, finely chopped**
6	**ounces spaghetti**
2	**cups (about 10 ounces) fresh or frozen green peas**
4	**large eggs**
⅓	**cup freshly grated pecorino Romano**
½	**teaspoon salt**
¼	**teaspoon ground black pepper**
2	**tablespoons chopped fresh parsley leaves**
	Cracked black pepper for serving

1 Heat oil in large nonstick skillet over medium heat. Add bacon, onion, and garlic. Cook, stirring occasionally, until onion is golden and bacon is crisp, about 15 minutes. Remove skillet from heat.

2 Meanwhile, cook spaghetti according to package directions, stirring in peas during last 1 minute of cooking time. Whisk together eggs, pecorino Romano, salt, and ground black pepper in medium bowl. Set aside.

3 Drain pasta and peas, reserving ¼ cup cooking liquid. Add pasta to skillet. Whisk cooking liquid into egg mixture. Quickly add egg mixture to hot pasta mixture, tossing to coat.

4 Place skillet over medium-low heat. Cook, stirring, until mixture is very creamy, about 1 minute. Divide pasta evenly among 4 plates or bowls and sprinkle with parsley. Serve with cracked black pepper on the side.

7 **SmartPoints value per serving** (1¼ cups): 373 Cal, 11 g Total Fat, 4 g Sat Fat, 582 mg Sod, 46 g Total Carb, 7 g Sugar, 5 g Fib, 19 g Prot.

Rigatoni with butternut, blue cheese, and walnuts

Serves 4

Here's an example of a few simple ingredients coming together to produce big, rich flavor: sweet roasted winter squash, tangy cheese, and earthy sage and walnuts. Gorgonzola is an ideal melting blue cheese with great depth of flavor and creamy texture, but you can also substitute Danish blue or Maytag blue for no change in SmartPoints.

6	**ounces rigatoni**
1	**(20-ounce) package peeled and cut butternut squash**
2	**teaspoons olive oil**
¼	**teaspoon salt**
1	**small red onion, thinly sliced**
1	**cup vegetable broth**
3	**ounces Gorgonzola, diced**
1	**tablespoon chopped fresh sage**
¼	**teaspoon black pepper**
2	**tablespoons toasted chopped walnuts**

1 Cook rigatoni according to package directions. Drain, reserving ½ cup cooking water. Keep warm.

2 Meanwhile, cut squash into ¾-inch chunks. Heat oil in large nonstick skillet over medium heat. Add squash and salt to skillet and cook, stirring occasionally, until squash is lightly browned, about 10 minutes. Add onion and cook, stirring occasionally, until tender, about 4 minutes. Add broth and bring to boil. Reduce heat, cover, and simmer until squash is fork-tender, about 6 minutes.

3 Add rigatoni to squash mixture and toss to combine. Stir in Gorgonzola, sage, and pepper. Stir in pasta cooking water as needed until creamy. Divide evenly among 4 plates or bowls and sprinkle with walnuts.

9 **SmartPoints value per serving** (1¼ cups pasta mixture and ½ tablespoon walnuts): 353 Cal, 12 g Total Fat, 5 g Sat Fat, 535 mg Sod, 52 g Total Carb, 5 g Sugar, 5 g Fib, 12 g Prot.

Linguine with red clam sauce

Serves 4

24 littleneck clams, scrubbed

½ cup dry white wine

1 tablespoon fresh thyme or 1 teaspoon dried

1 tablespoon chopped fresh oregano or 1 teaspoon dried

4 garlic cloves, finely chopped

6 ounces linguine

1 tablespoon olive oil

8 plum tomatoes, chopped

2 tablespoons chopped fresh basil

3 tablespoons chopped fresh parsley

¼ teaspoon red pepper flakes

½ teaspoon salt

1 (6.5-ounce) can chopped clams and juice

1 Scrub littleneck clams well under cold running water. Place in large pot of cold water; let soak a few minutes to release any residual grit, then drain. Repeat for several changes of water until no sand falls to bottom of pot.

2 Combine clams, wine, thyme, oregano, and garlic in large saucepan. Cover and cook over medium heat until clams open, about 5 minutes. Discard any clams that do not open. When cool enough to handle, remove clam meat from 12 shells and coarsely chop; set aside. Reserve remaining clams with meat still inside for garnish; reserve cooking liquid (including the garlic and herbs) separately.

3 Cook linguine according to package directions. Drain and place in warmed serving bowl; keep warm.

4 Meanwhile, heat oil in medium nonstick skillet over medium heat. Add tomatoes, 1 tablespoon basil, 2 tablespoons parsley, pepper flakes, and salt. Cook, stirring, over medium heat, until tomatoes begin to break down, 5–10 minutes. Add reserved clam cooking liquid and canned clams and juice; reduce heat and simmer until thickened. Stir in chopped clam meat and heat through, about 1 minute. Pour over linguine, toss to coat, and garnish with reserved clam shells. Sprinkle with remaining 1 tablespoon parsley and remaining 1 tablespoon basil and serve at once.

7 **SmartPoints value per serving** (about 1⅔ cups): 354 Cal, 5 g Total Fat, 1 g Sat Fat, 678 mg Sod, 44 g Total Carb, 5 g Sugar, 3 g Fib, 26 g Prot.

Freestyle it

Want a mixed-seafood dish? Add a dozen scrubbed mussels and a handful or two of peeled deveined medium shrimp to the skillet in Step 4 after the tomatoes are cooked through; cook, covered, until the mussels open and the shrimp are pink. You'll get a delicious linguine *frutti di mare* with no change in SmartPoints.

**Linguine with
red clam sauce**

Veggie Bolognese with soy and mushrooms

Serves 4

A mixture of dried porcini mushrooms and fresh cremini mushrooms gives this vegetarian penne deep, rich flavor while keeping it meatless.

½ **pound whole wheat penne**

½ **ounce dried porcini mushrooms**

¾ **cup boiling water**

1 **teaspoon olive oil**

4 **ounces cremini mushrooms, trimmed and thinly sliced**

1 **carrot, diced**

½ **onion, diced**

6 **ounces frozen soy crumbles, thawed**

2 **garlic cloves, finely chopped**

1½ **cups fat-free marinara sauce**

¼ **cup fresh basil leaves, thinly sliced**

1 Cook penne according to package directions. Drain and keep warm.

2 Meanwhile, put porcini mushrooms in measuring cup and pour boiling water over them. Let stand 5 minutes to soften. With slotted spoon, remove mushrooms from liquid; reserve liquid. Coarsely chop mushrooms.

3 Heat oil in large nonstick saucepan over medium heat. Add cremini mushrooms and cook, stirring frequently, until soft and brown, about 6 minutes. Add carrot and onion and cook 3 more minutes. Stir in porcini mushrooms, soy crumbles, and garlic; cook, stirring frequently, 2 minutes. Stir in marinara and carefully pour in reserved mushroom liquid, making sure to leave any grit in bottom of cup. Bring to boil. Reduce heat and simmer 5 minutes.

4 Remove saucepan from heat and stir in penne. Serve sprinkled with basil.

 9 **SmartPoints value per serving** (about 1⅔ cups): 359 Cal, 4 g Total Fat, 0 g Sat Fat, 453 mg Sod, 61 g Total Carb, 7 g Sugar, 6 g Fib, 20 g Prot.

Freestyle it
Soy crumbles are a tasty meat substitute and convenient to keep in the freezer. If you like, however, you can substitute a zero Points protein like diced smoked tofu and save 1 SmartPoints value.

Asian turkey noodle bowls with peanuts

Serves 6

Got leftovers? This noodle dish will keep refrigerated for up to 2 days. You don't even have to reheat it—enjoy it chilled, the way bowls of noodles are often served in Asian countries.

4	**ounces rice-stick noodles**
¼	**cup chicken broth**
	Grated zest and juice of 2 limes
1	**tablespoon packed brown sugar**
1	**tablespoon soy sauce**
2	**teaspoons Asian fish sauce**
1½	**teaspoons chili-garlic paste**
2	**teaspoons peanut oil**
1	**pound ground skinless turkey breast**
½	**teaspoon Chinese five-spice powder**
¼	**teaspoon salt**
3	**cups small broccoli florets**
3	**garlic cloves, minced**
1	**tablespoon minced peeled fresh ginger**
¼	**cup chopped fresh cilantro leaves**
4	**tablespoons dry-roasted peanuts, coarsely chopped**

1 Prepare rice stick noodles according to package directions. Drain well and transfer to medium bowl.

2 Meanwhile, whisk together broth, lime zest and juice, brown sugar, soy sauce, fish sauce, and chili-garlic paste in small bowl until brown sugar dissolves.

3 Heat 1 teaspoon oil in large skillet over medium-high heat. Add turkey, five-spice powder, and salt. Cook, breaking turkey apart with wooden spoon, until turkey is no longer pink and most liquid has evaporated, about 5 minutes. Add turkey mixture to noodles.

4 Heat remaining 1 teaspoon oil in same skillet over medium-high heat. Add broccoli, garlic, and ginger. Cook, stirring constantly, just until broccoli turns bright green, about 4 minutes. Add noodles and turkey mixture to broccoli in skillet and cook, tossing, until heated through. Remove from heat and stir in lime mixture. Sprinkle with cilantro and peanuts.

4 **SmartPoints value per serving** (1 cup noodles and broccoli and 1 tablespoon peanuts): 244 Cal, 8 g Total Fat, 1 g Sat Fat, 504 mg Sod, 24 g Total Carb, 4 g Sugar, 2 g Fib, 21 g Prot.

Ramen noodles with chicken and guachjong

Serves 4

If you know guachjong, the spicy Korean condiment made from chiles and fermented soybeans, you might already be a fan; if you don't, you should give it a try. Here it flavors tender chicken and veggies in a fantastic noodle dish.

2 **teaspoons sesame oil**

1 **teaspoon canola or safflower oil**

2 **garlic cloves, minced**

2 **teaspoons minced peeled fresh ginger**

1 **pound boneless skinless chicken breast, sliced crosswise into thin strips**

1 **pound baby bok choy, trimmed and stems sliced**

1 **(8-ounce) package cremini mushrooms, trimmed and halved**

2¼ **cups chicken broth**

2 **tablespoons reduced-sodium soy sauce**

2 **tablespoons guachjong (Korean chili-garlic sauce)**

4 **ounces dried ramen noodles, seasoning packet discarded**

4 **radishes, thinly sliced**

2 **tablespoons cilantro leaves**

2 **scallions, thinly sliced**

1 Heat sesame oil and canola oil in wok or large saucepan over medium-high heat. Add garlic and ginger; cook, stirring constantly, until fragrant, about 30 seconds. Add chicken and cook, stirring frequently, 2 minutes.

2 Stir in bok choy, mushrooms, ¼ cup broth, the soy sauce, and guachjong; cook until tender, about 2 minutes.

3 Bring remaining 2 cups broth to boil in small saucepan. Add noodles and cook, tossing with tongs occasionally, until tender, 2–3 minutes. Divide noodles evenly among 4 plates or bowls. Top evenly with chicken mixture, radishes, cilantro, and scallions.

5 **SmartPoints value per serving** (1 bowl): 334 Cal, 17 g Total Fat, 2 g Sat Fat, 868 mg Sod, 13 g Total Carb, 3 g Sugar, 2 g Fib, 32 g Prot.

Note from Chef Eric

The best part about a ramen is the intense richness of the broth. To pump it up, put the broth in a pressure cooker with chicken thighs or even chicken bones. Cook for an hour, then skim any fat, and you'll have a broth that screams "chicken!"

Warm udon salad with spicy pork

Serves 6

Thick udon noodles are a Japanese classic made from wheat flour and available at larger supermarkets or specialty stores. This recipe for udon with pork and veggies is delicious warm, but you can also enjoy it chilled or at room temperature, the way the Japanese often serve udon in the summer months.

4	**ounces udon noodles**
½	**pound green beans, sliced on diagonal into 1½-inch pieces**
1	**teaspoon canola oil**
¾	**pound pork tenderloin, trimmed and cut into thin 3-inch-long strips**
½	**teaspoon togarashi pepper or ⅛ teaspoon cayenne, or to taste**
¼	**teaspoon salt**
2	**tablespoons mirin**
2½	**tablespoons soy sauce**
1	**teaspoon finely grated peeled fresh ginger**
¾	**cup cilantro leaves**
1	**small avocado, pitted, peeled, and cut into ½-inch cubes**

1 Cook noodles according to package directions, adding green beans during last 3 minutes of cooking. Drain.

2 Meanwhile, heat oil in large wok or heavy skillet over medium-high heat until very hot. Add pork, togarashi, and salt and stir-fry just until pork is no longer pink, about 2 minutes. Add noodles and green beans, mirin, soy sauce, and ginger; stir-fry until heated through, about 2 minutes. Divide noodle mixture evenly among 6 bowls and garnish with cilantro and avocado.

 SmartPoints value per serving (1½ cups): 198 Cal, 7 g Total Fat, 1 g Sat Fat, 533 mg Sod, 19 g Total Carb, 1 g Sugar, 3 g Fib, 16 g Prot.

Freestyle it
For more vegetable goodness, add 2 grated carrots along with the noodles and green beans in Step 1.

Singapore rice noodles with seafood

Serves 4

This aromatic stir-fry features rice noodles tossed with a delicious mixture of spiced shrimp and scallops. Stir-fries cook quickly, making them great for weeknights, but be sure to have all ingredients chopped and measured before you start cooking.

4	**ounces thin rice noodles**
½	**cup vegetable broth**
¼	**cup soy sauce, or to taste**
1	**tablespoon Asian fish sauce**
2	**tablespoons curry powder**
2	**teaspoons sesame oil**
1	**pound medium shrimp, peeled and deveined**
½	**pound large sea scallops, halved**
1	**onion, thinly sliced**
1	**red bell pepper, cut into thin strips**
2	**celery stalks, cut into thin strips**
1	**serrano or Thai chile pepper, seeded and thinly sliced (leave seeds in for a hotter dish)**
1	**cup snow peas, trimmed**
1	**tablespoon minced peeled fresh ginger**
2	**garlic cloves, minced**
½	**cup lightly packed fresh cilantro leaves**
3	**scallions, sliced**
Lime wedges for serving	

1 Place rice noodles in large bowl and pour in boiling water to cover. Let stand until tender, about 6 minutes. Drain and set aside.

2 Combine broth, soy sauce, fish sauce, and curry powder in small bowl; set aside.

3 Heat oil in wok or large skillet over high heat. Add shrimp and scallops; stir-fry 30 seconds. Add onion, bell pepper, celery, and chile pepper; stir-fry 1 minute. Stir in snow peas, ginger, garlic, and broth mixture. Stir-fry until seafood is cooked through, 1–2 minutes.

4 Add noodles to pan, tossing to coat. Divide mixture evenly among 4 plates or bowls and sprinkle with cilantro and scallions. Serve with lime wedges.

 SmartPoints value per serving (1½ cups): 308 Cal, 5 g Total Fat, 1 g Sat Fat, 2,194 mg Sod, 40 g Total Carb, 5 g Sugar, 5 g Fib, 28 g Prot.

Singapore rice noodles
with seafood

Vegetable pad thai

Vegetable pad thai

Serves 6

Sweet-and-savory pad thai is a noodle favorite. Our version includes the classic rice noodles mixed with a rainbow of vegetables, tofu, and Sriracha topped with egg and peanuts.
Rice noodles can vary in thickness and softening time, so for best results start checking for doneness after 3 minutes of soaking. The texture should be flexible but firm, not mushy.

4	**ounces flat rice stick noodles**
2	**teaspoons canola oil**
1	**red bell pepper, cut into thin strips**
1	**small red onion, thinly sliced**
2	**carrots, cut into matchstick strips**
1½	**cups thinly sliced green cabbage**
2	**garlic cloves, finely chopped**
2	**tablespoons Asian fish sauce**
2	**tablespoons reduced-sodium soy sauce**
1	**tablespoon tamarind paste (optional)**
1	**tablespoon sugar**
8	**ounces baked or smoked tofu, cut into thin slices**
1½	**teaspoons Sriracha or other hot pepper sauce**
3	**large hard-cooked eggs, chopped**
½	**cup chopped fresh cilantro**
2	**tablespoons dry-roasted peanuts, chopped**
6	**lime wedges**

1 Place noodles in large bowl. Add enough boiling water to cover; let stand until noodles are softened but still firm at the center, 3–7 minutes. Drain in colander and rinse under cold running water. Drain again.

2 Meanwhile, heat oil in large skillet over medium-high heat. Add bell pepper, onion, and carrots; cook, stirring frequently, until vegetables are crisp-tender, 2–3 minutes. Add cabbage and garlic; cook, stirring frequently, until fragrant, about 1 minute. In small cup, stir together fish sauce, soy sauce, tamarind paste (if using), and sugar. Add to skillet and cook, stirring, 30 seconds. Add noodles and tofu; cook, tossing gently to mix, until heated through, 2–3 minutes.

3 Remove pan from heat. Add Sriracha and toss gently. Divide noodles evenly among 6 plates or bowls; sprinkle evenly with eggs, cilantro, and peanuts. Serve with lime wedges.

4 **SmartPoints value per serving** (about 1 cup noodle mixture and 1 teaspoon peanuts): 243 Cal, 9 g Total Fat, 2 g Sat Fat, 919 mg Sod, 28 g Total Carb, 7 g Sugar, 3 g Fib, 8 g Prot.

Note from Chef Eric
The optional tamarind paste brings authentic tang to this sweet-and-savory dish. Look for it at specialty stores.

Soba noodles with tofu, garlic, and spinach

Serves 4

6   **ounces soba noodles**

2   **tablespoons rice wine vinegar**

2   **tablespoons + 1 teaspoon soy sauce**

2   **teaspoons agave nectar**

6   **scallions, thinly sliced**

1   **teaspoon Asian (dark) sesame oil**

3   **garlic cloves, thinly sliced**

1   **(4-ounce) package fresh spinach leaves, rinsed but not dried**

1   **cup very thinly sliced red cabbage**

½   **cup sliced water chestnuts**

2   **(8-ounce) packages baked teriyaki tofu, cubed**

2   **teaspoons toasted sesame seeds**

1 Cook noodles according to package directions (do not overcook or noodles will be gummy). Drain and place in large bowl. While noodles are still warm, add vinegar, 2 tablespoons soy sauce, the agave nectar, and half the scallions; toss to coat.

2 Meanwhile, coat large skillet or wok with nonstick spray; add oil and place skillet over medium-high heat. When oil is hot, add garlic; cook, stirring, until fragrant, about 30 seconds. Add spinach; cook, stirring, until spinach wilts, 1–2 minutes. Stir in cabbage and water chestnuts. Add spinach mixture to noodle mixture and toss; keep warm.

3 Coat skillet again with nonstick spray. Add tofu to skillet and cook over medium-high heat, tossing, until tofu is browned and heated through, about 2 minutes. Sprinkle tofu with remaining 1 teaspoon soy sauce and toss. Divide noodles evenly among 4 bowls and top evenly with tofu and remaining scallions. Sprinkle with sesame seeds.

(5) **SmartPoints value per serving** (about 1⅓ cups noodles and tofu and ½ teaspoon sesame seeds): 401 Cal, 12 g Total Fat, 2 g Sat Fat, 1,372 mg Sod, 50 g Total Carb, 7 g Sugar, 4 g Fib, 14 g Prot.

Freestyle it

Get more protein and fiber by adding 1½ cups shelled cooked edamame to the skillet along with the spinach in Step 2 for no additional SmartPoints.

Shrimp scampi "zoodles" with garlic crumbs

Serves 4

Skip the rice or traditional pasta and try garlicky shrimp scampi with zucchini noodles instead. Be sure to cook "zoodles" just until barely tender; if they're cooked too long they can release a lot of liquid and make the dish watery.

4	teaspoons extra-virgin olive oil
½	cup panko (Japanese bread crumbs)
6	garlic cloves, minced
1¼	pounds large shrimp, peeled and deveined
3	shallots, chopped
1¼	teaspoons salt
⅛	teaspoon red pepper flakes, or to taste
⅓	cup dry white wine
1¼	pounds zucchini noodles (about 7 cups)
1	cup chopped ripe plum tomatoes
1	teaspoon finely grated lemon zest
1	tablespoon fresh lemon juice
¼	cup chopped fresh parsley or sliced basil

1 Heat ½ teaspoon oil in large skillet over medium heat. Add panko and 1 garlic clove and cook, stirring, until crumbs are golden, 2–3 minutes. Remove from skillet and set aside.

2 Heat 1 teaspoon oil in same skillet over medium-high heat. Add shrimp and shallots and sprinkle with ¼ teaspoon salt and the pepper flakes. Cook, stirring frequently, until shrimp are almost cooked through, about 3 minutes. Add wine and remaining 5 garlic cloves and cook, stirring, until shrimp are cooked through, about 2 minutes. Transfer shrimp to bowl.

3 Heat 1½ teaspoons oil in same skillet over medium-high heat. Add zucchini and sprinkle with ½ teaspoon salt. Cook, tossing, just until zucchini is crisp-tender, about 2 minutes.

4 Remove skillet from heat and stir in shrimp and juices, tomatoes, lemon zest and juice, parsley, and remaining ½ teaspoon salt. Divide evenly among 4 bowls or plates. Drizzle each serving with ¼ teaspoon of remaining oil and sprinkle each with 2 tablespoons crumbs.

4 **SmartPoints value per serving** (1¼ cups zoodles and shrimp, 2 tablespoons crumbs, and ¼ teaspoon oil): 264 Cal, 8 g Total Fat, 1 g Sat Fat, 1,636 mg Sod, 22 g Total Carb, 7 g Sugar, 3 g Fib, 24 g Prot.

Freestyle it
Vegetable "noodles" are a tasty zero Points alternative to pasta. Look for them in the produce section of larger supermarkets, or make your own with a spiralizer. See page 135 for another great veggie-noodle recipe.

Beet and butternut
"noodles" with kale
and feta

Beet and butternut "noodles" with kale and feta

Serves 4

(ⓥ) (ⓖ) (ⓢ)

We suggest a combination of beet and butternut noodles in this dish because of how brilliant they look together, but you can also use just one or the other. Lacinato kale, also known as dinosaur kale or Tuscan kale, is a variety with very dark blue-green leaves. You also use green kale instead.

6	**ounces beet noodles (about 3 cups)**
6	**ounces butternut noodles (about 3 cups)**
4	**teaspoons extra-virgin olive oil**
1	**onion, chopped**
3	**garlic cloves, minced**
2	**teaspoons fresh thyme leaves**
1	**bunch lacinato kale, tough ribs removed, leaves sliced (about 5 cups)**
¾	**teaspoon salt**
¼	**teaspoon black pepper**
1	**teaspoon lemon juice**
1½	**teaspoons balsamic vinegar**
⅔	**cup crumbled feta**
½	**cup toasted pumpkin seeds**

1 Bring 1 inch water to boil in large saucepan. Place beet noodles in one half of steamer basket and butternut noodles in the other half (keep them as separate as possible so beet juice won't stain the butternut noodles). Place basket over water; cover and steam until tender, about 9 minutes.

2 Meanwhile, heat 1 teaspoon oil in large nonstick skillet over medium heat. Add onion and cook, stirring occasionally, until golden, about 7 minutes. Add garlic and thyme and cook, stirring, until fragrant, about 30 seconds.

3 Add kale, ½ teaspoon salt, and ⅛ teaspoon pepper; cook over medium heat, covered, stirring occasionally, until kale is tender, about 6 minutes. Remove from heat.

4 Place hot beet and butternut noodles in large bowl and toss with lemon juice, 1 teaspoon oil, remaining ¼ teaspoon salt, and remaining ⅛ teaspoon pepper. Add kale mixture and balsamic and gently toss. Spoon evenly onto 4 plates; sprinkle evenly with feta and pumpkin seeds. Drizzle each serving with ½ teaspoon of remaining oil.

(7) **SmartPoints value per serving** (1½ cups vegetable noodles, 2½ tablespoons cheese, 2 tablespoons pumpkin seeds, and ½ teaspoon oil): 253 Cal, 18 g Total Fat, 5 g Sat Fat, 774 mg Sod, 17 g Total Carb, 6 g Sugar, 5 g Fib, 10 g Prot.

Freestyle it
Some great additions to this dish include diced hard-cooked egg or chickpeas—both zero Points foods.

Sweet-and-smoky
Sunday chicken,
page 143

Celery root and Yukon
Gold mash, page 209

Chapter 6

Roasts, casseroles, and other oven meals

Collard greens with
garlicky mojo, page 217

In this chapter

Ⓥ Vegetarian   Ⓥ Vegan   Ⓖ Gluten free   Ⓓ Dairy free   Ⓝ Nut free

Turkey and quinoa meat loaf

Serves 6

This crowd-pleasing meat loaf combines tasty turkey with nutty whole-grain quinoa and a good dose of veggies. Quinoa has a bitter protective coating called saponin, so giving it a good rinse in a fine-mesh sieve before cooking is essential—unless it says prerinsed on the package.

½ **cup quinoa, rinsed well**

1 **zucchini, shredded**

2 **large egg whites**

1 **small red onion, finely chopped**

1 **tablespoon chopped fresh parsley**

1 **teaspoon Italian seasoning blend**

½ **cup chili sauce or ketchup**

½ **teaspoon salt**

½ **teaspoon black pepper**

1 **pound ground skinless turkey breast**

1 Cook quinoa according to package directions. Fluff with fork; let cool slightly.

2 Meanwhile, preheat oven to 375°F. Line bottom of 9x13-inch baking pan with parchment paper.

3 Squeeze zucchini dry; combine in large bowl with egg whites, onion, parsley, Italian seasoning, ¼ cup chili sauce, the salt, and pepper. Add turkey and quinoa and mix well. Transfer mixture to baking pan; shape into 5x11-inch loaf. Brush remaining ¼ cup chili sauce over loaf.

4 Bake until instant-read thermometer inserted into center of meat loaf registers 165°F, 50–55 minutes. Let stand 5 minutes. Cut into 6 slices.

3 **SmartPoints value per serving** (1 slice): 177 Cal, 2 g Total Fat, 1 g Sat Fat, 773 mg Sod, 19 g Total Carb, 5 g Sugar, 3 g Fib, 21 g Prot.

Note from Chef Eric
I love making this updated classic at home when it's just me and the kids. It's so easy to throw together, and I get to play with them while the oven does the work.

Crunchy oven-fried drumsticks

Serves 6

1 **cup low-fat buttermilk**

2 **garlic cloves, crushed through garlic press**

1 **teaspoon salt**

½ **teaspoon black pepper**

6 **(¼-pound) skinless chicken drumsticks**

½ **cup whole wheat panko (Japanese bread crumbs)**

1 **teaspoon chili powder**

1 **teaspoon paprika**

¾ **teaspoon mustard powder**

½ **teaspoon garlic powder**

1 Combine buttermilk, garlic, ½ teaspoon salt, and pepper in large zip-close plastic bag; add chicken. Squeeze out air and seal bag; turn to coat chicken. Refrigerate at least 20 minutes or up to 1 day, turning bag occasionally.

2 Set oven rack in lower third of oven. Preheat oven to 400°F. Line baking sheet with foil; spray with nonstick spray.

3 Combine panko, chili powder, paprika, mustard powder, garlic powder, and remaining ½ teaspoon salt on sheet of wax paper. Drain chicken and discard marinade. Coat drumsticks, one at a time, in panko mixture, pressing so it adheres. Lightly spray each drumstick with nonstick spray and arrange on prepared baking sheet.

4 Bake chicken until browned and instant-read thermometer inserted into thickest part of drumstick (not touching bone) registers 165°F, about 35 minutes. Let stand 5 minutes before serving.

4 **SmartPoints value per serving** (1 piece chicken): 179 Cal, 5 g Total Fat, 1 g Sat Fat, 603 mg Sod, 10 g Total Carb, 2 g Sugar, 1 g Fib, 24 g Prot.

Crunchy oven-fried drumsticks

Sweet-and-smoky
Sunday chicken

Collard greens
with garlicky
mojo, page 217

Celery root and
Yukon Gold
mash, page 209

Sweet-and-smoky Sunday chicken

Serves 6

Nothing beats the aroma of a roasting chicken, and this foolproof recipe requires just a few ingredients and minimal prep. We call it Sunday chicken, but it's easy enough for any weeknight; just pop it in the oven and begin checking it for doneness after about an hour.

1 **tablespoon brown sugar**
1 **tablespoon smoked paprika**
1 **tablespoon hot pepper sauce**
1 **tablespoon balsamic vinegar**
2 **garlic cloves, minced**
½ **teaspoon salt**
1 **(3½-pound) whole chicken, giblets removed**

1 Preheat oven to 375°F. Spray roasting rack with nonstick spray and place in roasting pan.

2 Combine brown sugar, paprika, pepper sauce, vinegar, garlic, and salt in small bowl.

3 With fingers, gently separate chicken skin from breast and thigh meat. Rub seasoning mix onto meat under skin. Smooth skin back into place. Tuck wings under chicken and tie legs together with kitchen string.

4 Place chicken, breast side up, on prepared rack in roasting pan. Roast until instant-read thermometer inserted into thigh (not touching bone) registers 165°F, 1¼–1½ hours.

5 Transfer chicken to cutting board; let stand 10 minutes. Discard wings; cut chicken into 6 pieces. Remove skin before eating.

3 **SmartPoints value per serving** (1 piece chicken): 175 Cal, 4 g Total Fat, 1 g Sat Fat, 361 mg Sod, 4 g Total Carb, 3 g Sugar, 0 g Fib, 29 g Prot.

Stuffed cabbage

Serves 8

1 **tablespoon olive oil**

1 **cup finely chopped onion**

1 **(28-ounce) can crushed tomatoes**

2 **tablespoons red-wine vinegar**

2 **tablespoons brown sugar**

1 **cup seedless red grapes**

¾ **teaspoon salt**

¼ **teaspoon pepper**

1 **large head green cabbage (16 large leaves will be used)**

2 **pounds ground skinless turkey breast**

2 **large eggs, beaten**

½ **cup dried bread crumbs**

¼ **cup uncooked rice**

1 **teaspoon chopped fresh oregano, or ½ teaspoon dried**

1 To make sauce, heat oil in large saucepan over medium-low heat. Add ½ cup onion and cook, stirring occasionally, until translucent, about 8 minutes. Add tomatoes, vinegar, brown sugar, grapes, ½ teaspoon salt, and ⅛ teaspoon pepper. Bring to boil, lower heat, and simmer, uncovered, 30 minutes, stirring occasionally. Set aside.

2 Meanwhile, bring large pot of water to boil. Remove core from cabbage by cutting around it at an angle with a paring knife. Immerse head of cabbage in boiling water for a few minutes; remove with tongs as soon as outer few leaves are flexible. Peel off leaves, then return head to water. Repeat until you have 16 leaves. Let cool. Save remaining head of cabbage for another use.

3 To make filling, combine turkey, eggs, remaining ½ cup onion, the bread crumbs, rice, oregano, remaining ¼ teaspoon salt, and remaining ⅛ teaspoon pepper in large bowl and stir until combined. Add 1 cup of sauce to meat mixture and mix lightly with fork.

4 Preheat oven to 350°F. To assemble stuffed cabbage, place 1 cup sauce in bottom of large Dutch oven. Remove tough rib from the base of each cabbage leaf by cutting it out with a paring knife. Place ⅓ to ½ cup of filling in an oval shape near the bottom edge (where you cut out the rib) of 1 leaf. Tuck in sides and roll up to enclose filling. Repeat with remaining leaves and filling. Place 8 rolls, seam sides down, over sauce in Dutch oven. Cover with more sauce. Add remaining rolls and cover with remaining sauce. Cover pot and bake until meat is cooked and rice is tender, about 1 hour.

 2 **SmartPoints value per serving** (2 rolls and ⅓ cup sauce): 314 Cal, 8 g Total Fat, 2 g Sat Fat, 521 mg Sod, 31 g Total Carb, 14 g Sugar, 6 g Fib, 31 g Prot.

Note from Chef Eric

Comfort food is best when it evokes a feeling of family and tradition. Stuffed cabbage was a staple at holiday gatherings when I was growing up. For this version, I substitute ground turkey for beef. I also use grapes instead of the traditional raisins, bringing subdued sweetness and adding zero Points.

Stuffed
cabbage

Beef tenderloin with fingerlings
and horseradish cream

Beef tenderloin with fingerlings and horseradish cream

Serves 6

Here's a supereasy meal! Everything is roasted together in one pan: melt-in-your-mouth beef tenderloin (aka filet mignon), satisfying potatoes, and flavorful Brussels sprouts. Lining the pan with foil means cleanup is a snap.

¾ **cup plain low-fat Greek yogurt**

3 **tablespoons bottled horseradish**

2 **tablespoons chopped fresh chives**

1½ **teaspoons kosher salt**

1¼ **teaspoons Dijon mustard**

⅛ **teaspoon + ¼ teaspoon black pepper**

¼ **cup fresh rosemary leaves, chopped, plus a few sprigs for garnish**

2 **tablespoons olive oil**

3 **large garlic cloves, minced**

1 **teaspoon grated lemon zest**

1½ **pounds fingerling potatoes, scrubbed and halved or quartered if large**

¾ **pound Brussels sprouts, halved or quartered if large**

1 **(1½-pound) lean beef tenderloin, trimmed and tied**

1 To make horseradish cream, stir together yogurt, horseradish, chives, ½ teaspoon salt, mustard, and ⅛ teaspoon pepper in serving bowl. Cover and refrigerate.

2 Preheat oven to 450°F. Line large roasting pan or rimmed baking sheet with foil; spray with nonstick spray.

3 Stir together chopped rosemary, oil, garlic, lemon zest, remaining 1 teaspoon salt, and remaining ¼ teaspoon pepper in small bowl.

4 Combine potatoes and Brussels sprouts in prepared pan. Sprinkle with 2 tablespoons rosemary mixture and toss until coated evenly. Push vegetables to opposite sides of pan, forming even layer. Rub remaining rosemary mixture all over beef. Place beef in center of pan.

5 Roast, stirring vegetables once after 20 minutes, until instant-read thermometer inserted into center of beef registers 145°F, about 30 minutes. Transfer beef to cutting board; let stand 5 minutes. Cut into 12 slices and serve with potato mixture and horseradish cream. Garnish with rosemary sprigs.

8 **SmartPoints value per serving** (2 slices beef with 1¾ cups potato mixture and 2 tablespoons horseradish cream): 351 Cal, 12 g Total Fat, 4 g Sat Fat, 633 mg Sod, 27 g Total Carb, 3 g Sugar, 5 g Fib, 32 g Prot.

Note from Chef Eric

This horseradish cream is also delicious as a dip for raw or roasted vegetables. A ¼-cup serving of the sauce alone is 1 SmartPoints value.

Garlic-herb roasted pork loin with pears

Serves 12

This easy pork roast feeds a crowd, or plan for leftovers to serve during the week—it makes great pork sandwiches! We like it accompanied with brilliant red sauerkraut as a color and flavor contrast, but you could also serve it with pickled red onions.

6	**ripe pears, peeled, halved, and cored**
1	**(3-pound) lean boneless pork loin roast, trimmed**
3	**garlic cloves, cut into slivers**
2	**tablespoons chopped fresh rosemary**
2	**tablespoons chopped fresh thyme**
1	**tablespoon olive oil**
1	**teaspoon salt**
½	**teaspoon black pepper**

Red sauerkraut for serving (optional)

1 Preheat oven to 400°F. Spray medium roasting pan with nonstick spray. Lay pears across bottom of pan, overlapping if they won't fit in single layer.

2 With small knife, cut about 24 shallow slits in pork; insert garlic slivers into slits.

3 Mix together rosemary, thyme, oil, salt, and pepper in cup. Rub all over pork, pushing herb mixture into slits. Place pork in pan on top of pears and roast until instant-read thermometer inserted into center of roast registers 145°F, about 1 hour.

4 Transfer pork to cutting board and let stand 10 minutes. Arrange pears on platter. Cut pork into 24 slices and place on platter. Spoon any pan drippings over pork and serve sauerkraut (if using) alongside.

SmartPoints value per serving (2 slices pork and 1 pear half): 211 Cal, 6 g Total Fat, 2 g Sat Fat, 251 mg Sod, 13 Total Carb, 8 g Sugar, 3 g Fib, 26 g Prot.

Note from Chef Eric

Add a teaspoon or two of Dijon mustard to this rub to bring some heat to the party.

Miso-maple cod with red rice

Serves 4

4 (6-ounce) skinless cod fillets

2 tablespoons red or white miso paste

2 teaspoons maple syrup

1 tablespoon rice vinegar

1 tablespoon mirin

2 teaspoons reduced-sodium soy sauce

1 teaspoon Sriracha or other hot pepper sauce

1¼ cups water

¼ teaspoon salt

½ cup red rice

4 cups lightly packed baby arugula

2 seedless clementines, sectioned

¼ cup fresh cilantro leaves

1 small avocado, peeled, pitted, and thinly sliced

3 scallions, sliced

1 Bring water and salt to boil in small saucepan; stir in rice. Cover, adjust heat, and simmer until rice is tender and water is absorbed, about 50 minutes. Cover and keep warm.

2 Line baking sheet with foil; spray foil with nonstick spray and place cod on foil. Whisk miso, maple syrup, vinegar, mirin, soy sauce, and Sriracha in small bowl until smooth. Spread evenly over cod. Set aside.

3 Preheat broiler. Broil fish 5 inches from heat until browned and just opaque in center, 4–5 minutes.

4 Place 1 cup arugula in each of 4 bowls. Top evenly with rice, clementines, and cilantro. Place 1 fillet on each serving and top evenly with avocado slices. Sprinkle with scallions.

 SmartPoints value per serving (1 bowl): 336 Cal, 8 g Total Fat, 1 g Sat Fat, 668 mg Sod, 31 g Total Carb, 7 g Sugar, 5 g Fib, 35 g Prot.

Freestyle it

Want an easy vegan version of this dish? Just replace the cod with tofu, also a zero Points food. Drain a 16-ounce package of firm tofu, cut it into 4 slices, and press the slices between plates and drain to remove excess liquid. You can then top and broil it just like you would the cod.

Pomegranate-glazed branzino with spinach and potatoes

Serves 4

1 **pound Red Bliss potatoes, diced**

5 **ounces (about 8 cups) baby spinach**

1 **red onion, thinly sliced**

2 **tablespoons olive oil**

1 **whole 3-pound branzino, or 2 whole 1½- to 2-pound branzinos, cleaned by your fish seller**

½ **teaspoon salt**

1 **lemon, thinly sliced**

4 **sprigs fresh rosemary**

2 **tablespoons pomegranate molasses**

1 **teaspoon flaky sea salt (such as Maldon)**

3 **tablespoons pomegranate seeds**

1 Preheat oven to 400°F. In large bowl, toss potatoes, spinach, and onion with 1 tablespoon oil and arrange on baking sheet. Season fish with salt inside and out. Stuff cavity with lemon and rosemary and place on another baking sheet. Brush fish with remaining 1 tablespoon oil. Bake fish and vegetables 25 minutes.

2 Stir vegetables. Brush fish with pomegranate molasses and continue cooking until skin is lightly charred and flesh and backbone appear opaque, about 20 minutes. To ensure fish is cooked, gently push the tip of a knife through center of fish; if there is no resistance, fish is done.

3 Remove fish and vegetables from oven. Cover vegetables and keep warm. Let fish rest 10 minutes. Transfer fish to platter. Sprinkle fish with flaky salt and pomegranate seeds. Spoon vegetables around fish and serve.

6 **SmartPoints value per serving** (¼ of fish and ½ cup vegetables): 361 Cal, 11 g Total Fat, 2 g Sat Fat, 963 mg Sod, 32 g Total Carb, 9 g Sugar, 4 g Fib, 35 g Prot.

Note from Chef Eric

For me, there is no more rewarding, elegant family-style roast than a whole fish. I love to serve it with the head and tail on, but feel free to have your fishmonger remove them for you if you or your guests prefer. Don't be afraid to get a good char on the skin when you roast; it adds great flavor.

Pomegranate-glazed branzino with spinach and potatoes

Baked beer batter fish 'n' chips

Serves 4

- **2** **(½-pound) baking potatoes, scrubbed**
- **2** **teaspoons olive oil**
- **1** **teaspoon salt**
- **¾** **teaspoon paprika**
- **⅓** **cup light beer**
- **¼** **cup all-purpose flour**
- **1** **large egg white**
- **½** **teaspoon thyme**
- **¼** **teaspoon black pepper**
- **1** **cup panko (Japanese bread crumbs)**
- **1** **pound skinless cod fillet, cut crosswise into 8 pieces**

Malt vinegar or lemon wedges for serving (optional)

1 Adjust oven racks to upper and lower thirds of oven. Preheat oven to 475°F. Spray 2 medium rimmed baking sheets with olive oil nonstick spray.

2 Cut potatoes lengthwise in half; cut each half into 4 wedges. Toss together potatoes, oil, ½ teaspoon salt, and ½ teaspoon paprika in large bowl. Place potatoes, cut side down, on 1 prepared baking sheet. Roast on lower oven rack until bottoms of potatoes are deep golden and crisp, about 15 minutes. Turn potatoes over and roast until crisp outside and tender inside, about 15 minutes longer.

3 Meanwhile, to make batter, whisk together beer, flour, egg white, thyme, pepper, remaining ½ teaspoon salt, and remaining ¼ teaspoon paprika in medium bowl. Place panko on sheet of wax paper. Dip fish, one piece at a time, into batter and then into crumbs, pressing so they adhere.

4 Place fish on remaining prepared baking sheet; lightly spray with nonstick spray. About 10 minutes before potato baking time is up, place fish on upper oven rack. Bake until golden brown and just opaque in center, about 10 minutes. Serve with potatoes and malt vinegar or lemon wedges (if using).

 SmartPoints value per serving (2 pieces fish and 4 potato wedges): 336 Cal, 6 g Total Fat, 1 g Sat Fat, 848 mg Sod, 41 g Total Carb, 2 g Sugar, 4 g Fib, 27 g Prot.

Note from Chef Eric

Two ways to keep this fish-and-chips meal authentic without adding SmartPoints: Serve it wrapped in or on top of newspaper, and drizzle it with malt vinegar instead of lemon juice. That's British comfort food at its best!

Easy chicken sausage enchiladas

Serves 12

2   **teaspoons canola oil**

¾   **pound hot Italian chicken or turkey sausages, casings removed**

1   **large red bell pepper, chopped**

1   **large onion, chopped**

2   **garlic cloves, minced**

2½   **teaspoons chili powder**

1¼   **teaspoons ground cumin**

⅛   **teaspoon black pepper**

1   **(14½-ounce) can diced tomatoes**

1   **(15-ounce) can black beans, rinsed and drained**

1   **(15-ounce) can pinto beans, rinsed and drained**

12   **(6-inch) flour tortillas**

1   **(15½-ounce) jar or can enchilada sauce**

1¼   **cups shredded reduced-fat Cheddar**

1 Preheat oven to 350°F. Spray 9x13-inch baking dish with nonstick spray.

2 Heat oil in large nonstick skillet over medium heat. Add sausage, bell pepper, and onion; cook, breaking sausage apart with wooden spoon, until sausage is cooked through, vegetables are tender, and most liquid evaporates, about 15 minutes. Add garlic, chili powder, cumin, and black pepper; cook, stirring occasionally, just until fragrant, about 1 minute. Stir in tomatoes, black beans, and pinto beans; bring to boil. Reduce heat and simmer until flavors are blended, about 5 minutes.

3 Place tortillas on work surface. Evenly spoon sausage mixture down center of each tortilla; roll up to enclose filling. Place enchiladas, seam side down, in prepared baking dish; spread evenly with enchilada sauce and sprinkle with Cheddar.

4 Cover baking dish with nonstick foil. Bake until enchiladas are heated through and sauce is bubbly, 30–40 minutes. Let stand 5 minutes before serving.

5 **SmartPoints value per serving** (1 enchilada): 255 Cal, 7 g Total Fat, 2 g Sat Fat, 737 mg Sod, 32 g Total Carb, 3 g Sugar, 6 g Fib, 15 g Prot.

Note from Chef Eric

A great way to add even more bang and flavor to this dish is with a tomatillo sauce. Simply roast husked tomatillos with some garlic and onion until soft and browned, then puree with cilantro and a pinch or two of ground cloves. *Dios, mio amigos!*

Tuna, noodle, and green bean casserole

Serves 6

1 cup wide whole wheat egg noodles

½ pound green beans, trimmed, cut into 1-inch pieces, or left whole

2 teaspoons olive oil

½ pound cremini mushrooms, sliced

1 onion, finely chopped

2 garlic cloves, finely chopped

1 cup chicken broth

1 (10¾-ounce) can condensed cream of mushroom soup

¼ teaspoon salt, or to taste

¼ teaspoon black pepper, or to taste

2 (5-ounce) cans water-packed solid white tuna, drained and flaked

¼ cup chopped fresh parsley leaves

¾ cup canned French fried or crispy fried onions

12 pitted black olives, sliced

1 Preheat oven to 350°F.

2 Bring large saucepan filled two-thirds full of salted water to boil. Add noodles and cook until barely tender, about 9 minutes, adding green beans during last 3 minutes of cooking time. Drain and set aside.

3 Heat oil in large heavy ovenproof skillet over medium heat. Add mushrooms, chopped onion, and garlic. Cook, stirring, until vegetables are tender, about 8 minutes. Remove from heat and whisk in broth and soup. Gently stir in noodles and green beans, salt, and pepper. Fold in tuna and parsley.

4 Sprinkle fried onions on top and dot with sliced olives. Bake until filling is bubbly and top is golden, about 15 minutes. Cool 5 minutes before serving.

 5 **SmartPoints value per serving** (generous 1 cup casserole): 228 Cal, 10 g Total Fat, 2 g Sat Fat, 879 mg Sod, 19 g Total Carb, 3 g Sugar, 3 g Fib, 16 g Prot.

Freestyle it

Love green peas in tuna casserole? They're a zero Points food, so go for it! Add a cup of fresh or frozen peas along with the green beans in Step 2.

Eggplant parmesan

Serves 6

This version of the Italian favorite hits all the right cheesy, saucy notes for just a fraction of the calories and fat.

1   **(2-pound) eggplant, cut into ½-inch-thick rounds**

1   **teaspoon chopped fresh thyme leaves**

¾   **teaspoon salt**

¼   **teaspoon black pepper**

2   **teaspoons olive oil**

2   **large shallots, finely chopped**

Pinch red pepper flakes, or to taste

1   **(28-ounce) can whole peeled tomatoes, with juice**

¾   **cup part-skim ricotta**

¼   **cup + 2 tablespoons grated Parmesan**

¼   **cup chopped fresh basil leaves**

2   **tablespoons panko (Japanese bread crumbs)**

½   **cup shredded part-skim mozzarella**

1 Arrange oven racks in upper and lower thirds of oven. Preheat oven to 425°F. Line two large baking sheets with parchment paper.

2 Generously spray both sides of eggplant with nonstick spray. Arrange on prepared baking sheets in single layer. Sprinkle with thyme, ¼ teaspoon salt, and the black pepper, pressing so it adheres. Roast until eggplant is golden brown and very tender, about 20 minutes, turning eggplant over and rotating baking sheets after 10 minutes.

3 Meanwhile, heat oil in large skillet over medium heat. Add shallots and pepper flakes; cook, stirring, until shallots are softened, about 4 minutes. Add tomatoes and ¼ teaspoon salt; bring to boil over high heat, breaking up tomatoes with side of wooden spoon. Reduce heat and simmer until sauce is thickened, about 20 minutes.

4 Stir together ricotta, ¼ cup Parmesan, the basil, and remaining ¼ teaspoon salt in medium bowl. Stir together panko and remaining 2 tablespoons Parmesan in small bowl.

5 Increase oven temperature to 450°F. Lightly spray 10-inch square or 2-quart baking dish with nonstick spray.

6 Spread ½ cup sauce in bottom of prepared dish; top with single layer of eggplant. Dot eggplant with ½ cup ricotta mixture. Top evenly with ¼ cup mozzarella, another layer of eggplant, 1 cup sauce, and remaining ½ cup ricotta mixture. Repeat layering with remaining eggplant, remaining ¼ cup mozzarella, and remaining sauce. Sprinkle evenly with panko mixture. Bake on upper rack until top is golden and sauce is bubbly, about 15 minutes. Let stand 5 minutes before cutting into 6 portions.

 SmartPoints value per serving (⅙ of casserole): 185 Cal, 8 g Total Fat, 4 g Sat Fat, 655 mg Sod, 20 g Total Carb, 8 g Sugar, 6 g Fib, 11 g Prot.

Baked falafel with cucumber-yogurt sauce

Baked falafel with cucumber-yogurt sauce

Serves 4

FALAFEL

1	cup lightly packed fresh cilantro leaves
1	cup lightly packed fresh parsley leaves
3	garlic cloves, minced
1	teaspoon ground cumin
1	teaspoon chili powder
1	teaspoon ground coriander
1	(15½-ounce) can chickpeas, rinsed and drained
2½	tablespoons lemon juice
4	teaspoons olive oil
2	tablespoons all-purpose flour
2	teaspoons sesame seeds
½	teaspoon baking powder
½	teaspoon salt

YOGURT SAUCE

1	cup plain nonfat Greek yogurt
2	Kirby cucumbers, peeled and grated
2	tablespoons fresh lemon juice
1	cup fresh mint leaves, chopped
¼	teaspoon salt
¼	teaspoon cracked black pepper

Dried sumac for garnish (optional)

1 To make falafel, preheat oven to 400°F. Line large baking sheet with foil. Spray foil with nonstick spray.

2 Combine all falafel ingredients in food processor and pulse until coarse paste forms. Form mixture into 12 balls, each about the size of a golf ball. Place balls about 2 inches apart on baking sheet and press very lightly on each to form thick patty. Spray patties with nonstick spray. Bake 15 minutes. Flip patties very carefully with spatula and bake until crisped, about 10 minutes longer. Let cool slightly.

3 To make yogurt sauce, combine all yogurt sauce ingredients in medium bowl and mix thoroughly. Sprinkle with sumac (if using). To serve, place a pool of sauce on each of 4 plates and top with warm falafel patties.

2 **SmartPoints value per serving** (about ½ cup sauce and 3 patties): 276 Cal, 9 g Total Fat, 1 g Sat Fat, 819 mg Sod, 37 g Total Carb, 7 g Sugar, 10 g Fib, 16 g Prot.

Note from Chef Eric

Being a member of the WW community has reaffirmed my appreciation and love for the almighty chickpea. Falafel is the chickpea's best foot forward, but to make falafel healthier, I've begun preparing them baked instead of fried. A sauce of cucumber and yogurt is an ideal partner.

Texas-style
turkey chili,
page 167

Satisfying stews

In this chapter

Ⓥ Vegetarian   Ⓥ Vegan   Ⓖ Gluten free   Ⓓ Dairy free   Ⓝ Nut free

Bayou chicken sausage gumbo

Serves 4

2　teaspoons canola oil

6　ounces (2 links) chicken andouille sausage, sliced

1　onion, chopped

3　celery stalks, chopped

1　green bell pepper, chopped

4　garlic cloves, minced

2　tablespoons all-purpose flour

1　teaspoon Cajun seasoning

2　cups chicken broth

1　(14½-ounce) can diced tomatoes with green pepper, celery, and onions

1　cup frozen sliced okra

¼　teaspoon salt

1　cup chopped cooked chicken breast

2　cups hot cooked rice

Hot sauce for serving

1 Heat oil in large saucepan over medium-high heat. Add sausage, onion, celery, bell pepper, and garlic; cook, stirring often, until vegetables are softened, about 5 minutes. Add flour and Cajun seasoning; cook, stirring constantly, 1 minute.

2 Stir in broth, tomatoes, okra, and salt; bring to boil. Reduce heat and simmer, uncovered, until slightly thickened, about 15 minutes. Add chicken and simmer 2 minutes more. Divide gumbo evenly among 4 bowls and top each with ½ cup rice. Serve with hot sauce on the side.

8 **SmartPoints value per serving** (1¼ cups gumbo with ½ cup rice): 336 Cal, 8 g Total Fat, 2 g Sat Fat, 1,510 mg Sod, 43 g Total Carb, 11 g Sugar, 4 g Fib, 24 g Prot.

Freestyle it

Chicken and seafood combinations are popular in gumbo, and since most seafood is 0 SmartPoints, you can experiment, adding some without recalculating SmartPoints. Add peeled shrimp or crawfish tails with the chicken in Step 2 and cook until the shellfish is cooked through, 3 to 4 minutes.

Chicken stew with cornmeal-sage dumplings

Serves 4

Chicken and dumplings is a dish that got many Americans through hard times, including the Civil War and the Great Depression: It was an economical way to stretch a single chicken over several meals. Today it's a home and restaurant favorite, beloved for its combination of spoonable stew and tender biscuit-like dumplings.

STEW

2	teaspoons olive oil
1	onion, chopped
1	cup baby-cut carrots, sliced diagonally in half
3	celery stalks, thinly sliced on diagonal
1	garlic clove, minced
½	teaspoon salt
¼	teaspoon black pepper
1	tablespoon all-purpose flour
4	cups chicken broth
½	pound green beans, trimmed and cut into 1-inch pieces
2	cups cubed skinless boneless cooked chicken breast

DUMPLINGS

⅔	cup all-purpose flour
⅓	cup yellow cornmeal
¾	teaspoon baking powder
½	teaspoon dried sage, crumbled
¼	teaspoon salt
1	cup low-fat buttermilk
1	tablespoon finely chopped fresh parsley leaves, plus more for garnish

1 To make stew, heat oil in Dutch oven over medium heat. Add onion, carrots, celery, garlic, salt, and pepper; cook, stirring occasionally, until onion is softened, about 5 minutes. Stir in flour and cook, stirring, 1 minute. Slowly stir in broth. Add green beans and chicken and bring to boil. Reduce heat and simmer, covered, until beans are crisp-tender, about 5 minutes.

2 Meanwhile, to make dumplings, whisk together flour, cornmeal, baking powder, sage, and salt in medium bowl. Add buttermilk and 1 tablesoon parsley, stirring just until flour mixture is moistened. Drop batter by rounded teaspoonfuls into simmering stew, making 16 dumplings. Cook 8 minutes; gently turn dumplings over. Cook, covered, until dumplings are light and fluffy, 8–10 minutes longer. Sprinkle with parsley. Ladle stew and dumplings evenly into 4 bowls.

6 **SmartPoints value per serving** (about 1½ cups stew and 4 dumplings): 342 Cal, 6 g Total Fat, 2 g Sat Fat, 1,570 mg Sod, 41 g Total Carb, 9 g Sugar, 5 g Fib, 30 g Prot.

Chicken stew with cornmeal-sage dumplings

Mexican-spiced shredded chicken and hominy

Serves 8

Stews with shredded chicken (particularly thigh meat) are a classic when it comes to comfort food. This recipe combines it with traditional Mexican seasonings and hominy, a deliciously toothsome corn product popular South of the border.

2	**teaspoons olive oil**
1	**large onion, chopped**
2	**garlic cloves, finely chopped**
2	**teaspoons dried oregano**
1½	**teaspoons ground coriander**
1½	**teaspoons chili powder**
1½	**teaspoons ground cumin**
¾	**teaspoon salt, or to taste**
1	**(14½-ounce) can petite diced tomatoes with chipotle**
2	**cups chicken broth**
1½	**pounds skinless boneless chicken thighs**
1	**(29-ounce) can hominy, rinsed and drained**
2	**small zucchini, quartered lengthwise and cut into 1-inch pieces**
¼	**cup chopped fresh cilantro**
	Lime wedges

1 Heat oil in large skillet over medium-high heat. Add onion and cook, stirring occasionally, until golden, about 5 minutes.

2 Add garlic, oregano, coriander, chili powder, cumin, and salt to skillet; cook, stirring, 1 minute.

3 Add tomatoes, broth, and chicken to skillet; bring to boil over high heat, scraping bottom of pan. Reduce heat and simmer, covered, until chicken is cooked through, about 20 minutes (if liquid in pan doesn't cover chicken, turn chicken halfway through cooking). Transfer chicken to plate.

4 Add hominy and zucchini to pan and increase heat to medium-high; cook until zucchini is tender and liquid is reduced, stirring occasionally, about 15 minutes.

5 Shred or thinly slice chicken and return to pan. Ladle into 8 bowls and top with cilantro. Serve with lime wedges.

 SmartPoints value per serving (generous 1 cup): 216 Cal, 6 g Total Fat, 1 g Sat Fat, 1,083 mg Sod, 21 g Total Carb, 2 g Sugar, 4 g Fib, 20 g Prot.

Note from Chef Eric

Living in Los Angeles, I'm surrounded by some of the finest Mexican food in the United States, and nothing warms the *corazón* like a great *pozole*. Serve this dish with sliced radish and shredded cabbage for authentic crunch. Maybe top it with sliced avocado, too (one quarter of a small Hass avocado has 2 SmartPoints).

Turkey mole

Serves 6

Recipes for mole (pronounced MO-lay), Mexico's famous chili sauce, can call for up to 40 ingredients and take days to prepare. Our version streamlines the prep and focuses on the delicious basics.

1	**tablespoon ground cumin**
2	**teaspoons dried oregano**
½	**teaspoon salt**
¼	**teaspoon black pepper**
¼	**teaspoon ground allspice**
2	**pounds skinless turkey thighs, trimmed**
2	**teaspoons safflower oil or canola oil**
1	**large onion, chopped**
3	**carrots, sliced**
3	**garlic cloves, finely chopped**
2	**cups chicken broth**
1	**(14½-ounce) can diced tomatoes**
¼	**cup raisins**
3	**dried apricot halves, chopped**
1	**tablespoon finely chopped chipotles en adobo, or to taste**
1	**ounce bittersweet chocolate, chopped**
⅓	**cup pepitas (shelled green pumpkin seeds), toasted**
2	**tablespoons sesame seeds, toasted**

Thinly sliced red onion and fresh cilantro sprigs for garnish

1 Combine cumin, oregano, salt, pepper, and allspice in large bowl. Add turkey and toss to coat. Spray large Dutch oven with nonstick spray and set over medium-high heat. Add turkey and cook until browned, about 4 minutes on each side; transfer turkey to plate.

2 Heat oil in same pot over medium heat. Add chopped onion, carrots, and garlic; cover and cook, stirring occasionally, until vegetables are tender, about 5 minutes. Return turkey and any accumulated juices to pot. Stir in broth, tomatoes, raisins, apricots, and chipotle en adobo, scraping up browned bits from bottom of pan. Bring to boil over high heat. Cover, lower heat, and simmer until turkey is fork-tender, about 1½ hours.

3 Remove pot from heat. With slotted spoon, transfer turkey to cutting board; when cool enough to handle, discard bones and shred turkey. Cover and keep warm. Stir chocolate, pepitas, and 1 tablespoon sesame seeds into sauce mixture. Let sauce cool 5 minutes. Transfer one half of sauce to blender and puree; pour into medium bowl. Puree remaining sauce. Return sauce to pot; stir in turkey. Cook over medium heat until hot, about 3 minutes. Ladle into 6 bowls; top each bowl with ½ teaspoon of remaining sesame seeds and garnish with red onion and cilantro.

7 **SmartPoints value per serving** (1 cup mole and ½ teaspoon sesame seeds): 306 Cal, 13 g Total Fat, 4 g Sat Fat, 869 mg Sod, 20 g Total Carb, 9 g Sugar, 5 g Fib, 32 g Prot.

Note from Chef Eric

One thing I'll never do is sacrifice flavor in my dishes. This SmartPoints-friendly recipe is everything WW Freestyle is about: healthy, creative, and flavorful food. And using chocolate in a dish while keeping it low in SmartPoints? Yes, please!

Texas-style
turkey chili

Texas-style turkey chili

Serves 6

Forget chili powder: Texas-style chili uses dried whole chilies and spices for rich flavor, not a store-bought mix. We add a bit of tomato puree to our version for body (many purists wouldn't) and a few aromatic veggies because we love them. Go forth and simmer, then garnish the chili as you like—our recommendations are all 0 SmartPoints.

3   **mild dried whole chiles (such as ancho, pasilla, or Anaheim)**

1   **cup boiling water**

2   **tablespoons sunflower oil**

2½ **pounds boneless skinless turkey breast, trimmed and cut into ½-inch cubes**

1   **teaspoon salt, plus more to taste**

1   **onion, diced**

1   **celery stalk, diced**

4   **garlic cloves, chopped**

1½ **tablespoons ground cumin**

3   **tablespoons tomato paste**

1½ **cups tomato puree**

¾   **cup lager or other beer**

2   **cups beef broth**

⅛   **teaspoon–¼ teaspoon ground habanero chile pepper or other very hot ground chile**

Chopped cilantro, plain fat-free Greek yogurt, diced red onion, and lime wedges for serving on the side (optional)

1 In small bowl, combine dried chilies and boiling water and let soak 30 minutes. Remove and discard stems and seeds; transfer chiles and soaking liquid to blender. Puree and set aside.

2 Meanwhile, heat 1 tablespoon oil in very large pot over high heat. Sprinkle turkey with salt. Working in 3 batches, add turkey and cook, turning occasionally, until browned, about 4 minutes per batch. Remove with slotted spoon.

3 Add remaining 1 tablespoon oil to same pot . Add onion, celery, and garlic and cook, stirring frequently, until softened, about 5 minutes. Stir in cumin and cook 30 seconds. Stir in tomato paste and cook 2 minutes longer. Stir in tomato puree, beer, broth, pureed dried chile mixture, and ground habanero. Bring to boil, reduce heat, cover, and simmer until turkey is very tender, about 1 hour.

4 Simmer chili, uncovered, until thickened slightly, about 10 minutes. Taste and season with more salt and ground chile, if desired. Ladle evenly into 6 bowls. Serve with toppings of choice on the side for diners to customize their bowls.

② **SmartPoints value per serving** (1⅓ cups): 289 Cal, 8 g Total Fat, 1 g Sat Fat, 1,118 mg Sod, 11 g Total Carb, 5 g Sugar, 2 g Fib, 43 g Prot.

Note from Chef Eric
Some purists say *no* to beans in chili, but they're such a great zero Points way to add body and flavor—I can't resist them. Add a can of your favorite variety to this stew for 0 additional SmartPoints.

Caribbean beef stew with coconut basmati rice

Serves 6

Jerk seasoning gives this luscious stew heat and spice, and chunks of sweet potato are an unexpected highlight. We pair it with aromatic coconut rice for a tropical treat.

1	**pound lean boneless beef bottom round, trimmed and cut into 1-inch chunks**
1	**tablespoon jerk seasoning, or to taste**
2	**teaspoons olive oil**
1	**onion, thinly sliced**
2	**garlic cloves, minced**
1	**(14½-ounce) can diced tomatoes**
1	**(14½-ounce) can beef broth**
½	**teaspoon salt**
2	**sweet potatoes (about 12 ounces), peeled and cubed**
½	**pound fresh green beans, trimmed and cut into 1-inch pieces**
1½	**cups water**
1	**cup brown basmati rice**
½	**cup light (low-fat) coconut milk**
1	**cup finely diced pineapple for serving (optional)**
	Cilantro leaves

1 Sprinkle beef with jerk seasoning. Heat oil in Dutch oven over medium-high heat. Add beef and cook, stirring occasionally, until browned, about 4 minutes. Add onion and garlic and cook, stirring occasionally, until onion is softened, about 5 minutes. Add tomatoes, broth, and ¼ teaspoon salt; bring to boil. Reduce heat and simmer, covered, until beef is almost tender, about 45 minutes. Add sweet potatoes and simmer, covered, until potatoes are almost tender, about 15 minutes. Add green beans and simmer, covered, until beans are tender, about 6 minutes longer.

2 Meanwhile, to make rice, bring water and remaining ¼ teaspoon salt to boil in medium saucepan. Add rice and coconut milk; return to boil. Reduce heat and simmer, covered, until rice is tender, about 40 minutes. Divide rice and stew evenly among 6 bowls. Top with pineapple (if using) and cilantro.

 SmartPoints value per serving (generous 1 cup stew with ½ cup rice): 335 Cal, 8 g Total Fat, 3 g Sat Fat, 693 mg Sod, 45 g Total Carb, 7 g Sugar, 5 g Fib, 22 g Prot.

Note from Chef Eric

I'm always looking for a low SmartPoints way to satisfy my sweet tooth, and adding sweet potato and pineapple to this savory dish is a great way to do just that. And the coconut evokes flavors of the islands every time.

Caribbean beef stew with coconut basmati rice

Brandy-laced beef and mushroom stroganoff

Serves 4

This speedy version of Hungarian stroganoff uses beef tenderloin, a naturally tender cut that doesn't require long cooking. With mushrooms, brandy, and paprika, the flavor is delicious and the aroma intoxicating!

6	**ounces wide egg noodles**
2	**tablespoons all-purpose flour**
¾	**teaspoon salt**
¼	**teaspoon black pepper, or to taste**
1	**pound lean beef tenderloin, trimmed, cut into thin slices, slices cut into strips**
2	**teaspoons olive oil**
1	**large red onion, thinly sliced**
1	**tablespoon sweet paprika, preferably Hungarian**
1	**pound mixed mushrooms, sliced (if using shiitakes, remove stems)**
3	**tablespoons brandy**
1	**cup beef broth**
½	**cup reduced-fat sour cream**
2	**tablespoons chopped fresh parsley**

1 Cook noodles according to package directions. Drain and keep warm.

2 Combine flour, ¼ teaspoon salt, and the pepper in large zip-close plastic bag. Add beef; seal bag and shake until beef is coated evenly.

3 Heat oil in large heavy skillet over medium-high heat. Working in 2 batches, cook beef until lightly browned, stirring once or twice, about 2 minutes per batch. Transfer beef to plate.

4 Add onion to skillet and cook, stirring, until softened, about 5 minutes; stir in paprika. Add mushrooms and remaining ½ teaspoon salt; cook, stirring frequently, until mushrooms soften, about 6 minutes. Add brandy and bring to boil; cook, stirring, until almost evaporated. Add broth and bring to boil; reduce heat and simmer until liquid is slightly reduced, 2–3 minutes.

5 Return beef and any accumulated juices to skillet; cook, stirring, until heated through, about 2 minutes. Remove skillet from heat; stir in sour cream. Divide noodles evenly among 4 plates or bowls and top with stroganoff and parsley.

12 **SmartPoints value per serving** (about 1 cup beef with sauce and ⅓ cup noodles): 488 Cal, 16 g Total Fat, 6 g Sat Fat, 725 mg Sod, 43 g Total Carb, 5 g Sugar, 4 g Fib, 38 g Prot.

Note from Chef Eric
This classic and decadent dish is perfect, luxurious comfort food to warm the soul.

Classic firehouse chili

Serves 4

2 teaspoons sunflower oil or canola oil

1 pound ground lean beef (7% fat or less)

1 cup diced onion

1 small green bell pepper, chopped

2 garlic cloves, finely chopped

1 tablespoon chili powder

½ teaspoon cayenne, or to taste

½ teaspoon salt

2 tablespoons tomato paste

1 (15-ounce) can kidney beans, rinsed and drained

1 (15-ounce) can diced fire-roasted tomatoes

1 cup beef broth

½ cup shredded reduced-fat Cheddar

1 Heat oil in large saucepan over medium-high heat. Add beef; cook, stirring occasionally and breaking chunks apart with spoon, until browned, about 8 minutes. Reserve ¼ cup diced onion for garnish. Add remaining ¾ cup onion, bell pepper, garlic, chili powder, cayenne, and salt. Cook, stirring frequently, until vegetables soften, about 5 minutes.

2 Stir in tomato paste; cook, stirring, 2 minutes. Add beans, tomatoes, and broth; bring to boil. Reduce heat to medium-low. Simmer, uncovered, stirring occasionally, until chili thickens, about 10 minutes.

3 Ladle chili evenly into 4 bowls and serve garnished with reserved onion and Cheddar.

7 **SmartPoints value per serving** (1¼ cups chili and 2 tablespoons cheese): 389 Cal, 14 g Total Fat, 5 g Sat Fat, 1,309 mg Sod, 30 g Total Carb, 9 g Sugar, 8 g Fib, 36 g Prot.

Freestyle it

Serve your chili with a variety of zero Points toppings for everyone to customize their own bowl: Plain fat-free Greek yogurt, chopped cilantro, sliced scallions, sliced radishes, diced tomato, pickled jalapeños, and lime wedges are all excellent additions.

Slow-cooker veal stew with mushrooms

Serves 4

Tender veal meat is excellent in stews, and here it's paired with root vegetables and earthy mushrooms for a hearty dish that's big on flavor but low in fat.

1	**pound lean veal stew meat, cut into 1-inch chunks**
¾	**teaspoon salt**
¼	**teaspoon black pepper**
3	**teaspoons olive oil**
1	**onion, finely chopped**
1	**tablespoon all-purpose flour**
1	**cup chicken broth**
½	**pound small red potatoes, cut into ½-inch-thick slices**
1	**large carrot, cut into ½-inch-thick slices**
2	**large garlic cloves, minced**
2	**teaspoons grated lemon zest**
½	**teaspoon dried thyme**
2	**(4-ounce) packages assorted sliced mixed mushrooms**
2	**tablespoons chopped fresh chives**

1 Sprinkle veal with ½ teaspoon salt and ⅛ teaspoon pepper. Heat 2 teaspoons oil in large skillet over medium-high heat. Working in two batches, add veal and cook until browned on all sides, about 3 minutes per batch. With slotted spoon, transfer veal to 5- to 6-quart slow cooker.

2 Heat remaining 1 teaspoon oil in same skillet over medium heat. Add onion; cover, and cook, stirring occasionally, until golden, about 3 minutes. Add flour and cook, uncovered, stirring constantly, 1 minute. Stir in broth and bring to boil, scraping up browned bits from bottom of pan.

3 Transfer onion mixture to slow cooker. Add potatoes, carrot, garlic, lemon zest, thyme, remaining ¼ teaspoon salt, remaining ⅛ teaspoon pepper, and the mushrooms to slow cooker. Cover and cook on Low until veal is fork-tender, 5–6 hours. Ladle evenly into 4 bowls and sprinkle with chives.

 SmartPoints value per serving (1¼ cups): 234 Cal, 6 g Total Fat, 1 g Sat Fat, 746 mg Sod, 18 g Total Carb, 4 g Sugar, 3 g Fib, 28 g Prot.

Note from Chef Eric

One of my all-time favorite veal dishes is a *blanquette de veau*, a creamy French version of this stew. Want to recreate it with some zero Points ingredients? Add peas and stir in some plain nonfat Greek yogurt or unsweetened plain soy yogurt at the end of cooking. *Voilà!*

Venison stew with root vegetables

Serves 4

Lean, flavorful venison is a stewing favorite, available fresh or frozen in much of the country or from specialty stores. If you can't find it, or if you prefer beef, the recipe is equally delicious prepared with lean round steak; use ¾ pound cubed beef round for no change in SmartPoints value.

1	**pound venison tenderloins, cut into 1½-inch cubes**
¾	**teaspoon salt**
¼	**teaspoon black pepper**
4	**teaspoons olive oil**
1	**large onion, diced**
1	**fennel bulb, chopped**
2	**large garlic cloves, minced**
2	**teaspoons chopped fresh rosemary**
2	**teaspoons chopped fresh thyme**
1½	**tablespoons tomato paste**
1	**cup dry red wine**
2½	**cups beef broth**
¾	**pound red potatoes, cut into 1½-inch chunks**
¾	**pound carrots, sliced on diagonal 1½-inch thick**
¼	**cup chopped fresh parsley leaves**

1 Sprinkle venison with ½ teaspoon salt and the pepper. Heat 2 teaspoons oil in medium Dutch oven over medium-high heat. Add one half of venison and cook until browned, about 8 minutes, turning cubes occasionally. Transfer to plate and repeat with remaining venison.

2 Heat remaining 2 teaspoons oil in same pot over medium heat. Add onion and fennel; cover and cook, stirring occasionally, until vegetables are tender, about 5 minutes. Add garlic, rosemary, and thyme; cook, stirring frequently, until fragrant, about 1 minute. Return venison and any accumulated juices to pot. Stir in tomato paste, wine, broth, and remaining ¼ teaspoon salt, scraping up browned bits from bottom of pan. Bring to boil over high heat. Cover, lower heat, and simmer 45 minutes.

3 Stir in potatoes and carrots. Return to boil; cover, adjust heat, and simmer until venison and vegetables are fork-tender, about 45 minutes. Stir in parsley.

 SmartPoints value per serving (1¾ cups): 372 Cal, 8 g Total Fat, 2 g Sat Fat, 1,122 mg Sod, 34 g Total Carb, 10 g Sugar, 7 g Fib, 32 g Prot.

Slow-cooker
lamb couscous

Slow-cooker lamb couscous

Serves 6

Leg of lamb is popular for its rich, bold flavor, and slow cooking keeps it fantastically moist and tender in this couscous dish. Most slow cookers heat more evenly on Low, and most foods will be tastier with longer cooking, so that's how we recommend cooking this stew. If you're pressed for time, however, use the High setting and the stew should be done in 3–3½ hours.

2   **pounds lean leg of lamb, trimmed and cut into 1-inch cubes**

¼   **cup all-purpose flour**

1½   **teaspoons kosher salt, or to taste**

½   **teaspoon black pepper**

2   **teaspoons olive oil**

3   **leeks, halved lengthwise and cut into 1½-inch pieces, rinsed well**

1   **pound baby-cut carrots, halved**

1   **cup chicken broth**

3   **tablespoons Dijon mustard**

2   **tablespoons minced fresh rosemary**

2   **garlic cloves, finely chopped**

1   **cup couscous**

Parsley for garnish (optional)

1 Toss lamb with flour, 1 teaspoon salt, and ¼ teaspoon pepper in large bowl. Heat oil in large skillet over medium-high heat. Working in batches, add lamb to skillet and brown on all sides; add to 4- or 5-quart slow cooker.

2 Add leeks and carrots to slow cooker; stir to combine. Whisk broth, mustard, rosemary, and garlic in small bowl. Pour over lamb and vegetables; cover and cook on Low until lamb shreds easily with fork, about 6 hours.

3 Prepare couscous according to package directions.

4 Stir remaining ½ teaspoon salt and remaining ¼ teaspoon pepper into stew. Garnish with parsley (if using). Divide couscous and stew between 6 plates or bowls.

 SmartPoints value per serving (1 cup stew and ½ cup couscous): 391 Cal, 7 g Total Fat, 2 g Sat Fat, 986 mg Sod, 40 g Total Carb, 6 g Sugar, 5 g Fib, 38 g Prot.

Note from Chef Eric

When I was training in Paris, a restaurant in my predominantly immigrant neighborhood gave out free lamb couscous to all the residents every Sunday. To this day, it personifies community and comfort to me.

Haddock-and-potato stew with saffron

Serves 4

This brightly flavored stew takes inspiration from Scandinavian seafood dishes that pair chunks of sweet fish with saffron and potatoes. Saffron adds a brilliant golden color to the broth and a deep, earthy flavor. It's a bit expensive, however, so feel free to substitute a few pinches of turmeric instead.

½	**fennel bulb, finely chopped**
2	**garlic cloves, chopped**
1½	**cups canned crushed tomatoes**
½	**cup dry white wine**
¼	**teaspoon saffron threads**
½	**teaspoon salt, or to taste**
¼	**teaspoon black pepper**
2	**(8-ounce) russet potatoes, peeled and cut into ½-inch cubes**
1	**pound skinless haddock fillet or other firm white fish, cut into large chunks**
1	**tablespoon chopped fresh dill or parsley**
4	**lemon wedges**

1 Coat large saucepan with nonstick spray and place over medium-high heat. Add fennel and garlic and cook, stirring, until fennel is just softened, about 5 minutes. Stir in tomatoes, wine, saffron, salt, and pepper and bring to boil.

2 Stir in potatoes, cover pan, and simmer until potatoes are just tender, about 12 minutes.

3 Gently stir in haddock, cover, and simmer until fish is firm and opaque, about 6 minutes. Ladle stew evenly into 4 serving bowls and sprinkle with dill or parsley. Serve with lemon wedges

 SmartPoints value per serving (1½ cups): 231 Cal, 1 g Total Fat, 0 g Sat Fat, 685 mg Sod, 29 g Total Carb, 4 g Sugar, 4 g Fib, 22 g Prot.

**Haddock-and-potato
stew with saffron**

One-pot
clambake

One-pot clambake

Serves 8

32 littleneck clams

1   tablespoon cornmeal

2   tablespoons unsalted butter

2   large onions, chopped

1   teaspoon kosher salt

4   parsley sprigs, plus chopped parsley for garnish

4   garlic cloves, minced

1   tablespoon Old Bay Seasoning

1   bay leaf

½   cup dry white wine

¾   cup chicken broth

2   pounds baby potatoes, scrubbed

4   links (¾ pound) cooked chicken chorizo, each cut into 4 pieces

4   ears sweet corn, husks and silk removed and ears halved

1   large lemon, cut into 8 wedges

1 Scrub clams and place in large bowl of cold water. Add cornmeal to help clams release any grit; let soak about 15 minutes. Lift clams from water and rinse. Set aside.

2 Melt butter in large soup pot or stockpot over medium heat. Add onion and salt; cook, stirring frequently, until onion is softened, about 10 minutes. Stir in parsley sprigs, garlic, Old Bay Seasoning, and bay leaf; cook, stirring, 1 minute. Add wine and cook 1 minute. Add broth and increase heat to medium-high.

3 Add potatoes to pot and top with chorizo; place corn over chorizo, then add clams. Cover and cook until clams are opened and corn and potatoes are fork-tender, 15–20 minutes.

4 With slotted spoon, transfer clams to large platter (discard bay leaf and any clams that do not open). Use slotted spoon to transfer chorizo, corn, and potatoes to platter with clams; drizzle some broth from pot over clams, sausage, and vegetables. Serve with remaining broth on the side and lemon wedges. Sprinkle with chopped parsley.

6 **SmartPoints value per serving** (4 clams, 2 slices sausage, ½ ear corn, ¼ pound potatoes, ¼ cup broth): 312 Cal, 9 g Total Fat, 3 g Sat Fat, 1,185 mg Sod, 37 g Total Carb, 6 g Sugar, 5 g Fiber, 20 g Prot.

Note from Chef Eric

With the WW Freestyle program, using zero Points ingredients like clams and corn gives you the wiggle room you need to invite chorizo to this party. What a treat!

Mussels with leeks and white wine

Serves 4

Silken tofu, a zero Points ingredient, imparts creaminess and richness to the mussel broth and also adds protein.

2	**teaspoons olive oil**
2	**large leeks (white and light green parts only), halved lengthwise, thinly sliced, and rinsed well**
3	**garlic cloves, minced**
1	**cup dry white wine**
½	**cup chicken broth**
2	**tomatoes, chopped**
½	**teaspoon saffron threads, crumbled**
⅛	**teaspoon cayenne, or to taste**
3	**pounds mussels, scrubbed and debearded**
½	**cup silken tofu**
⅛	**teaspoon salt, or to taste**
1	**tablespoon chopped fresh parsley leaves**

1 Heat oil in large Dutch oven over medium-low heat. Add leeks and cook, stirring occasionally, until softened, about 6 minutes. Stir in garlic and cook until fragrant, about 30 seconds.

2 Stir wine, broth, tomatoes, saffron, and cayenne into Dutch oven and bring to boil. Add mussels; cook, covered, until mussels open, about 4 minutes. Discard any mussels that do not open. With slotted spoon, transfer mussels to large bowl; cover with foil to keep warm.

3 Return Dutch oven to medium heat and simmer until mixture is slightly thickened, about 6 minutes. Pour ½ cup pan juices into blender. Add tofu and salt and puree. Return mixture to Dutch oven and bring to boil.

4 Divide mussels evenly among 4 bowls. Pour pan juices over mussels, dividing evenly. Sprinkle with parsley.

 SmartPoints value per serving (about 20 mussels with pan juices): 424 Cal, 11 g Total Fat, 2 g Sat Fat, 1,170 mg Sod, 25 g Total Carb, 5 g Sugar, 2 g Fib, 44 g Prot.

Slow-cooker vegetable and farro stew

Serves 8

Want this hearty vegetarian stew to have the most flavor possible? Use whole peeled San Marzano tomatoes. This variety of plum tomato is grown in the rich volcanic soil at the base of Mount Vesuvius in Italy, which gives them their sweet flavor and low acidity. They are coveted for their meaty texture, low seed count, and easy-to-remove skin.

6	garlic cloves, chopped
½	cup coarsely chopped fresh parsley leaves
½	teaspoon + pinch salt
¼	teaspoon + pinch black pepper
2	tablespoons olive oil
2	teaspoons fennel seeds
10	ounces cremini mushrooms, halved or quartered depending on size
1	fennel bulb, chopped
1	onion, diced
1	(2-pound) kabocha or butternut squash, peeled, seeded, and cut into ½-inch dice
1	(28-ounce) can whole peeled tomatoes, broken up
1	(32-ounce) carton reduced-sodium vegetable broth
¾	cup farro, rinsed
¾	cup brown lentils, rinsed
½	cup Parmesan shavings

1 Stir together one third of the garlic and the parsley in cup. Season with pinch salt and pinch pepper. Cover and refrigerate.

2 Heat oil in flameproof slow-cooker insert or large heavy nonstick skillet over medium-high heat. Add fennel seeds and remaining garlic; cook, stirring frequently, until fragrant, about 30 seconds. Add mushrooms, chopped fennel, and onion; sprinkle with ¼ teaspoon salt and ⅛ teaspoon pepper. Cook, stirring occasionally, until vegetables are softened and begin to brown, about 10 minutes. Return insert with vegetables to slow cooker (or spoon vegetable mixture into slow cooker).

3 Add squash, tomatoes, broth, farro, and lentils to slow cooker and sprinkle with remaining ¼ teaspoon salt and ⅛ teaspoon pepper; stir well to combine. Cover and cook until farro, lentils, and squash are tender, about 4 hours on High. Divide stew evenly among 8 large shallow bowls. Sprinkle evenly with garlic-parsley mixture and Parmesan shavings.

4 **SmartPoints value per serving** (scant 2 cups stew and 1 tablespoon cheese): 272 Cal, 6 g Total Fat, 2 g Sat Fat, 562 mg Sod, 47 g Total Carb, 7 g Sugar, 8 g Fib, 12 g Prot.

Note from Chef Eric

Since I joined the WW community, my love for and attention to vegetables has been heightened in my cooking. This stew is an ideal example of how WW Freestyle has pushed me to include more veggies in my recipes.

Middle Eastern eggplant and chickpea stew

Serves 4

This fragrant stew is packed with flavor, texture, and color from an assortment of classic Middle Eastern produce and other ingredients. Love spice? The recipe calls for a hit of fiery harissa, a traditional Middle Eastern blend of hot chiles, but you can also serve more harissa on the side if you like: Just thin some paste with a bit of water or lemon juice and pass it around.

1	medium (1¼-pound) eggplant, trimmed and cut into ¾-inch cubes
4	teaspoons olive oil
¾	teaspoon salt
1	large onion, diced
2	bell peppers (any color), cut into 1-inch pieces
2	garlic cloves, minced
2	teaspoons ground cumin
2	teaspoons dried mint
1	teaspoon smoked mild paprika
¼	teaspoon black pepper
1	(15-ounce can) chickpeas, rinsed and drained
1	(14½-ounce) can diced tomatoes
1½	cups vegetable broth
2	tablespoons tomato paste
2	teaspoons harissa paste
2	tablespoons chopped fresh parsley leaves

Lemon wedges for serving

1 Preheat oven to 425°F. Line large rimmed baking sheet with foil.

2 Toss eggplant with 2 teaspoons oil and ¼ teaspoon salt in large bowl; spread in even layer on prepared baking sheet. Roast, stirring once or twice, until lightly browned and tender, 20–25 minutes.

3 Meanwhile, in medium Dutch oven, heat remaining 2 teaspoons oil over medium-high heat. Add onion and bell peppers; cover and cook, stirring occasionally, until onions are golden brown, about 8 minutes. Add garlic, cumin, mint, paprika, and black pepper; cook, stirring frequently, until fragrant, about 1 minute.

4 Stir in eggplant, chickpeas, tomatoes, broth, tomato paste, harissa, and remaining ½ teaspoon salt, scraping up browned bits from bottom of pan. Bring to boil over high heat. Lower heat and simmer until flavors blend, about 10 minutes. Ladle evenly into 4 bowls and top with parsley. Serve with lemon wedges.

 SmartPoints value per serving (1¾ cup): 277 Cal, 8 g Total Fat, 1 g Sat Fat, 1,128 mg Sod, 45 g Total Carb, 15 g Sugar, 14 g Fib, 11 g Prot.

Note from Chef Eric

For breakfast, I often put leftovers from this stew in a casserole dish, crack in some eggs, and bake it until the eggs just set. The result? A fantastically nourishing shakshuka!

Middle Eastern eggplant and chickpea stew

Curried lentil stew
with butternut,
kale, and coconut

Curried lentil stew with butternut, kale, and coconut

Serves 4

Here's a fantastic way to use red lentils, a quick-cooking variety that boasts a striking deep-orange hue. This stew features them with sweet butternut squash, earthy kale, and creamy coconut milk for a totally satisfying vegan dish.

2   teaspoons olive oil

1   large onion, chopped

1   leek, halved lengthwise, rinsed, thinly sliced, and rinsed again

1   (32-ounce) container vegetable broth

1   pound peeled, halved, seeded, and diced butternut squash (about 2½ cups)

1   tablespoon curry powder

½   teaspoon ground cumin

½   teaspoon salt

Pinch cayenne

1   cup red lentils, picked over, rinsed, and drained

3   cups lightly packed coarsely chopped kale leaves

½   cup light (low-fat) coconut milk

1 Heat oil in Dutch oven over medium-high heat. Add onion and leek and cook, stirring, until softened, about 3 minutes. Stir in broth, squash, curry powder, cumin, salt, and cayenne. Bring to boil. Adjust heat and simmer until squash begins to soften, about 10 minutes.

2 Stir in lentils and kale and cook until lentils begin to fall apart and vegetables are tender, 10–12 minutes. Stir in coconut milk and heat through. Ladle evenly into 4 bowls.

 SmartPoints value per serving (1½ cups): 315 Cal, 6 g Total Fat, 2 g Sat Fat, 840 mg Sod, 55 g Total Carb, 7 g Sugar, 10 g Fib, 14 g Prot.

Freestyle it
Top each serving with a dollop of plain fat-free Greek yogurt or plain unsweetened soy yogurt (both zero Points foods) and a sprinkle of chopped fresh cilantro if you like.

Flash-cooked
peppered
tuna with
Mediterranean
salad, page 199

Chapter 8
Skillet dinners

In this chapter

Vegetarian   Vegan   Gluten free   Dairy free   Nut free

Shrimp and chicken chorizo paella

Serves 8

This traditional one-skillet Spanish meal has it all: tasty proteins, lots of veggies, and a hearty portion of rice. Make it to serve a crowd, or refrigerate leftovers for up to 2 days.

½	teaspoon saffron threads
¼	cup hot water
2	teaspoons olive oil
1	pound large shrimp, peeled and deveined
¾	pound chicken chorizo, sliced
1	large onion, thinly sliced
1	(8-ounce) package cremini mushrooms, sliced
4	scallions, white and green parts sliced and kept separate
1	teaspoon kosher salt
1	tablespoon minced garlic
2	cups Arborio rice
1	(14½-ounce) can diced tomatoes, drained
¼	teaspoon paprika
2½	cups reduced-sodium chicken broth
1	cup jarred roasted piquillo or regular peppers, drained and sliced
1	cup frozen baby peas
16	mussels, scrubbed
¼	cup chopped fresh parsley leaves

1 Crumble saffron threads into water in cup and stir well.

2 Heat 1 teaspoon oil in large heavy skillet over medium-high heat. Add shrimp and cook until almost opaque in center, about 2 minutes per side; transfer to plate. Add remaining 1 teaspoon oil, the chorizo, onion, mushrooms, white parts of scallions, and salt to skillet; cook, stirring often, until mushrooms begin to brown, about 5 minutes.

3 Add garlic to skillet; cook, stirring constantly, 1 minute. Add rice, tomatoes, and paprika, stirring to mix well. Add broth and saffron water; bring to boil. Reduce heat and simmer 15 minutes.

4 Stir peppers into rice mixture along with peas and shrimp. Nestle mussels into rice; cover pan and cook until rice is tender and mussels open, about 5 minutes (discard any mussels that don't open). Sprinkle paella with parsley and green part of scallions.

 SmartPoints value per serving (1½ cups): 389 Cal, 7 g Total Fat, 2 g Sat Fat, 1,311 mg Sod, 54 g Total Carb, 6 g Sugar, 4 g Fib, 26 g Prot.

Note from Chef Eric

Paella has everything I learned to love about food during my time in Spain, particularly the combination of rich seafood, like shrimp, and the flavorful punch of chorizo. You can also make a version using cauliflower "rice" instead of regular rice. Cauliflower rice is a zero Points food and available in some groceries.

Iron skillet chicken potpie

Serves 4

Save on kitchen time by using supermarket or takeout rotisserie chicken for the roasted chicken breast that studs the filling.

FILLING

- 2 **carrots, halved lengthwise and chopped**
- 1 **celery stalk, chopped**
- 1 **teaspoon canola oil**
- 1 **cup reduced-sodium chicken broth**
- 1 **cup low-fat (1%) milk**
- 2 **tablespoons cornstarch**
- ½ **teaspoon salt**
- ¼ **teaspoon poultry seasoning**
- ¼ **teaspoon black pepper**
- 2 **cups diced skinless roasted chicken breast**

BISCUITS

- 1 **cup + 2 tablespoons all-purpose flour**
- 2 **tablespoons yellow cornmeal**
- 1 **teaspoon baking powder**
- ¼ **teaspoon baking soda**
- ¼ **teaspoon salt**
- ⅔ **cup low-fat buttermilk**
- 1 **tablespoon + 1 teaspoon unsalted butter, melted**
- 2 **tablespoons snipped fresh chives**

1 Preheat oven to 400°F.

2 To make filling, place carrots and celery in 9-inch cast-iron skillet. Drizzle with oil and toss. Roast in oven, stirring once or twice, until just tender, about 15 minutes. Transfer to plate and set aside.

3 In same skillet, whisk together broth, milk, cornstarch, salt, poultry seasoning, and pepper. Bring to boil over medium-high heat, stirring constantly, until sauce is bubbly and thickens. Stir in chicken and vegetables; return to boil. Remove skillet from heat and keep warm.

4 To make biscuits, whisk together flour, cornmeal, baking powder, baking soda, and salt in medium bowl. Stir together buttermilk and 1 tablespoon melted butter in small bowl; stir in chives. Add buttermilk mixture to flour mixture, stirring just until flour mixture is moistened.

5 Drop dough by scant 2-tablespoon dollops over chicken mixture, making 12 biscuits. Brush biscuits with remaining 1 teaspoon melted butter. Bake until biscuits are golden and filling is bubbly, 25–30 minutes. Let stand 10 minutes. Ladle into 4 bowls.

9 **SmartPoints value per serving** (3 biscuits and about 1 cup filling): 379 Cal, 9 g Total Fat, 4 g Sat Fat, 945 mg Sod, 43 g Total Carb, 7 g Sugar, 2 g Fib, 30 g Prot.

Note from Chef Eric

When I need something warm and nourishing for body and soul, chicken potpie is my go-to. And I like to bulk up my pies with excellent zero Points vegetables like leeks and snap peas.

Iron skillet
chicken potpie

Chicken fajita rice bowls

Serves 4

These easy rice bowls feature spiced fajita-style chicken and a mix of colorful veggies for a crowd-pleasing meal. Look for precooked brown rice in the freezer section of large supermarkets.

½ teaspoon chili powder

½ teaspoon paprika

½ teaspoon garlic powder

½ teaspoon ground cumin

¼ teaspoon dried oregano

½ teaspoon salt

⅛ teaspoon black pepper

¾ pound skinless boneless chicken breast, cut into strips

1 teaspoon olive oil

2 cups frozen cooked brown rice, reheated according to package instructions

2 cups diced peeled jicama

1 small red or yellow bell pepper, diced

1 avocado, peeled, pitted, and diced

¼ cup sliced pickled jalapeño peppers

½ cup pico de gallo or salsa

4 lime wedges

1 Combine chili powder, paprika, garlic powder, cumin, oregano, salt, and black pepper in small bowl. Sprinkle mixture over chicken and toss to coat. Heat oil in medium skillet over medium-high heat. Add chicken and cook, stirring occasionally, until chicken is no longer pink, 4–5 minutes.

2 Place ½ cup rice in each of 4 bowls. Top each bowl evenly with jicama, bell pepper, avocado, pickled jalapeño, and chicken. Spoon on pico de gallo and serve with a lime wedge.

5 **SmartPoints value per serving** (1 bowl): 324 Cal, 10 g Total Fat, 2 g Sat Fat, 457 mg Sod, 36 g Total Carb, 3 g Sugar, 8 g Fib, 23 g Prot.

Freestyle it
Add a few spoonfuls of cooked and drained black beans to the bowls for no change in SmartPoints value.

Moussaka in minutes

Serves 4

1½ teaspoons olive oil

1   small (1-pound) eggplant, cut into ½-inch chunks

1   large onion, diced

½   pound lean ground beef (7% fat or less)

3   large garlic cloves, minced

1   (14½-ounce) can diced fire-roasted tomatoes

1   (8-ounce) can tomato sauce

2½ teaspoons dried oregano

½   teaspoon cinnamon

½   teaspoon salt

½   teaspoon black pepper

¼   teaspoon ground allspice

1   cup reduced-fat ricotta

1   large egg

¼   cup crumbled feta

2   tablespoons chopped fresh parsley leaves

1 Heat oil in large ovenproof skillet over medium-high heat. Add eggplant and onion; cover and cook, stirring occasionally, until vegetables are softened and lightly browned, 6–8 minutes. Transfer to medium bowl.

2 Add beef and garlic to skillet. Cook, breaking beef apart with wooden spoon, until beef is no longer pink, about 3 minutes.

3 Return eggplant mixture to skillet. Add tomatoes, tomato sauce, oregano, cinnamon, salt, pepper, and allspice and bring to simmer. Reduce heat; cover and simmer, stirring occasionally, until eggplant is tender, about 5 minutes.

4 Meanwhile, preheat broiler. Stir together ricotta, egg, and feta in small bowl. When eggplant is tender, spoon ricotta mixture over top and spread evenly (mixture will not completely cover top). Broil until topping is puffed and browned in spots, about 5 minutes. Spoon evenly onto 4 plates and top with parsley.

6   **SmartPoints value per serving** (1¼ cups): 320 Cal, 14 g Total Fat, 7 g Sat Fat, 1,010 mg Sod, 25 g Total Carb, 11 g Sugar, 7 g Fib, 25 g Prot.

Note from Chef Eric
I like to toss chopped drained spinach with nutmeg into this classic comfort dish for an added layer of freshness—and no additional SmartPoints!

Vietnamese beef and broccoli with jasmine rice

Vietnamese beef and broccoli with jasmine rice

Serves 4

Need a palate-pleaser? The bright flavors of Vietnamese food take center stage in this colorful meal-in-a-bowl recipe. Lime, fish sauce, and peanuts give it wonderful tang and depth of flavor, while cilantro, mint, and watercress keep it fresh and light.

1	**pound lean flank steak, trimmed and thinly sliced**
1	**teaspoon salt**
¼	**teaspoon black pepper**
3	**teaspoons sesame oil**
4	**cups broccoli florets**
1	**tablespoon minced peeled fresh ginger**
3	**garlic cloves, finely chopped**
2	**tablespoons water**
1½	**tablespoons lime juice**
1½	**tablespoons fish sauce**
2	**cups cooked jasmine rice, warmed**
2	**cups watercress sprigs, chopped**
½	**cup thinly sliced red onion**
¼	**cup cilantro leaves**
¼	**cup mint leaves**
¼	**cup roasted salted peanuts, chopped**
4	**lime wedges**

1 Sprinkle steak with salt and pepper. Heat 1 teaspoon oil in large skillet over high heat; add steak and cook, stirring 2 or 3 times, until browned on all sides, about 5 minutes. Transfer steak to plate and keep warm.

2 Add remaining 2 teaspoons oil and broccoli to same skillet; cook, stirring frequently, until broccoli begins to brown, 3–4 minutes. Reduce heat to medium and stir in ginger and garlic; cook, stirring a few times, until fragrant, about 30 seconds. Add water to skillet; continue to cook, stirring a few times, until broccoli is crisp-tender, 2–3 minutes. Stir in lime juice and fish sauce. Remove from heat.

3 Add steak to skillet. Top with watercress, onion, cilantro, and mint. Add rice to skillet, or divide among 4 bowls and top with steak mixture. Sprinkle with peanuts and serve with lime wedges on the side.

8 **SmartPoints value per serving** (1 bowl): 383 Cal, 13 g Total Fat, 3 g Sat Fat, 1,301 mg Sod, 36 g Total Carb, 3 g Sugar, 5 g Fib, 32 g Prot.

Note from Chef Eric

I've discovered new ways on my WW Freestyle journey to add depth and flavor to my food. Instead of using less-healthy fallbacks like high-fat ingredients, I've found that spice and heat can bring complexity and satisfying flavor to dishes while keeping SmartPoints low. Add a sliced mild or hot chile to this dish and see if you agree.

Coconut-curry salmon stir-fry

Serves 4

This recipe is a must-try for those looking to eat more heart-healthy salmon. Stir-frying it in a tropical curry sauce rich with the flavor and aroma of coconut is both speedy and wonderfully unexpected.

2	**teaspoons coconut oil**
2	**garlic cloves, finely chopped**
2	**teaspoons minced peeled fresh ginger**
2	**jalapeño peppers, seeded and finely chopped, or to taste**
¼	**cup Thai green curry paste**
¾	**pound skinless wild salmon fillet, cut into ¾-inch cubes**
2	**red bell peppers, thinly sliced**
2	**yellow bell peppers, thinly sliced**
3	**cups sugar snap peas, trimmed**
½	**cup light (low-fat) coconut milk**
½	**cup chicken broth**
1	**teaspoon salt**
⅓	**cup chopped fresh cilantro leaves**
⅓	**cup chopped scallions**
2	**tablespoons lime juice**
¼	**cup toasted coconut chips**

1 Heat oil in large skillet or wok over medium heat. Add garlic, ginger, and jalapeños and stir-fry until fragrant, 2–3 minutes.

2 Add curry paste, salmon, bell peppers, and sugar snap peas to pan and cook, stirring frequently, until salmon browns, about 5 minutes. Stir in coconut milk, broth, and salt and bring to boil. Simmer until salmon is cooked through and vegetables are crisp-tender, about 5 minutes.

3 Stir in cilantro, scallions, and lime juice. Serve sprinkled with coconut chips.

 6 **SmartPoints value per serving** (2 cups stir-fry and 1 tablespoon coconut chips): 316 Cal, 15 g Total Fat, 10 g Sat Fat, 776 mg Sod, 26 g Total Carb, 8 g Sugar, 6 g Fib, 23 g Prot.

Freestyle it

Love seafood? Add ½ pound of either medium peeled and deveined shrimp or bay scallops along with the coconut milk in Step 2 for no change in SmartPoints value.

**Coconut-curry
salmon stir-fry**

Flash-cooked peppered tuna with Mediterranean salad

Flash-cooked peppered tuna with Mediterranean salad

Serves 4

Rich, meaty tuna steak seared with a savory crust is the star of this easy seafood-and-salad recipe. Got leftovers? It makes an ideal pack-and-go lunch.

4	**ounces orzo**
2	**teaspoons cracked black pepper**
1	**teaspoon ground coriander**
½	**teaspoon ground cumin**
¼	**teaspoon coarse sea salt**
4	**(6-ounce) tuna steaks, each about 1 to 1½ inches thick**
3½	**teaspoons olive oil**
1	**(15½-ounce) can cannellini (white kidney) beans, rinsed and drained**
1	**cup loosely packed fresh parsley leaves**
¼	**cup crumbled feta**
1	**shallot, finely chopped**
⅓	**cup Kalamata olives, pitted and coarsely chopped**
4	**sun-dried tomato halves (not packed in oil), chopped**
2	**tablespoons lemon juice**
2	**teaspoons chopped fresh oregano leaves**

1 Cook orzo according to package directions. Drain and transfer to large bowl.

2 Meanwhile, combine pepper, coriander, cumin, and salt in small bowl. Sprinkle mixture evenly over tuna. Heat 1½ teaspoons oil in large skillet over medium-high heat. When very hot, add tuna and cook 3 minutes. Flip tuna and cook until browned and tuna is just dark red in center, 2–3 minutes more. Transfer to cutting board and thinly slice each steak.

3 Add beans, parsley, feta, shallot, olives, sun-dried tomatoes, lemon juice, oregano, and remaining 2 teaspoons oil to bowl; toss to coat. Divide mixture evenly among 4 plates. Top each with a sliced tuna steak.

6 **SmartPoints value per serving** (1 tuna steak and 1 cup bean salad): 470 Cal, 9 g Total Fat, 2 g Sat Fat, 773 mg Sod, 42 g Total Carb, 2 g Sugar, 6 g Fib, 53 g Prot.

Note from Chef Eric
This is another terrific dish that eats just as delicious hot and cold. Try it both ways!

Pan-seared mahimahi with herb sauce and mushroom orzo

Serves 4

Get ready for big flavor from this skillet dinner. Meaty mahimahi is drizzled with a fresh herb sauce you can make in the blender and accompanied by quick-cooking orzo. Use tricolor orzo, available at larger supermarkets, for more visual appeal.

2	tablespoons all-purpose flour
1¼	teaspoons + ⅛ teaspoon kosher salt
¼	teaspoon + ⅛ teaspoon black pepper
4	(6-ounce) mahimahi fillets
2	cups chicken broth
1	cup orzo
1	teaspoon olive oil
1	(8-ounce) package cremini mushrooms, sliced
1	large shallot, minced
4	cups lightly packed baby spinach
1	cup grape tomatoes, halved
1	large garlic clove, minced
¼	teaspoon grated lemon zest
1	cup lightly packed basil leaves, plus more for garnish
½	cup lightly packed fresh parsley leaves
3	tablespoons warm water
1	teaspoon lemon juice
¼	cup grated Parmesan

1 Stir together flour, 1 teaspoon salt, and ¼ teaspoon pepper in shallow dish. Dredge fish in seasoned flour, pressing gently so it adheres. Let fish stand in dish.

2 Combine broth and orzo in medium saucepan and set over high heat. Bring to boil. Reduce heat to medium-low and simmer, stirring frequently, until al dente, about 10 minutes. Drain and transfer to medium bowl. Cover to keep warm.

3 Heat oil in large skillet over medium-high heat. Add mushrooms, shallot, ¼ teaspoon salt, and ⅛ teaspoon pepper. Cook, stirring frequently, until mushrooms begin to brown, 8–10 minutes. Stir in spinach, tomatoes, and all but ⅛ teaspoon garlic; cook, stirring, until spinach is wilted, about 2 minutes longer. Add to orzo along with lemon zest. Transfer to serving bowl and cover to keep warm.

4 Wipe out skillet. Spray with nonstick spray and set over medium-high heat. Add fish to skillet and cook until browned and just opaque in center, about 5 minutes per side.

5 Meanwhile, to make herb sauce, combine 1 cup basil, parsley, reserved ⅛ teaspoon garlic, water, lemon juice, and remaining ⅛ teaspoon salt in blender or food processor and puree.

6 Serve fish drizzled with herb sauce. Sprinkle Parmesan and basil leaves over orzo mixture.

6 **SmartPoints value per serving** (1 mahimahi fillet, 1½ tablespoons sauce, and 1 cup orzo mixture): 399 Cal, 5 g Total Fat, 2 g Sat Fat, 1,341 mg Sod, 43 g Total Carb, 5 g Sugar, 4 g Fib, 44 g Prot.

Crunchy pan-fried fish fillets

Serves 4

A classic mixture of cornmeal and bread crumbs makes an exceptionally crisp coating for tender fish fillets. Leftovers make an ideal sandwich filling.

¼　cup yellow cornmeal

2　tablespoons plain dried bread crumbs

¾　teaspoon dried oregano

½　teaspoon salt

¼　teaspoon black pepper

Pinch cayenne

2　large egg whites

1　tablespoon water

½　teaspoon hot pepper sauce, or to taste

4　(¼-pound) thin skinless tilapia or catfish fillets

2　teaspoons canola oil

Lemon wedges

1 Mix together cornmeal, bread crumbs, oregano, salt, black pepper, and cayenne on sheet of wax paper. Whisk egg whites, water, and pepper sauce in pie plate or large shallow bowl.

2 Dip fish fillets, one at a time, into egg-white mixture, allowing excess to drip off. Coat each fillet with cornmeal mixture, shaking off excess. Spray tops of fillets with nonstick spray.

3 Heat oil in large heavy nonstick skillet over medium-high heat. Place fish in skillet, sprayed side down, in batches if needed, and cook until golden on bottom, about 4 minutes. Spray fish with nonstick spray and turn fish over; cook just until opaque throughout, about 3 minutes longer. Serve with lemon wedges.

 SmartPoints value per serving (1 fish fillet): 176 Cal, 4 g Total Fat, 1 g Sat Fat, 400 mg Sod, 12 g Total Carb, 1 g Sugar, 1 g Fib, 24 g Prot.

Note from Chef Eric

This fish is great when I'm cooking for the whole family: It's light on SmartPoints for me, heavy in flavor and crunch for the kids!

Spicy shrimp with creamy cheese grits

Serves 4

Grits, finely ground hulled corn kernels, are an institution in the South. They're prepared in a variety of ways, including as a side dish, pudding, or soufflé, as well as for breakfast. The savory combination of shrimp and grits is particularly popular in the Carolinas.

2	teaspoons canola oil
1	small onion, finely chopped
3	cups chicken broth
¾	cup quick-cooking grits
½	cup shredded reduced-fat sharp Cheddar
2	garlic cloves, minced
1¼	pounds medium shrimp, peeled and deveined
½	teaspoon smoked paprika
¼	teaspoon red pepper flakes
1½	teaspoons lemon juice
2	tablespoons coarsely chopped fresh parsley leaves or cilantro leaves

1 Heat 1 teaspoon oil in medium saucepan over medium heat. Add all but 2 tablespoons onion to saucepan. Cook, stirring, until softened, about 3 minutes. Add broth and bring to boil. Stir in grits. Cook, stirring constantly, until thickened, 4–5 minutes. Remove saucepan from heat; stir in Cheddar until melted. Keep warm.

2 Heat remaining 1 teaspoon oil in large skillet over medium-high heat. Add reserved 2 tablespoons onion and cook, stirring, until softened, about 3 minutes. Add garlic and cook, stirring, until fragrant, about 30 seconds. Add shrimp, paprika, and pepper flakes. Cook, stirring constantly, until shrimp are just opaque in center, 4–5 minutes. Sprinkle with lemon juice. Divide grits evenly among 4 plates or bowls and top with shrimp and parsley.

6 **SmartPoints value per serving** (about 12 shrimp and ¾ cup grits): 279 Cal, 7 g Total Fat, 2 g Sat Fat, 1,506 mg Sod, 28 g Total Carb, 2 g Sugar, 2 g Fib, 26 g Prot.

Spicy shrimp with creamy cheese grits

Arepas with
black bean-and-
corn salad

Arepas with black bean-and-corn salad

Serves 4

(Ⓥ) (Ⓦ) (Ⓢ)

AREPAS

2 cups masarepa or regular cornmeal

2 teaspoons salt

2½ cups warm water

1 seeded and diced Hatch or Anaheim chile (optional)

1 tablespoon canola oil

TOPPING

1½ teaspoons canola oil

1 garlic clove, minced

½ red onion, thinly sliced

2 ears sweet corn, roasted and shucked

1 teaspoon chili powder

1 (15-ounce) can black beans, rinsed and drained

Juice of 1 lime

¼ cup fresh cilantro leaves

Plain nonfat Greek yogurt for serving (optional)

1 For arepas, combine masarepa and salt in a medium bowl. Make well in center and pour in water. Using wooden spoon, gradually incorporate masarepa into water, stirring until no dry lumps remain. Stir in chile (if using). Let rest 5 minutes.

2 Heat ½ tablespoon oil in large nonstick skillet over medium heat. Pour in batter to form 4 arepas. Cook until golden brown on bottom, about 5 minutes. Flip and cook until other side is golden brown, about 5 minutes longer. Transfer to plate or platter and keep warm. Repeat with remaining ½ tablespoon oil and remaining batter.

3 For topping, heat oil in medium saucepan over medium heat. Add garlic and onion, reduce heat to low, and cook until onion is translucent, about 5 minutes. Increase heat to medium and add corn, chili powder, and beans. Cook until all ingredients are heated through. Stir in lime juice and cilantro and remove from heat.

4 Spoon topping mixture evenly over arepas and serve with yogurt if diners would like a dollop on top+.

8 **SmartPoints value per serving** (2 arepas and generous ½ cup topping): 434 Cal, 8 g Total Fat, 1 g Sat Fat, 1,616 mg Sod, 82 g Total Carb, 4 g Sugar, 14 g Fib, 14 g Prot.

Note from Chef Eric

Arepas are one of the deliciously simple comfort foods of South America. Using precooked cornmeal like masarepa is preferred, although traditional cornmeal will do in a pinch. The topping takes advantage of zero Points stars like beans and corn. Add shredded chicken breast or steamed shrimp too for no additional SmartPoints.

Creole-style red beans and rice, page 212

Chapter 9
Soulful sides

In this chapter

Ⓥ Vegetarian   Ⓥ Vegan   Ⓖ Gluten free   Ⓓ Dairy free   Ⓝ Nut free

Celery root and Yukon Gold mash

Serves 8

(icons)

Combining celery root (also known as celeriac or knob celery) with flavorful Yukon Gold potatoes is the secret to one of the tastiest mashes around. The addition of caramelized onions makes them irresistible.

2	**tablespoons canola oil**
2	**onions, chopped**
1	**pound celery root, trimmed, peeled, and cut into 1-inch chunks**
1	**pound Yukon Gold potatoes, scrubbed and cut into 1-inch chunks**
1	**teaspoon salt**
½	**teaspoon ground white pepper or ¼ teaspoon black pepper**
¼	**cup low-fat buttermilk, warmed**
2	**tablespoons chopped fresh parsley**

1 Heat oil in large skillet over medium heat. Add onions and cook, stirring frequently, until softened, about 5 minutes. Cover skillet and cook, stirring occasionally, until onions are golden and tender, about 20 minutes.

2 Meanwhile, combine celery root and potato chunks in large saucepan and add enough water to cover. Bring to boil over medium-high heat; reduce heat and simmer until tender, about 15 minutes. Drain.

3 Return celery root and potatoes to saucepan and sprinkle with salt and pepper; stir in buttermilk. With potato masher or wooden spoon, coarsely mash potato mixture; stir in onions and parsley.

2 **SmartPoints value per serving** (about ½ cup): 107 Cal, 4 g Total Fat, 0 g Sat Fat, 372 mg Sod, 17 g Total Carb, 3 g Sugar, 3 g Fib, 2 g Prot.

Note from Chef Eric

Mashed potatoes are my go-to for a crowd-pleasing side. Adding the celery root here not only stretches the potatoes without increasing the SmartPoints, but also injects a great flavor.

Yellow corn bread with buttermilk and thyme

Serves 12

Buttermilk is a baker's secret to tender, flavorful corn bread. We suggest using stoneground yellow cornmeal in this recipe, but you can use white cornmeal (favored in the South) interchangeably.

1¼	**cups yellow cornmeal, preferably stoneground**
¾	**cup all-purpose flour**
1	**tablespoon + 1 teaspoon sugar**
2	**teaspoons baking powder**
½	**teaspoon baking soda**
¾	**teaspoon fine salt**
¼	**teaspoon black pepper**
1	**cup low-fat buttermilk**
1	**large egg**
2	**tablespoons canola oil**
1	**cup yellow corn kernels, thawed and drained if frozen**
1	**tablespoon thyme leaves**
	Flaky sea salt (optional)

1 Preheat oven to 400°F. Spray 8-inch square baking pan with nonstick spray. Set aside.

2 Whisk together cornmeal, flour, sugar, baking powder, baking soda, fine salt, and pepper in large bowl. Beat buttermilk, egg, and oil in small bowl until mixed well. Add buttermilk mixture to cornmeal mixture, stirring just until cornmeal mixture is moistened; fold in corn and thyme. Pour into prepared baking pan. Sprinkle with flaky sea salt (if using).

3 Bake until golden brown and toothpick inserted into center comes out clean, about 20 minutes. Let cool in pan on wire rack 10 minutes. Cut into 12 pieces. Serve warm.

4 **SmartPoints value per serving** (1 piece): 131 Cal, 3 g Total Fat, 0 g Sat Fat, 316 mg Sod, 22 g Total Carb, 3 g Sugar, 1 g Fib, 3 g Prot.

Roasted vegetable ratatouille, page 213

Creole-style red beans and rice, page 212

Yellow corn bread with buttermilk and thyme

Creole-style red beans and rice

Serves 6

Red beans and rice is an integral part of Louisiana's Creole cuisine. It was typically prepared on Mondays, as the pork bones left over from Sunday's dinner were used to flavor the dish. Monday was also wash day, which meant that a pot of red beans could sit on the stove and bubble away for hours while the household was busy scrubbing clothes.

½ **cup brown rice**

1 **tablespoon canola oil**

1 **small green bell pepper, chopped**

1 **onion, finely chopped**

1 **celery stalk, chopped**

3 **garlic cloves, minced**

1 **(14½-ounce) can diced fire-roasted tomatoes**

1 **cup vegetable broth**

1 **teaspoon dried thyme**

1 **teaspoon hot pepper sauce, or to taste**

¼ **teaspoon salt**

⅛ **teaspoon cayenne, or to taste**

2 **(15½-ounce) cans small red beans or red kidney beans, rinsed and drained**

3 **scallions, thinly sliced**

1 Cook rice according to package directions.

2 Meanwhile, heat oil in large nonstick skillet over medium heat. Add bell pepper, onion, celery, and garlic; cook, stirring, until vegetables are softened, about 8 minutes.

3 Add tomatoes, broth, thyme, pepper sauce, salt, and cayenne to skillet; bring to boil. Reduce heat and simmer, covered, stirring occasionally, until flavors are blended, about 6 minutes. Stir in cooked rice and beans. Cook, stirring, until heated through, about 3 minutes longer. Sprinkle with scallions.

3 **SmartPoints value per serving** (1½ cups): 234 Cal, 4 g Total Fat, 0 g Sat Fat, 798 mg Sod, 41 g Total Carb, 7 g Sugar, 8 g Fib, 10 g Prot.

Roasted vegetable ratatouille

Serves 4

Roasting a mix of sunny ratatouille-style vegetables for this dish concentrates their flavor and makes a luscious side dish.

1   **medium Vidalia onion, chopped**

1   **small eggplant (about 10 ounces), cut into ¾-inch cubes**

1   **zucchini, halved and cut into ¾-inch-thick slices**

1   **yellow bell pepper, cut into ¾-inch dice**

1   **pint grape tomatoes**

2   **teaspoons olive oil**

¼   **teaspoon salt**

¼   **teaspoon black pepper**

2   **garlic cloves, finely chopped**

3   **tablespoons chopped fresh basil**

2   **tablespoons grated Parmesan**

1 Preheat oven to 425°F.

2 Place onion, eggplant, zucchini, bell pepper, and tomatoes on large rimmed baking sheet lined with parchment paper. Drizzle with oil, sprinkle with salt and pepper, and toss. Spread in even layer and roast, stirring once or twice, until tender and browned, about 40 minutes. Stir in garlic and roast 2 more minutes.

3 Sprinkle with basil and Parmesan and serve.

1 **SmartPoints value per serving** (1 cup vegetables and ½ tablespoon Parmesan): 95 Cal, 4 g Total Fat, 1 g Sat Fat, 213 mg Sod, 15 g Total Carb, 8 g Sugar, 5 g Fib, 4 g Prot.

Note from Chef Eric

Some people think that to decrease the fat in their cooking, they need to steam everything. But there are many other techniques that build depth and keep recipes healthy. Roasting is one of my favorite methods of cooking; it works fabulously to caramelize and deepen the flavor of the vegetables in this recipe.

Whole wheat crescent
rolls with poppy seeds

Whole wheat crescent rolls with poppy seeds

Serves 12

Nothing beats the flavor and aroma of freshly baked rolls, and they're probably easier to make than you think! These traditional crescent-shaped rolls get deep flavor from white whole wheat flour (a variety that's a bit lighter in color and texture than regular whole wheat) and a touch of honey.

1   **cup warm water (105°F–115°F)**

1   **tablespoon honey**

2½ **cups white whole wheat flour**

1   **package quick-rise yeast**

1¼ **teaspoons salt**

1   **large egg, beaten with
1 teaspoon water**

2½ **teaspoons poppy seeds**

1 Stir together water and honey in large glass measuring cup. Combine flour, yeast, and salt in food processor; pulse until mixed. With machine running, pour honey mixture through feed tube; process until dough pulls away from sides of bowl, about 1 minute. Turn dough onto lightly floured surface and knead a few times until smooth. Cover with clean kitchen towel and let rest 15 minutes.

2 Spray large baking sheet with nonstick spray. Lightly sprinkle work surface with flour. Divide dough in half. Roll one piece of dough into 10-inch round; with pizza cutter or knife, cut into 6 wedges. Starting at wide end, roll up each wedge and bend ends in to form crescents. Place crescents seam side down, 2 inches apart, on baking sheet. Repeat with remaining dough, making 12 crescents. Cover rolls loosely with plastic wrap and let rise in warm place until almost doubled in size, 40–50 minutes.

3 Meanwhile, preheat oven to 375°F.

4 Remove plastic wrap; gently brush tops of rolls with beaten egg and sprinkle with poppy seeds. Bake until rolls are golden brown, about 15 minutes. Transfer rolls to wire rack. Serve warm or at room temperature.

SmartPoints value per serving (1 roll): 112 Cal, 1 g Total Fat, 0 g Sat Fat, 250 mg Sod, 20 g Total Carb, 4 g Sugar, 1 g Fib, 5 g Prot.

Roasted vegetable and herb sourdough dressing

Serves 10

We've incorporated tons of fresh veggies and herbs into this lightened-up dressing for a fabulous side dish. Think Thanksgiving, or anytime you've got pork chops, roast chicken, or another dish that could use a great parsley-sage-rosemary-and-thyme-flavored accompaniment.

9	ounces sourdough bread, cut into ½-inch cubes
1	(1-pound) butternut squash, peeled, seeded, and cut into ½-inch dice
1	pound Brussels sprouts, halved or quartered if large
2	Gala apples, cut into ½-inch dice
1	fennel bulb, coarsely chopped
4	shallots, sliced
2	tablespoons olive oil
½	teaspoon salt
¼	teaspoon black pepper
3	slices turkey bacon
1⅔	cups chicken broth
2	celery stalks, thinly sliced
1	large egg, beaten
1½	teaspoons chopped fresh sage
1½	teaspoons chopped fresh rosemary
1½	teaspoons chopped fresh thyme
⅓	cup chopped pecans
1	tablespoon chopped fresh parsley

1 Preheat oven to 425°F. Spray shallow 2½-quart baking dish with nonstick spray; set aside.

2 Put bread on large rimmed baking sheet and spray with nonstick spray; spread evenly. Bake until toasted, about 10 minutes.

3 Meanwhile, toss together squash, Brussels sprouts, apples, fennel, shallots, 1 tablespoon oil, the salt, and pepper in large bowl until mixed well; divide between 2 large rimmed baking sheets, spreading to form even layer. Spray with nonstick spray. Roast until browned and tender, about 25 minutes, stirring once and switching pans between oven racks halfway through roasting time.

4 Spray large skillet with nonstick spray and set over medium heat. Add bacon and cook, turning once or twice, until crisp, 4–5 minutes. Transfer to paper towels to drain; coarsely chop.

5 Spoon roasted vegetables into large bowl; add bread, bacon, remaining 1 tablespoon oil, the broth, celery, egg, sage, rosemary, and thyme, and stir well. Spoon stuffing into prepared baking dish; spray with nonstick spray. Cover dish with foil; bake until heated through, about 30 minutes. Uncover and sprinkle evenly with pecans. Bake until top is crispy, about 10 minutes longer; sprinkle with parsley.

4 **SmartPoints value per serving** (¾ cup): 211 Cal, 8 g Total Fat, 1 Sat Fat, 501 mg Sod, 32 g Total Carb, 9 g Sugar, 6 g Fib, 7 g Prot.

Note from Chef Eric

Some people's favorite part of Thanksgiving is the turkey, but for me it's the sides. In my opinion, a great dressing can make the difference between a good Thanksgiving meal and an outstanding one.

Collard greens with garlicky mojo

Serves 6

Citrusy, garlicky mojo is traditionally drizzled over starchy tubers like yucca or over roast meats. Here we substitute hearty collard greens for a terrific dish that's big on flavor but low in SmartPoints.

2   **(1-pound) bunches collard greens, stems removed, leaves cut into ribbons**

1   **tablespoon olive oil**

2   **garlic cloves, minced**

3   **tablespoons fresh orange juice**

3   **tablespoons lime juice**

½   **teaspoon dried oregano or 1½ teaspoons chopped fresh oregano leaves**

¼   **teaspoon salt, or to taste**

1   Place collards in large steamer basket set inside large pot of simmering water; cover and steam until tender, 5–10 minutes.

2   Meanwhile, heat oil in small saucepan over low heat; add garlic and cook, stirring, until garlic softens, about 1 minute. Stir in orange juice, lime juice, oregano, and salt; serve sauce over steamed greens.

 SmartPoints value per serving (⅔ cup greens and 1 tablespoon mojo): 51 Cal, 3 g Total Fat, 0 g Sat Fat, 109 mg Sod, 6 g Total Carb, 1 g Sugar, 3 g Fib, 2 g Prot.

Note from Chef Eric

Wanna jazz up these greens even more? Hit 'em with your favorite hot sauce. You won't regret it!

Super-crispy onion rings

Serves 4

Although recipes for fried onion rings appeared around 1900, they didn't really take off until fast-food restaurants put them on their menus almost a half century later. The best news is that deep-frying isn't the only way to cook this treat. A bit of baking powder in our oven-fried recipe ensures that they bake up light and crisp.

2	**large Vidalia or other sweet onions**
½	**cup all-purpose flour**
1½	**teaspoons baking powder**
3	**large eggs**
2	**teaspoons water**
1	**cup plain dried whole wheat bread crumbs**
2	**teaspoons Cajun seasoning, or to taste**

Flaky sea salt (such as Maldon, optional)

1 Preheat oven to 450°F. Spray 2 large baking sheets with nonstick spray.

2 Cut onions into ½-inch rounds and separate into rings. Set aside 32 of largest rings; reserve remaining onion for another use.

3 Combine flour and baking powder in large zip-close plastic bag. Whisk together eggs and water in shallow bowl. Mix together bread crumbs and Cajun seasoning in another shallow bowl.

4 Add onion rings, a few at a time, to flour mixture; shake until coated. Dip rings, one at a time, into egg mixture, then coat with bread crumbs, transferring rings as they are coated to prepared baking sheets. Bake 10 minutes; turn rings over and bake until deep golden and crispy, about 10 minutes longer. Serve warm, sprinkled with flaky salt (if desired).

(4) **SmartPoints value per serving** (8 onion rings): 225 Cal, 4 g Total Fat, 1 g Sat Fat, 886 mg Sod, 35 g Total Carb, 4 g Sugar, 5 g Fib, 11 g Prot.

Note from Chef Eric
This is one of those sides I always crave. Try dunking the rings in a ranch dip made with Greek yogurt.

Brussels sprouts with grapes and capers, page 221

Super-crispy onion rings

Green bean casserole, page 220

Green bean casserole

Serves 8

1½ pounds green beans, trimmed
   and halved lengthwise or
   left whole

2 teaspoons olive oil

3 large shallots, 1 finely chopped
   and 2 thinly sliced

1 cup coarse fresh bread crumbs

1 teaspoon chopped fresh thyme

¾ teaspoon salt

¼ teaspoon black pepper

2 tablespoons grated
   pecorino Romano

2 cups low-fat (1%) milk

1 tablespoon unsalted butter

10 ounces cremini mushrooms,
   sliced

3 tablespoons all-purpose flour

Pinch ground nutmeg or cayenne

1 Preheat oven to 350°F. Spray 1½-quart baking dish with nonstick spray.

2 Bring 1 inch water to boil in large saucepan. Put green beans in steamer basket and set basket in saucepan. Cover tightly and steam until green beans are crisp-tender, about 4 minutes; rinse well under cold running water. Spread green beans on large clean kitchen towel; pat dry. Transfer to prepared baking dish.

3 To make topping, heat oil in large nonstick skillet over medium heat; add chopped shallot. Cook, stirring occasionally, until browned and tender, about 4 minutes. Add bread crumbs and cook, stirring occasionally, until golden, about 3 minutes. Transfer to large bowl; stir in thyme, ¼ teaspoon salt, and the pepper. Set aside to cool; stir in pecorino Romano.

4 To make sauce, in microwavable measuring cup, microwave milk on High until hot, about 3 minutes; cover to keep warm. (Or heat milk in small saucepan over medium-high heat just until small bubbles appear around edge, about 5 minutes. Remove pan from heat; cover and keep warm.)

5 Meanwhile, melt butter in same skillet over medium heat; add sliced shallots. Cook, stirring occasionally, until golden, about 4 minutes. Add mushrooms; increase heat to medium-high and cook, stirring occasionally, until tender, about 5 minutes. Stir in flour and cook, stirring frequently, 1 minute. Slowly add warm milk, stirring constantly to prevent lumps; bring to boil over medium heat, whisking constantly. Cook 1 minute; stir in remaining ½ teaspoon salt and the nutmeg.

6 Pour sauce evenly over green beans; toss gently until coated evenly. Sprinkle casserole evenly with bread crumb mixture; bake until topping is golden and sauce is bubbling, 25–30 minutes.

3 **SmartPoints value per serving** (generous ¾ cup): 128 Cal, 4 g Total Fat, 2 g Sat Fat, 318 mg Sod, 18 g Total Carb, 8 g Sugar, 4 g Fib, 6 g Prot.

Brussels sprouts with grapes and capers

Serves 4

1	pound Brussels sprouts, trimmed, tough outer leaves removed, halved if large
3	garlic cloves, chopped
2	tablespoons capers
1	tablespoon olive oil
1	cup red seedless grapes
½	teaspoon salt
¼	teaspoon black pepper

Preheat oven to 400°F. Toss all ingredients together in large bowl. Place in single layer on rimmed baking sheet. Roast until sprouts are browned and grapes are very soft, 25–30 minutes.

1 **SmartPoints value per serving** (¾ cup): 113 Cal, 4 g Total Fat, 1 g Sat Fat, 425 mg Sod, 19 g Total Carb, 9 g Sugar, 4 g Fib, 4 g Prot.

Note from Chef Eric

I've been serving versions of this side dish for years at my restaurants. I love how the sweetness of the roasted grapes mixes with the brininess of the capers. These two contrasting tastes combine with crunchy Brussels sprouts for a low SmartPoints flavor explosion.

Honey mustard
chicken bites,
page 226

Hot spinach-
artichoke dip,
page 228

Chapter 10

Easy snacks and munchies

Crispy
jalapeño
poppers,
page 229

In this chapter

Vegetarian   Vegan   Gluten free   Dairy free   Nut free

Slow-cooker shredded chicken nachos

Serves 6

We love these loaded nachos as a hearty snack, but with an awesome 44 grams of protein per serving, they can also serve as a light meal.

1 **tablespoon ground cumin**

1½ **teaspoons ancho chile powder**

1 **teaspoon dried oregano**

½ **teaspoon salt**

1¾ **pounds skinless boneless chicken breasts**

1 **large red bell pepper, cut into 1½-inch pieces**

1 **(14½-ounce) can petite diced tomatoes with jalapeños**

1 **(15½-ounce) can black beans, rinsed and drained**

6 **(6-inch) corn tortillas**

1½ **cups shredded reduced-fat Mexican cheese blend**

6 **tablespoons reduced-fat sour cream**

⅓ **cup lightly packed fresh cilantro leaves**

⅓ **cup sliced pickled jalapeño pepper**

1 **lime, cut into 6 wedges**

1 Stir together cumin, chile powder, oregano, and salt in cup. Place chicken in 5-quart slow cooker. Sprinkle with spice mixture and toss until coated evenly. Arrange chicken in single layer. Top with bell pepper and tomatoes. Cover and cook until chicken is fork-tender, about 3 hours on High. Using two forks, shred chicken in slow cooker; stir in beans. Cover and cook until heated through, about 20 minutes on High.

2 Meanwhile, preheat oven to 425°F.

3 Lightly spray both sides of tortillas with nonstick spray. Stack tortillas and cut into 6 wedges; unstack wedges (you should have 36). Arrange wedges in single layer on large rimmed baking sheet. Bake until lightly browned and crisp, about 12 minutes, turning chips over halfway through baking time. Transfer chips to wire rack and let cool completely.

4 Preheat broiler. Arrange chips, slightly overlapping, on same baking sheet. Using slotted spoon, spoon chicken mixture on top of chips; sprinkle evenly with cheese blend. Broil 4 inches from heat until cheese is melted and mixture is bubbly, about 1 minute. Top evenly with sour cream, cilantro, and jalapeño. With wide spatula, transfer nachos to 6 small plates. Serve with lime wedges.

5 **SmartPoints value per serving** (6 nacho chips): 406 Cal, 12 g Total Fat, 5 g Sat Fat, 977 mg Sod, 32 g Total Carb, 4 g Sugar, 8 g Fib, 44 g Prot.

Note from Chef Eric

Make these nachos with blue corn tortillas for an earthier flavor and unique color.

Honey mustard chicken bites

Serves 24

These easy snack treats look a little like pigs in blankets but feature tender strips of chicken thigh instead of franks.

1 **(8-ounce) tube refrigerated breadstick dough**

1 **pound skinless boneless chicken thighs, cut into 24 chunks**

¼ **cup Dijon mustard**

3 **tablespoons honey**

Flaky sea salt (optional)

1½ **teaspoons reduced-sodium soy sauce**

2 **teaspoons chopped fresh chives, plus more for garnish**

1 Preheat oven to 375°F. Line large baking sheet with parchment paper.

2 Unroll dough and cut into 24 strips; place strips horizontally on work surface in front of you. Top each strip with 1 piece chicken. Combine mustard and honey in a small bowl; set half aside to use as dip. Use pastry brush to brush each piece of chicken with some of the remaining honey-mustard. Roll dough around chicken (chicken will stick out on ends). Sprinkle with flaky salt (if using).

3 Arrange chicken bites on prepared baking sheet. Bake until dough is golden brown and chicken is cooked through, 15–20 minutes. Let cool 5 minutes.

4 Meanwhile, stir together reserved honey-mustard mixture and soy sauce in small serving bowl; stir in chives. Sprinkle chicken bites with more chives and serve with sauce.

 SmartPoints value per serving (1 chicken bite and scant ½ teaspoon sauce): 58 Cal, 1 g Total Fat, 0 g Sat Fat, 156 mg Sod, 6 g Total Carb, 3 g Sugar, 0 g Fib, 4 g Prot.

Note from Chef Eric

Boost this dip with a dash of horseradish to make it both sweet and extra spicy. About 1 teaspoon will do the trick.

Honey mustard chicken bites

Crispy jalapeño poppers, page 229

Hot spinach-artichoke dip, page 228

Hot spinach-artichoke dip

Serves 18

Love a hot dip? Give this rich, creamy veggie-packed version a try. It's great with classic dippers like carrot and celery sticks, or you can serve it with crackers or tortilla chips and calculate the additional SmartPoints.

1	**tablespoon unsalted butter**
1	**small onion, finely chopped**
2	**garlic cloves, finely chopped**
1	**(10-ounce) package frozen spinach, thawed and squeezed dry**
1	**(8-ounce) can water chestnuts, drained and chopped**
1	**(14-ounce) can artichoke hearts in water, drained and chopped**
1	**(8-ounce) package reduced-fat cream cheese (Neufchâtel)**
1	**cup reduced-fat sour cream**
1	**cup shredded reduced-fat Cheddar**
1	**teaspoon hot pepper sauce**
½	**teaspoon salt**
¼	**teaspoon black pepper**

Finely chopped parsley for garnish

1 Preheat oven to 350°F. Coat an 1½-quart casserole or 11x7-inch baking dish with nonstick spray.

2 Melt butter in large nonstick skillet over medium heat. Add onion and garlic; cook, stirring, until tender, about 5 minutes. Add spinach, water chestnuts, and artichoke hearts; cook 2 minutes. Stir in cream cheese, sour cream, ½ cup Cheddar, the pepper sauce, salt, and black pepper, stirring until cheese melts.

3 Spoon dip mixture into prepared baking dish. Sprinkle with remaining ½ cup Cheddar. Bake until heated through, about 20 minutes. Sprinkle with parsley.

SmartPoints value per serving (¼ cup): 97 Cal, 6 g Total Fat, 4 g Sat Fat, 211 mg Sod, 8 g Total Carb, 2 g Sugar, 2 g Fib, 4 g Prot.

Crispy jalapeño poppers

Serves 8

Enjoy this lightened-up classic anytime you need a finger-food treat: game day, cocktail parties, or movie nights. It's best to wear disposable gloves when you prepare the jalapeños; the oils in chile peppers can cause skin irritation. Wash your hands well after removing the gloves, and avoid touching your face for a few hours afterward just in case residue lingers on your fingers.

½ **cup shredded reduced-fat Mexican cheese blend**

¼ **cup reduced-fat whipped cream cheese**

1 **tablespoon fat-free mayonnaise**

8 **small jalapeño peppers**

1 **large egg**

1 **teaspoon cold water**

7 **tablespoons cornflake crumbs**

1 Preheat oven to 350°F. Spray large rimmed baking sheet with nonstick spray.

2 Stir together cheese blend, cream cheese, and mayonnaise in medium bowl.

3 Halve each jalapeño lengthwise and remove seeds. Fill evenly with cheese mixture.

4 Place egg in shallow bowl. Add water and beat with a fork until the egg is smooth and frothy. Place cornflake crumbs in separate shallow bowl. Dip stuffed jalapeños, one at a time, into egg and roll in cornflake crumbs until coated on all sides.

5 Arrange jalapeños on prepared baking sheet. Spray with nonstick spray. Bake until filling is bubbly and crumbs begin to brown, about 30 minutes. Serve hot.

2 **SmartPoints value per serving** (2 poppers): 68 Cal, 3 g Total Fat, 2 g Sat Fat, 152 mg Sod, 6 g Total Carb, 2 g Sugar, 0 g Fib, 4 g Prot.

Note from Chef Eric

I used to drown my poppers in fruit preserves because I love spice balanced with sweetness. But with WW Freestyle, I can drizzle these bites with a touch of honey and still stick to my eating plan. One teaspoon of honey for each serving will add just 1 SmartPoints value.

**"Umami bomb"
stuffed mushrooms**

"Umami bomb" stuffed mushrooms

Serves 8

Umami is the savory "fifth flavor" that excites our taste buds and heightens our enjoyment of food. It's found famously in roast meat and soy sauce, but also in mushrooms and garlic. We suggest you serve these stuffed treats with truffle salt, another umami-rich ingredient, but you can also use a sprinkling of flaky sea salt.

16	**cremini mushrooms, stems removed and reserved**
¼	**teaspoon fine sea salt, or to taste**
⅛	**teaspoon black pepper, or to taste**
2	**shallots, minced**
¼	**pound mixed wild mushrooms, finely chopped**
1	**teaspoon minced garlic**
1	**teaspoon minced fresh rosemary**
1	**teaspoon minced fresh thyme, plus additional for garnish**
2	**tablespoons minced red bell pepper**
	Truffle salt to taste (optional)

1 Preheat oven to 350°F. Line shallow baking pan with foil.

2 Place cremini mushroom caps in prepared pan, rounded side down. Lightly spray with nonstick spray; sprinkle with fine sea salt and black pepper. Roast until mushrooms are tender, about 15 minutes. Pat mushrooms with paper towels to remove any juices.

3 Chop reserved mushroom stems. Spray medium skillet with nonstick spray and set over medium-high heat. Add shallots and chopped mushrooms and chopped stems; cook, stirring frequently, until softened, about 10 minutes. Add garlic, rosemary, thyme, and bell pepper; cook, stirring, 1 minute. Season to taste with sea salt and black pepper or sprinkle with truffle salt (if using).

4 Spoon mushroom mixture evenly into mushroom caps. Sprinkle with thyme.

 SmartPoints value per serving (2 stuffed mushrooms): 19 Cal, 0 g Total Fat, 0 g Sat Fat, 76 mg Sod, 3 g Total Carb, 2 g Sugar, 1 g Fib, 2 g Prot.

Parmesan-thyme popcorn

Serves 4

Using aged Parmigiano-Reggiano cheese is what makes this popcorn mix special: Reggiano is denser and more flavorful than regular Parmesan, so you get big impact from a relatively small amount.

¼ **cup grated Parmigiano-Reggiano (use a microplane or a box grater)**

1 **teaspoon dried thyme**

½ **teaspoon garlic powder**

½ **teaspoon salt**

8 **cups hot 94% fat-free popped microwave popcorn**

1 Mix together Parmigiano-Reggiano, thyme, garlic powder, and salt in cup.

2 Put hot popcorn in large bowl; spray with nonstick spray, tossing to coat evenly. Sprinkle with cheese mixture, tossing until coated evenly.

 SmartPoints value per serving (2 cups): 70 Cal, 3 g Total Fat, 1 g Sat Fat, 520 mg Sod, 10 g Total Carb, 0 g Sugar, 2 g Fib, 3 g Prot.

Note from Chef Eric

Snacks like this help when I'm cuddling with my wife at home watching a movie: It's a WW Freestyle–friendly way to nosh your way through a rom-com.

Parmesan-thyme
popcorn

Crispy chickpea-
and-peanut snack
mix, page 236

Peppery
kale chips,
page 235

Sweet-and-spicy
wasabi snack mix,
page 234

Sweet-and-spicy wasabi snack mix

Serves 8

Want an alternative to greasy movie-house popcorn? Try this super-flavorful mix of crunchy low-fat popcorn and wheat cereal squares tossed with spicy wasabi, ginger, and garlic.

4	**cups hot 94% fat-free popped microwave popcorn**
⅔	**cup corn nuts**
½	**cup honey-roasted peanuts**
1½	**teaspoons wasabi paste**
1	**teaspoon granulated garlic, or to taste**
½	**teaspoon ground ginger**
⅓	**cup wasabi peas**

1 Combine hot popcorn, corn nuts, and peanuts in medium bowl; spray with nonstick spray, tossing to coat evenly.

2 Mix together wasabi paste, garlic, and ginger in large bowl; add popcorn mixture and toss to coat evenly. Stir in wasabi peas.

 SmartPoints value per serving (about ½ cup): 114 Cal, 5 g Total Fat, 1 g Sat Fat, 117 mg Sod, 14 g Total Carb, 2 g Sugar, 2 g Fib, 3 g Prot.

Note from Chef Eric

At my first restaurant, The Foundry on Melrose, we used to serve what we called the GOAT mix. Not because it was the Greatest Of All Time snack, but because we stored it in a container that once contained goat cheese ice cream. This mix is a full-flavored but slightly healthier version of that one. Long live the GOAT.

Peppery kale chips

Serves 6

Ⓥ Ⓥ Ⓥ

A perfect snack: crunchy and peppery, with a hint of cheese flavor from salty, tangy pecorino cheese. Drying the kale leaves carefully is important to make sure your chips come out crisp, not soggy. Use a salad spinner to dry the leaves first, if you have one, then be sure to pat them very dry before tearing them into pieces.

2 **(½-pound) bunches kale, tough stems removed and discarded**

1 **tablespoon extra-virgin olive oil**

½ **teaspoon kosher salt**

½ **teaspoon cracked black pepper**

3 **tablespoons grated pecorino Romano**

1 Adjust oven racks to upper and lower thirds of oven. Preheat oven to 300°F. Line 2 large baking sheets with parchment paper.

2 Pat kale leaves dry with clean kitchen towel and tear into 3-inch pieces. Toss kale in large bowl with oil, salt, and pepper, massaging oil onto leaves. Sprinkle kale with pecorino Romano and toss again.

3 Divide kale among prepared baking sheets (work in batches if necessary so kale is in a single layer). Bake just until kale is crisp but not browned, about 25 minutes, stirring kale and switching pans between oven racks halfway through baking. Cool on baking sheets on racks. Store in an airtight container for up to 2 days.

1 **SmartPoints value per serving** (2 cups): 55 Cal, 4 g Total Fat, 1 g Sat Fat, 251 mg Sod, 3 g Total Carb, 1 g Sugar, 3 g Fib, 3 g Prot.

Crispy chickpea-and-peanut snack mix

Serves 6

This savory mix is ideal for parties, game day, or anytime you need a little crunch that also packs fiber and protein. It's best served the day it's made. Otherwise, store in a zip-close plastic bag and, if you like, recrisp it in a 350°F oven on a baking sheet for about 10 minutes, then cool before serving.

1	**(15-ounce) can chickpeas, rinsed and drained**
2	**teaspoons canola oil**
¼	**teaspoon salt**
¼	**teaspoon chili powder**
⅛	**teaspoon black pepper**
1	**tablespoon maple syrup**
1	**teaspoon brown sugar**
½	**teaspoon cinnamon**
⅛	**teaspoon ground nutmeg**
1½	**cups toasted wheat squares cereal (such as Wheat Chex)**
⅓	**cup roasted peanuts**

1 Preheat oven to 425°F. Line large rimmed baking sheet with foil.

2 Pat chickpeas dry with paper towels; discard any loose skins. Toss chickpeas on prepared baking sheet with oil, salt, chili powder, and pepper. Roast, shaking pan occasionally, until crisp, about 25 minutes.

3 Combine maple syrup, brown sugar, cinnamon, and nutmeg in large bowl. Add hot chickpeas, cereal, and peanuts; toss to coat.

4 Spread mixture on same baking sheet. Bake until golden and crisp, about 5 minutes. Cool on baking sheet on rack.

 SmartPoints value per serving (scant ½ cup): 223 Cal, 8 g Total Fat, 1 g Sat Fat, 360 mg Sod, 33 g Total Carb, 7 g Sugar, 7 g Fib, 9 g Prot.

Figs with honey and goat cheese

Serves 8

Here's a supereasy way to prepare fresh figs when they're in season. These bites are special enough to serve as an appetizer with white-wine spritzers, or make them up just to snack on anytime you need a sweet and savory treat; they'll keep refrigerated in an airtight container for about 2 days.

16 **medium fresh figs, washed and patted dry, each sliced in half lengthwise**

6 **tablespoons part-skim ricotta**

2 **tablespoons crumbled goat cheese**

2 **tablespoons chopped fresh thyme**

2 **tablespoons honey**

½ **teaspoon black pepper, or to taste**

Place figs on large serving platter, cut side up. Combine ricotta, goat cheese, and thyme in small bowl. Spoon about ¾ teaspoon cheese mixture over each fig half; drizzle with honey and sprinkle with pepper.

 SmartPoints value per serving (4 fig halves): 117 Cal, 2 g Total Fat, 1 g Sat Fat, 31 mg Sod, 24 g Total Carb, 21 g Sugar, 3 g Fib, 3 g Prot.

Note from Chef Eric
These figs make a tasty, easy hors d'oeuvre for any cocktail party, or even a light mid-afternoon snack.

Roasted grapes with rosemary and yogurt

Serves 4

Grapes roasted with rosemary and a touch of brown sugar become unexpectedly rich-tasting. Yogurt provides a slightly tart contrast, and since it's a zero Points food, it makes the whole dish particularly appealing as a between-meals snack.

5   cups seedless red grapes, stems removed

1½ teaspoons extra-virgin olive oil

1   tablespoon light brown sugar

1½ teaspoons chopped fresh rosemary, plus 4 small sprigs

Pinch coarsely ground black pepper

½   cup plain fat-free Greek yogurt

1½ teaspoons honey

⅛   teaspoon ground nutmeg

¼   cup dry white wine

1 Preheat oven to 425°F.

2 Put grapes on large rimmed baking sheet; drizzle evenly with oil and stir to coat. Spread grapes to form single layer. Roast 15 minutes. Sprinkle grapes with brown sugar, chopped rosemary, and pepper, gently tossing to coat. Roast until grapes start to burst and give off juice, about 15 minutes longer.

3 Meanwhile, stir together yogurt, honey, and nutmeg in small bowl.

4 When grapes are roasted, pour wine over and roast until wine is bubbling, about 1 minute longer. Stir grapes to release thick, sweet juices on baking sheet, turning grapes to coat.

5 Divide grapes and sauce evenly among 4 small dishes. Spoon yogurt mixture alongside and garnish with rosemary sprigs.

2 **SmartPoints value per serving** (½ cup grapes with sauce and 2 tablespoons yogurt mixture): 191 Cal, 2 g Total Fat, 0 g Sat Fat, 15 mg Sod, 40 g Total Carb, 35 g Sugar, 2 g Fib, 4 g Prot.

Frozen cappuccino

Serves 2

Replacing full-fat dairy with slimmer, healthier options and pumping up the volume with crushed ice makes a thick, creamy treat for a fraction of the SmartPoints of a standard milkshake. Share it with someone you love!

1½ **teaspoons instant espresso powder**

1 **teaspoon hot water**

⅓ **cup ice cubes**

1 **cup vanilla low-fat frozen yogurt**

⅔ **cup fat-free milk**

Pinch cinnamon

1 Combine espresso powder and water in cup and stir until espresso dissolves.

2 Crush ice in blender. Add frozen yogurt and milk; blend until smooth. Reserve one quarter of the yogurt mixture. Add dissolved espresso to remaining yogurt mixture and blend just until mixed.

3 Divide espresso mixture between 2 glasses; top each with one half of the reserved yogurt mixture and sprinkle with cinnamon.

7 **SmartPoints value per serving** (1 cup): 139 Cal, 2 g Total Fat, 1 g Sat Fat, 96 mg Sod, 23 g Total Carb, 21 g Sugar, 0 g Fib, 7 g Prot.

Note from Chef Eric

Here's a perfectly refreshing treat for hot days. This recipe also works well with matcha green tea powder in place of espresso powder.

Raspberries-and-cream shortcakes, page 261

Decadent desserts

In this chapter

Vegetarian   Vegan   Gluten free   Dairy free   Nut free

Angel food cake with peach-bourbon sauce

Serves 16

1¼ cups sugar

1   cup cake flour

¼   teaspoon salt

12 large egg whites

1½ teaspoons cream of tartar

1½ teaspoons vanilla extract

¼   teaspoon almond extract

6   cups thinly sliced peaches

2   tablespoons packed brown sugar

1   tablespoon bourbon

1 Position oven rack in lower third of oven; preheat oven to 350°F.

2 Put sugar in food processor and process for 1 minute. Remove and reserve ¾ cup. Add flour and salt to remaining sugar in processor and process for about 30 seconds.

3 With electric mixer on medium-low speed, beat egg whites in large bowl until foamy, about 1 minute. Beat in cream of tartar. Increase speed to medium and beat in reserved ¾ cup sugar, 1 tablespoon at a time, beating well after each addition. Once all sugar has been added, increase speed to medium-high and beat until stiff peaks form when beaters are lifted. Beat in vanilla and almond extracts.

4 Sift flour mixture, one third at a time, over beaten egg whites, gently folding in with rubber spatula just until blended. (Be careful not to overmix.) Scrape batter into ungreased 10-inch tube pan with removable bottom. Spread evenly. Bake until cake springs back when lightly pressed, 35–40 minutes.

5 Meanwhile, combine peaches, brown sugar, and bourbon in medium bowl. Let stand for at least 10 minutes, or refrigerate for up to 2 days.

6 When cake is done, immediately invert pan onto its legs or over neck of bottle and let cool completely. Run thin knife around sides and center tube of pan. Remove cake from pan and transfer to serving plate. Cut into 16 slices and serve with peach mixture.

(5) **SmartPoints value per serving** (1 slice cake and ⅓ cup peaches): 137 Cal, 0 g Total Fat, 0 g Sat Fat, 78 mg Sod, 30 g Total Carb, 22 g Sugar, 1 g Fib, 4 g Prot.

Note from Chef Eric
Grinding sugar in a food processor makes it superfine, which gives this cake a softer texture. Fresh peaches macerated with bourbon make a flavorful topping for this particularly light angel food. Top with a dollop of plain nonfat Greek yogurt or plain unsweetened soy yogurt for a zero Points addition.

Flourless chocolate-almond cake

Serves 12

Unleavened cakes like this one are a tradition for Passover, but this recipe is so rich and comforting you can turn to it any time of the year.

3 **tablespoons unsweetened Dutch process cocoa powder**

3 **ounces bittersweet chocolate, coarsely chopped**

1 **tablespoon unsalted butter**

½ **cup reduced-fat sour cream**

3 **large eggs, yolks and whites separated, + 2 large egg whites**

⅓ **cup + ½ cup granulated sugar**

1½ **teaspoons vanilla extract**

⅔ **cup almond flour (meal)**

¼ **teaspoon salt**

2 **teaspoons confectioners' sugar**

3 **cups fresh raspberries (about two 6-ounce containers)**

1 Preheat oven to 350°F. Spray 9-inch springform pan with nonstick spray. Sift 1 tablespoon cocoa powder into pan; tilt pan to coat bottom and side with cocoa, shaking out any excess.

2 Combine chocolate and butter in medium microwavable bowl; cover with sheet of wax paper and microwave on High until chocolate is softened and butter begins to melt, about 1 minute. Stir until smooth.

3 Sift remaining 2 tablespoons cocoa into small bowl; add sour cream, stirring until smooth. Set aside. Using whisk attachment of electric mixer, beat 3 egg yolks and ⅓ cup granulated sugar in large bowl at medium-high speed until thick and lemon-colored. Reduce speed to low. Beat in chocolate mixture and the vanilla. With rubber spatula, fold in sour cream mixture until blended; fold in almond flour until blended.

4 Wash whisk attachment. Using clean whisk attachment, beat 5 egg whites and the salt in another large bowl at medium speed until soft peaks form when beaters are lifted. With mixer at medium-high speed, add remaining ½ cup granulated sugar, 2 tablespoons at a time, beating until firm, glossy peaks form, about 2 minutes.

5 Spoon one third of beaten egg whites over chocolate mixture, gently folding in just until whites are incorporated. Repeat with remaining egg whites. Pour batter into prepared pan and gently smooth top. Bake until toothpick inserted into center comes out clean, about 40 minutes.

6 Let cake cool completely in pan on wire rack, about 1 hour. Run thin knife around edge of pan; release and remove pan side. Dust cake with confectioners' sugar; cut into 12 slices with knife dipped into hot water and dried. Serve with raspberries.

 7 **SmartPoints value per serving** (1 slice cake and ¼ cup raspberries): 181 Cal, 10 g Total Fat, 4 g Sat Fat, 81 mg Sod, 22 g Total Carb, 16 g Sugar, 4 g Fib, 5 g Prot.

Flourless chocolate-almond cake

**Banana-raspberry
graham cracker
icebox cake**

Banana-raspberry graham cracker icebox cake

Serves 10

Icebox cakes are some of the very easiest cakes you can put together—some have as few as two ingredients. Lots of great fruit and low-fat yogurt added to this recipe make it particularly tasty and low in SmartPoints while still keeping prep time to about 15 minutes.

1 **cup plain low-fat Greek yogurt**

2 **tablespoons confectioners' sugar**

2 **cups light whipped topping**

15 **reduced-fat graham cracker squares (7½ whole crackers)**

⅓ **cup low-sugar seedless raspberry jam**

3 **bananas, thinly sliced**

½ **cup fresh blackberries or raspberries**

1 Line 5x9-inch loaf pan with plastic wrap, allowing excess to overhang on two long sides.

2 Whisk together yogurt and sugar in medium bowl. With rubber spatula, gently fold in whipped topping. Set aside. Spread graham crackers evenly with raspberry jam.

3 Line bottom of prepared pan with 3 graham crackers, jam side up; top evenly with one quarter of the sliced bananas. Spread one quarter of the yogurt mixture over bananas. Repeat layers three more times. Top with remaining graham crackers, jam side down.

4 Cover top of cake with overhanging plastic wrap; gently mold with your hands to form even shape. Refrigerate until crackers soften, at least 8 hours or up to 1 day.

5 To serve, uncover cake and invert onto platter; remove plastic wrap and scatter berries over top. With serrated knife, gently cut cake into 10 slices.

5 **SmartPoints value per serving** (1 slice): 147 Cal, 3 g Total Fat, 2 g Sat Fat, 88 mg Sod, 27 g Total Carb, 14 g Sugar, 2 g Fib, 4 g Prot.

Note from Chef Eric

Baking isn't my strength, so an icebox cake this easy is a key arrow to have in my quiver. And my boys love it, too. I really appreciate eating dessert with my family without worrying about how to fit it into my SmartPoints Budget.

Apple-blueberry streusel pie

Serves 12

The classic combination of apples and blueberries makes one of the best pies we know. A quick topping of oats, cinnamon, and brown sugar becomes deliciously nutty and crisp as it browns.

1   **refrigerated pie crust (from 14.1-ounce package of 2)**

½   **cup + 2 tablespoons all-purpose flour**

3   **tablespoons cold unsalted butter, diced**

2   **tablespoons ground almonds or finely chopped almonds**

1   **teaspoon cinnamon**

⅛   **teaspoon salt**

½   **cup old-fashioned oats**

1½   **tablespoons light brown sugar**

2   **tablespoons granulated sugar**

3   **medium tart apples (such as Granny Smith or Braeburn), peeled, cored, and sliced about ½-inch thick**

1   **cup fresh blueberries**

1   Place baking sheet on middle rack of oven. Preheat oven to 375°F. Soften pie crust according to package directions.

2   On lightly floured surface, roll pie crust into 13-inch circle. Ease it into and up side of 9-inch pie plate; flute edge. Refrigerate while you prepare topping and filling.

3   For topping, put ½ cup flour, the butter, almonds, cinnamon, and salt in medium bowl. Work butter into dry ingredients with pastry cutter or your fingertips to make coarse crumbs. Stir in oats and brown sugar until clumps form. Set aside.

4   For filling, combine remaining 2 tablespoons flour and the granulated sugar in large bowl. Add apples and blueberries; toss until coated. Pile fruit into crust. Scatter topping over fruit.

5   Sit pie on hot baking sheet and bake until apples are tender and juices start to bubble, 1 hour 15 minutes (cover loosely with foil if top browns too quickly). Cool pie for at least 30 minutes. Cut into 12 slices and serve warm or at room temperature.

7   **SmartPoints value per serving** (1 slice): 199 Cal, 9 g Total Fat, 4 g Sat Fat, 104 mg Sod, 29 g Total Carb, 10 g Sugar, 3 g Fib, 2 g Prot.

Note from Chef Eric

Streusel is a great way to add texture and flavor to any pie, and it generally lowers the SmartPoints because you don't need to cover the top with crust. Half the crust, all the flavor!

Frozen peanut butter–toffee pie

Serves 12

Peanut butter is a comfort favorite in everything from sandwiches and sauces to smoothies and desserts. If you love it too, you should get to know peanut butter powder, a lower-fat ingredient that's excellent in desserts like this luscious pie.

¾ **cup powdered peanut butter**

½ **cup water**

6 **tablespoons plain fat-free Greek yogurt**

2 **tablespoons confectioners' sugar**

2 **cups light whipped topping**

1 **(6-ounce) prepared chocolate cookie crust**

2 **tablespoons chopped salted dry-roasted peanuts**

¼ **cup milk chocolate–covered toffee bits, chopped**

1 Stir together powdered peanut butter and water in medium bowl until smooth. Stir in yogurt and confectioners' sugar until combined.

2 Gently whisk whipped topping into peanut butter mixture; spoon into crust. Sprinkle with peanuts and toffee bits. Freeze pie until completely frozen, at least 4 hours or up to 2 days ahead.

3 Let pie soften at room temperature 15 minutes. Cut into 12 slices and serve.

6 **SmartPoints value per serving** (1 slice): 159 Cal, 8 g Total Fat, 2 g Sat Fat, 185 mg Sod, 17 g Total Carb, 9 g Sugar, 1 g Fib, 5 g Prot.

Note from Chef Eric
The tang of yogurt is the perfect foil to the sweetness of the toffee in this recipe, and it's a zero Points ingredient. WW Freestyle magic!

Triple-chocolate cream pie

Serves 12

This delicious pie features a rich filling of chocolate and cocoa powder. A topping of pomegranate seeds adds color and crunch, but you can also use raspberries or sliced strawberries.

14	chocolate graham cracker squares (7 whole crackers)
1½	tablespoons light stick butter
1	tablespoon egg white, beaten
½	cup sugar
⅓	cup cornstarch
¼	cup unsweetened Dutch process cocoa powder
Pinch salt	
½	cup low-fat (1%) milk
1	large egg
1	pint fat-free half-and-half
1	ounce unsweetened chocolate, chopped
1½	teaspoons vanilla extract
¼	cup aerosol whipped topping
2	tablespoons pomegranate seeds (arils)

1 Preheat oven to 350°F. Spray 9-inch pie plate with nonstick spray.

2 To make crust, put crackers in food processor; process until finely ground. Add butter; pulse to combine. Add egg white; pulse a few times until evenly moistened. Firmly press crumb mixture onto bottom and against side of prepared pie plate. Bake 12 minutes; transfer to wire rack and let cool.

3 To make filling, whisk together sugar, cornstarch, cocoa powder, and salt in medium bowl; whisk in milk and egg until blended.

4 Heat half-and-half in large saucepan over medium heat until small bubbles appear around edge of pan, about 6 minutes. Gradually whisk one half of hot half-and-half into cocoa mixture until blended. Whisk hot cocoa mixture into remaining half-and-half in pan. Cook, stirring frequently with heatproof spatula, until mixture comes to boil, about 4 minutes; boil 1 minute. Remove pan from heat and stir in chocolate and vanilla extract until chocolate is melted; pour into cooled crust.

5 Press plastic wrap onto surface of pie filling; refrigerate until filling is firm, for at least 4 hours or up to overnight. Remove pie from refrigerator; uncover. Garnish with whipped topping and sprinkle with pomegranate seeds. Cut into 12 slices and serve.

6 **SmartPoints value per serving** (1 slice): 128 Cal, 5 g Total Fat, 2 g Sat Fat, 98 mg Sod, 21 g Total Carb, 12 g Sugar, 1 g Fib, 3 g Prot.

Note from Chef Eric

The chocolate graham cracker crust in this recipe is one of my favorite baking treats. You could use a similar crust for a low-fat cheesecake filling, or even a curd pie.

Triple-chocolate cream pie

Mini-apple pies

Serves 6

As the pies bake, the walnuts toast, giving these free-form pies great crunch and flavor. They're best served warm, but you can store cooled pies in an airtight container for up to a day.

1   **tablespoon granulated sugar**

2   **teaspoons light brown sugar**

¼   **teaspoon cinnamon**

3   **small Golden Delicious apples, peeled and thinly sliced**

3   **sheets phyllo dough (14 × 18 inches), thawed if frozen**

2   **tablespoons finely chopped walnuts**

1 Set oven rack in lower third of oven. Preheat oven to 400°F. Spray large baking sheet with nonstick spray.

2 To make filling, stir together granulated sugar, brown sugar, and cinnamon in large bowl. Add apples and toss to coat.

3 To make crust, place 1 phyllo sheet on large cutting board; spray with nonstick spray. (Keep remaining phyllo covered with damp paper towel and plastic wrap to prevent it from drying out.) Top with another phyllo sheet; spray with nonstick spray. Top with third phyllo sheet; spray with nonstick spray.

4 Cut phyllo crosswise into thirds; cut lengthwise in half to form 6 pieces (6 × 6½ inches each). Arrange about ½ cup apple mixture, in overlapping slices, down center of one phyllo stack, leaving ¾-inch border; fold edges of phyllo up and over edge of filling, gently pressing against filling. Repeat with remaining ingredients to make 6 pies. Lightly spray with nonstick spray.

5 Using wide spatula, transfer pies to prepared baking sheet, placing them about 2 inches apart; sprinkle filling evenly with walnuts. Bake until edges of phyllo are golden and apples are tender, about 30 minutes. Transfer pies to wire racks. Serve warm.

2 **SmartPoints value per serving** (1 pie): 98 Cal, 3 g Total Fat, 0 g Sat Fat, 47 mg Sod, 19 g Total Carb, 11 g Sugar, 2 g Fib, 1 g Prot.

Note from Chef Eric

Play around with different varieties of apples until you find one you love. Whether it's the heightened sweetness of Red Delicious, the firm texture of Fuji, or the tartness of Granny Smith, there's a baking apple that fits everyone's flavor preference.

Strawberry–white chocolate bread pudding

Serves 6

Turn to this recipe whenever you have a surplus of sweet, juicy strawberries. We suggest using airy ciabatta in this pudding, but any light, soft bread will work well.

5   **ounces ciabatta bread, cut into 1-inch chunks (about 4 cups total)**

3   **tablespoons raisins**

½   **pound strawberries, hulled, halved if small or quartered if large**

1   **teaspoon unsalted butter, melted**

3   **large eggs**

2   **cups reduced-fat (2%) milk**

1   **tablespoon granulated sugar**

¾   **teaspoon vanilla extract**

1½ **ounces white chocolate, chopped**

1   **teaspoon confectioners' sugar**

1   Spray 1-quart casserole dish with nonstick spray. Put one half of bread into dish, then scatter with one half of raisins and one half of strawberries. Scatter remaining bread on top and drizzle with melted butter. Top with remaining raisins and strawberries.

2   Beat eggs in medium bowl until frothy. Beat in milk, granulated sugar, and vanilla. Pour egg mixture over bread, making sure each piece is coated. Gently press bread into the liquid to saturate. Set dish aside 15 minutes to allow bread to soak up liquid.

3   Preheat oven to 350°F.

4   Bake pudding for 30 minutes. Scatter white chocolate over top of pudding. Continue to bake until custard is softly set and bread is golden and crisped, 15–20 minutes longer. Let cool 5 minutes. Place confectioners' sugar in small sieve and dust top of pudding. Divide evenly among 6 bowls and serve warm.

 SmartPoints value per serving (1 cup): 218 Cal, 8 g Total Fat, 4 g Sat Fat, 225 mg Sod, 29 g Total Carb, 17 g Sugar, 1 g Fib, 9 g Prot.

Note from Chef Eric

Bread pudding has always been one of my go-to desserts. It's a great way to use up leftover bread, and it's supereasy to put together.

Mini-chocolate-banana cupcakes with peanut butter frosting

Mini–chocolate-banana cupcakes with peanut butter frosting

Serves 24

Everyone loves minis! These two-bite cupcakes are excellent for every occasion, from birthdays to tea parties and cocktail parties.

¾ **cup all-purpose flour**

⅓ **cup unsweetened cocoa powder**

1 **teaspoon baking powder**

1 **teaspoon baking soda**

¼ **teaspoon fine salt**

3 **ripe small bananas, mashed (about 1½ cups)**

¼ **cup plain low-fat Greek yogurt**

⅓ **cup sugar**

1 **large egg**

1 **teaspoon vanilla extract**

⅔ **cup mini–semisweet chocolate chips**

1 **cup frozen light whipped topping, thawed**

3 **tablespoons creamy peanut butter**

Flaky sea salt (optional)

1 Preheat oven to 350°F.

2 Whisk together flour, cocoa powder, baking powder, baking soda, and fine salt in small bowl. Mix together bananas, yogurt, sugar, egg, and vanilla in large bowl. With rubber spatula, fold flour mixture into banana mixture just until combined; gently stir in chocolate chips.

3 Spray 24-cup mini-muffin pan with nonstick spray (or line with paper liners); fill each with 1 heaping tablespoon batter. Bake until toothpick inserted into center of muffin comes out clean, about 13 minutes. Let cool in pan on wire rack, about 45 minutes.

4 Meanwhile, to make frosting, whisk together whipped topping and peanut butter until light and fluffy (whisk in a teaspoon of hot water if frosting is too thick). Frost each cupcake with 1 rounded teaspoon frosting; refrigerate until ready to serve. Sprinkle tops with a few grains sea salt (if using).

3 **SmartPoints value per serving** (1 cupcake): 92 Cal, 4 g Total Fat, 2 g Sat Fat, 112 mg Sod, 13 g Total Carb, 7 g Sugar, 1 g Fib, 2 g Prot.

Note from Chef Eric
Grab one of these quick bites to end another successful WW Freestyle day. They're also a perfect 3 SmartPoints late-afternoon sweet and chocolatey delight.

Pineapple-rhubarb crumble

Serves 12

The combination of tart rhubarb and sweet pineapple is outstandingly delicious in this unusual crumble. Oats, walnuts, and brown sugar are combined for a classic crunchy topping.

¼ **cup granulated sugar**

3 **tablespoons instant tapioca**

¼ **teaspoon salt**

1 **pound fresh rhubarb, trimmed and cut into 1-inch pieces**

4 **cups fresh pineapple chunks, cut into 1-inch pieces**

1 **teaspoon vanilla extract**

⅓ **cup packed brown sugar**

¼ **cup all-purpose flour**

¼ **cup old-fashioned oats**

¼ **cup finely chopped walnuts**

2 **tablespoons melted butter**

1 Preheat oven to 375°F. Spray 10-inch square baking dish or shallow 2-quart gratin dish with nonstick spray.

2 Mix together granulated sugar, tapioca, and ⅛ teaspoon salt in large bowl. Stir in rhubarb, pineapple, and vanilla. Scrape into prepared baking dish and level top.

3 Stir together brown sugar, flour, oats, walnuts, and remaining ⅛ teaspoon salt in medium bowl. Drizzle melted butter over top and stir until clumps form. Sprinkle oat mixture evenly over rhubarb mixture.

4 Bake until filling bubbles in center and topping is golden, about 45 minutes. Cool at least 30 minutes before serving.

4 **SmartPoints value per serving** (½ cup): 133 Cal, 4 g Total Fat, 1 g Sat Fat, 53 mg Sod, 25 g Total Carb, 16 g Sugar, 2 g Fib, 2 g Prot.

Pineapple-rhubarb crumble

Lemony tapioca pudding

Serves 6

This wonderfully creamy pudding is speckled with tender white tapioca pearls and enlivened by the taste of fresh lemon.

2¼ cups low-fat (1%) milk

½ cup half-and-half

¼ cup + 1 tablespoon sugar

3 tablespoons quick-cooking tapioca

⅛ teaspoon salt

2 large eggs, beaten

2 teaspoons finely grated lemon zest

1½ teaspoons vanilla extract

½ pound fresh strawberries, hulled and sliced

2 teaspoons fresh lemon juice

1 Stir together milk, half-and-half, ¼ cup sugar, tapioca, and salt in medium saucepan. Let stand 5 minutes.

2 Set pan over medium heat and cook, stirring constantly, until mixture reaches full boil, 10–15 minutes. Reduce heat and simmer 5 minutes.

3 Meanwhile, whisk eggs in medium bowl.

4 Whisk 1 cup hot milk mixture into beaten eggs. Whisk egg mixture into remaining milk mixture in saucepan. Return to medium-low heat. Cook, stirring, until mixture becomes thick enough to coat back of spoon, about 2 minutes. Remove pan from heat; stir in lemon zest and vanilla.

5 Transfer to bowl; cover with plastic wrap and refrigerate until chilled, for at least 3 hours or overnight. Meanwhile, toss strawberries in another bowl with remaining 1 tablespoon sugar. Stir lemon juice into pudding. Ladle pudding into serving bowls and top with strawberries.

6 **SmartPoints value per serving** (½ cup pudding and ½ cup strawberries): 161 Cal, 5 g Total Fat, 2 g Sat Fat, 124 mg Sod, 23 g Total Carb, 18 g Sugar, 1 g Fib, 6 g Prot.

Freestyle it
Take advantage of red, white, and blue zero Points foods to serve this pudding with more sliced strawberries, some fat-free Greek yogurt, and fresh blueberries.

Coconut rice pudding

Serves 8

4 tablespoons toasted shredded coconut

5 tablespoons sugar

2 cups low-fat (1%) milk

1 (13½-ounce) can light (low-fat) coconut milk

⅔ cup Arborio rice

½ teaspoon finely grated orange zest

⅛ teaspoon finely grated nutmeg

Pinch salt

2 teaspoons vanilla extract

1 Chop 2 tablespoons coconut; place in 5- to 6-quart slow cooker. Add sugar, milk, coconut milk, rice, orange zest, nutmeg, and salt; stir until combined. Cover and cook until rice is very tender, 2–2½ hours on High or 4–5 hours on Low.

2 Stir in vanilla. Serve warm or chilled, ladled into bowls and topped with remaining coconut.

8 **SmartPoints value per serving** (scant ½ cup pudding and scant 1 teaspoon coconut): 171 Cal, 6 g Total Fat, 5 g Sat Fat, 64 mg Sod, 26 g Total Carb, 11 g Sugar, 1 g Fib, 3 g Prot.

Note from Chef Eric

I sometimes like to top this rice pudding with diced mango and crushed peanuts—it reminds me of the sticky rice with mango that my wife and I ate everywhere on our honeymoon in Thailand. Half a tablespoon of chopped roasted peanuts per serving increases the SmartPoints by just 1.

Raspberries-and-cream shortcakes

Raspberries-and-cream shortcakes

Serves 14

2   **(6-ounce) containers fresh raspberries**

2   **cups all-purpose flour**

2½ **teaspoons baking powder**

1   **tablespoon + 5 teaspoons sugar**

¼   **teaspoon salt**

3   **tablespoons cold unsalted butter, cut into small pieces**

1   **large egg**

¾   **cup low-fat buttermilk**

½   **cup plain fat-free Greek yogurt**

6   **tablespoons crème fraîche**

¼   **teaspoon vanilla extract**

1   **teaspoon confectioners' sugar**

1 Preheat oven to 425°F. Line baking sheet with parchment paper.

2 To make shortcakes, cut ½ cup raspberries in half. Whisk flour, baking powder, 1 tablespoon sugar, and the salt together in large mixing bowl. Add butter and work it into flour mixture with your fingertips or pastry cutter just until it forms coarse crumbs. Add halved raspberries and gently toss.

3 Beat egg in medium bowl, then stir in buttermilk; pour over flour mixture. Stir dough gently just until blended, being careful not to crush raspberries. On lightly floured surface, knead a few times until mixture forms soft dough. Pat dough into disk about 7 inches in diameter and about ¾-inch thick.

4 Cut out 10 rounds using 2-inch round cookie cutter. Gently gather scraps and pat out again to ¾-inch thickness. Cut out 4 more shortcakes. Place shortcakes 2 inches apart on prepared baking sheet. Sprinkle tops of shortcakes with 1 teaspoon sugar. Bake until tops are golden, 13–14 minutes. Transfer shortcakes to wire rack to cool.

5 For filling, roughly crush remaining raspberries with side of spoon in medium bowl, keeping a few chunky pieces of fruit. Stir in 2 teaspoons sugar. Stir yogurt, crème fraîche, remaining 2 teaspoons sugar, and the vanilla together in another bowl. Split shortcakes using serrated knife. Spoon berries and a little juice onto bottom half of each shortcake, top with spoonful of cream mixture, and cover with shortcake tops. Sprinkle with confectioners' sugar.

5 **SmartPoints value per serving** (1 filled shortcake): 147 Cal, 6 g Total Fat, 3 g Sat Fat, 159 mg Sod, 20 g Total Carb, 5 g Sugar, 2 g Fib, 4 g Prot.

Freestyle it

Serve shortcakes with extra raspberries or other colorful berries on the side for no additional SmartPoints. Red currants are a festive choice if they're in season.

Berry angel food trifle

Serves 10

3   **cups plain low-fat yogurt**

¼   **cup honey**

2   **teaspoons vanilla extract**

1   **(10-ounce) package frozen mixed unsweetened berries**

1   **(10-ounce) store-bought vanilla angel food cake, cut into large chunks**

6   **cups fresh strawberries, hulled and thickly sliced**

1 Combine yogurt, honey, and vanilla in medium bowl.

2 In shallow dish, gently mash frozen berries with their juice.

3 Arrange half of cake in bottom of large glass bowl or trifle bowl; top with half of mashed frozen berries and half of fresh strawberries, placing prettiest fresh berries against side of bowl. Spoon half of yogurt mixture over berries, beginning against side of bowl and working inward. Repeat layers. Serve immediately or refrigerate up to 2 hours.

6   **SmartPoints value per serving** (1 cup): 163 Cal, 2 g Total Fat, 1 g Sat Fat, 94 mg Sod, 33 g Total Carb, 25 g Sugar, 3 g Fib, 6 g Prot.

Freestyle it

Add some diced pineapple to the trifle for more sweetness and 0 additional SmartPoints.

Pizzelle cookie cannolis

Serves 8

Pizzelle cookies are heated and formed into cannoli shells, a type of shell that is usually deep-fried. Creamy low-fat ricotta, dark chocolate, and orange zest make the filling absolutely delicious but keep the SmartPoints in check.

1	**cup + 2 tablespoons part-skim ricotta**
½	**cup light whipped topping**
3	**tablespoons confectioners' sugar**
¾	**teaspoon vanilla extract**
¼	**teaspoon grated orange zest**
¾	**ounce 60%–69% dark chocolate, finely chopped**
8	**vanilla pizzelle cookies (3–4 inches in diameter)**

1 Line sieve with paper coffee filter or piece of cheesecloth; set over small bowl. Add ricotta; cover with plastic wrap and place heavy can on top. Refrigerate for at least 1 hour to drain.

2 Mix together drained ricotta, whipped topping, confectioners' sugar, vanilla, and orange zest in another small bowl. Fold in chocolate and set aside.

3 Microwave cookies, one at a time, on paper plate, 20–30 seconds. Immediately remove warm cookie and wrap around handle of utensil, such as a vegetable peeler, to form cylinder shell (or carefully shape with your hands). Let cool; repeat with remaining cookies.

4 Spoon or pipe 2 tablespoons filling into each cookie shell; serve immediately.

4 **SmartPoints value per serving** (1 cannoli): 109 Cal, 5 g Total Fat, 3 g Sat Fat, 46 mg Sod, 10 g Total Carb, 6 g Sugar, 0 g Fib, 5 g Prot.

Note from Chef Eric

I like to fold chopped toasted pistachios into the filling here. It brings extra texture and matches perfectly with the orange zest. Stirring ¼ cup shelled roasted pistachios, chopped, into the ricotta filling will add only 1 SmartPoints value per serving.

Bananas
Foster

Bananas Foster

Serves 4

This classic dessert tastes truly decadent, but don't worry: We've made just enough tweaks to the traditional recipe, credited to New Orleans' fabled Brennan's Restaurant, to make it super-friendly to your SmartPoints Budget.

2   **tablespoons unsalted butter**

4   **teaspoons dark brown sugar**

3   **slightly under-ripe bananas, cut in half crosswise and each piece split lengthwise (12 pieces total)**

¼   **teaspoon cinnamon**

3   **tablespoons dark rum**

⅛   **teaspoon fine salt**

1   **pint vanilla reduced-calorie, high-protein ice cream (such as Halo Top)**

Flaky sea salt (optional)

1 Put butter and brown sugar in large skillet and cook over medium heat, stirring, until butter melts and mixture is blended, about 2 minutes.

2 Add bananas; sprinkle with cinnamon and cook over medium-low heat, turning bananas occasionally, until bananas soften slightly, about 1 minute.

3 Remove skillet from heat. Drizzle in rum and ignite using a long match or lighter. When the flames die down, return to medium heat and let mixture thicken slightly, about 1 minute. Remove from heat; sprinkle with fine salt and gently toss.

4 Place ½ cup ice cream in each of 4 bowls. Top each serving with 3 banana pieces and 1 tablespoon sauce. Sprinkle with a few grains flaky salt (if using).

6   **SmartPoints value per serving** (½ cup ice cream, 3 banana slices, 1 tablespoon sauce): 231 Cal, 8 g Total Fat, 5 g Sat Fat, 185 mg Sod, 38 g Total Carb, 18 g Sugar, 5 g Fib, 6 g Prot.

Freestyle it

Serve each bowl with a garnish of fresh berries for no additional SmartPoints.

Food truck souvlaki salad, page 30

Recipes by SmartPoints value

Index

Eric Greenspan is among Los Angeles' most popular and celebrated chefs. He graduated from Berkeley's Haas School of Business and Le Cordon Bleu culinary school in Paris before training with such renowned chefs as Alain Ducasse and Joachim Splichal. He opened The Foundry on Melrose to rave reviews, followed by several other successful eateries. Eric has appeared on countless programs. He has hosted shows for The Food Network and the National Geographic Channel; he is a regular judge on "Guy's Grocery Games"; and has judged and competed in numerous food competitions, including "Iron Chef America," on which he defeated Bobby Flay, and "Cutthroat Kitchen All-Stars," which he won. Eric is the Executive Chef and Owner of The Roof on Wilshire and owner of the Alt Grub Faction, a collection of delivery-only virtual restaurant concepts including Brekkie Breakfast Burritos, 2 on a Roll, and Chino Latino. He became a WW Member and the Brand Ambassador for WW Healthy Kitchen™ in 2018.